MARRIAGES
OF
LUNENBURG COUNTY, VIRGINIA,

1746-1853

Compiled by
EMMA R. MATHENY
and
HELEN K. YATES

CLEARFIELD

Matheny & Yates
Reprinted for
Clearfield Company, Inc. by
Genealogical Publishing Co., Inc.
Baltimore, Maryland
1990, 1997

Originally Published. Richmond, Virginia, 1967
© 1967 Emma R. Matheny and Helen K. Yates
All Rights Reserved
Reprinted, with permission, by the
Genealogical Publishing Co., Inc.
Baltimore, 1979
Library of Congress Catalogue Card Number 78-71107
International Standard Book Number 0-8063-0833-8
Made in the United States of America

Dedicated to

Mrs. Jewell T. Clark

Archival Assistant
Virginia State Library

without whose encouragement
and interest this compilation
would not have been completed

Know all men by these presents that we Joseph
Minor and Thomas Stith are held and firmly bound unto
our Sovereign Lord George the second by the Grace of
God of Great Britain France and Ireland King Defender
of the faith etc. in the sum of Fifty pounds, current
money to be paid to our said Lord the King his Heirs,
and Successors to the which payment well and truly
to be made, we bind ourselves our Heirs, Executors,
and Administrators jointly and severally firmly by
these presents Sealed with our Seals Dated this
Eleventh day of October 1750.

Whereas there is a marriage suddenly intended
to be solemnized Between the above bound Joseph Miner
and Edith Cox, Spinster, Daughter of John Cox,

The Condition of this present Obligation is such
that if there be no lawfull cause to obstruct the
same then this obligation to be void else to remain
in full force.

Sealed and Delivered   Joseph Minor (SEAL)

In Presence of: Thos. Stith (SEAL)

Clem. Read

Sample of the typed marriage bond on file at the
Courthouse, giving the original wording on the
early bonds.

"The Courthouse" Lunenburg County, Virginia
1827

Courtesy of the Altar Guild,
St. Paul's Episcopal Church
Kenbridge, Virginia

Lunenburg County formed from Brunswick 1746

Halifax 1752	Bedford 1754	Charlotte 1765	Mecklenburg 1765
Pittsylvania 1767	Campbell 1782		
Henry 1777	Franklin 1786		
Patrick 1791			

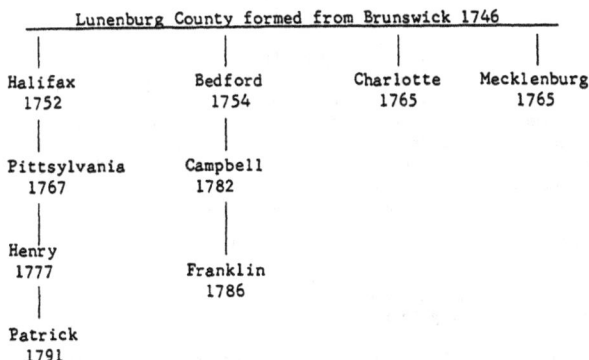

From the above chart, one can see at a glance the territory comprising Lunenburg County in 1746. The early marriages in this book cover the above area.

The existing marriage register of Lunenburg, 1746-1850, is in the form of an index with only the names of the contracting parties and the dates of marriages recorded. In copying this information from the original bonds, or from the typed copy thereof, a number of years ago, the compiler of this register omitted the names of the sureties, witnesses, and other genealogical information. The researcher experiences difficulty in finding a marriage in Lunenburg County as this so-called register is not set up in an organized manner. Apparently it was intended to be in alphabetical order, but as the years rolled by, not enough space was allowed for the many marriages to be added, and as a result, there are, for instance, two pages of "A's" then "H" continued from page 34, then "G" continued from 151, followed by more "A's" with two entries of "S's" at the bottom of the page, etc. A note written in front states, "Look all the way through this register" which means just that. The microfilm is in four sections according to dates, and each section starts with page 1, which explains why a marriage in 1750 is page 1, and a marriage in 1850 might also be page 1. The marriages found in the Will Books are minister's returns only. It is believed that the marriage bonds and/or licenses were recorded from loose papers a number of years after the event took place, and that some were not recorded at all. The copyist recorded a marriage wherever space allowed and therefore we have today an incomplete marriage register which makes it a difficult source for research.

The original marriage bonds are missing. In 1926 when Landon C. Bell wrote the history of Lunenburg County, The Old Free State, he mentioned that some of the early bonds were not extant. There are typed copies of approximately 1500 bonds on file in the Clerk's office, but the original bonds cannot be found. It was from these typed copies that the present compilers checked the marriages as recorded in the marriage register. These typed bonds enabled the compilers to include additional information to the marriages such as the names of the sureties, witnesses, and in some cases, the names of the parents, all of which help to identify the family.

About 1780 a law was enacted requiring ministers to submit to the court a list of marriages performed by them within the three months just past. However, the law was not strictly enforced, as we find some ministers very lax in making their returns. In some cases, the returns were dated a number of years after the ceremony was performed, thus accounting for the differences in names and dates between the Marriage Register and the Minister's Return, indicating that the minister recorded his marriages mostly from memory. A good example of this is a note written to the Clerk of the Court by Rev. Daniel Petty:

> "P.S. In examining my license I find that some copies in the above list bear a date which would have justified their being returned sooner but not having my return mark on them I could not depend on my memory. I therefore concluded to send them on in the list it being the most certain way to remove the doubt." [W.B. 13, page 15]

This was true also of some of the other ministers serving Lunenburg. Rev. Charles Ogburn returned a list with the first marriage dated 1795 and the last marriage on his long list dated 1831. Ministers' Returns were accurate in many instances, and are valuable records, especially when the marriage license or bond is missing.

The researcher will note that many discrepancies exist between Old Free State and this compilation due to different interpretation of the illegible handwriting. One example is the name Moon and Moor(e). It was difficult to distinguish between the "n" and the "r". Most of the serious discrepancies between the bond, the marriage index, and the minister's return, are brought to the attention of the reader. In some cases the spellings of names were corrected by the compilers through tax records and other sources. For this reason both the Marriage Register page number is given, as well as the Will Book reference.

In order to include all extant marriages, Will Book No. 3 to Will Book No. 14 were searched page by page for all marriages reported by the ministers which might not be included in the register. Deed Books were also examined for marriage contracts. A few such marriages were found in both books of records.

St. John's Church Register 1831-1948 is extant and the early marriages recorded therein, which were not found in the marriage index, are included in this book. St. John's Church is no longer in existence, but this register has been preserved by a Board of Trustees. Mr. William Neblett, a member of this board was kind enough to permit the compilers to bring the original register to the Virginia State Library where a photostat copy was made, thus preserving this old record, and making it available to more people.

The names of the Sureties were taken from the typed marriage bond, and in some cases, from Bell's The Old Free State. Apparently Mr. Bell had more information available to him in 1926 than now exists, and any name connected with a marriage can be an important clue.

(ii)

Mr. William Armstrong Crozier in his Early Virginia Marriages, about 50 marriage records from Lunenburg, some of which includes the parents' names as taken from letters of consent. This would indicate that Mr. Crozier also had information which is not extant today.

The compiling of all the information from these various sources into one marriage record makes for a more valuable instrument, and a more accurate record than now exists. All possible spellings of a name are grouped in alphabetical order according to the first name. There were many apparent errors in the existing records, and the compilers have no doubt added a few of their own in compiling over 2400 marriages. However, care has been taken and corrections and additions can still be made. The compilers invite the reader to submit any information, properly documented, which will make this record more complete and accurate. It is the hope that this might be the beginning of a true marriage register for Lunenburg County, Virginia.

By 1853, the Bureau of Vital Statistics came into being, and the County Clerk was required to submit to that agency a list of marriage licenses as issued by the Court Clerk. Not all such licenses for 1853 are on file at the Bureau for Lunenburg. Therefore, the compilers included the entire year in this publication.

Our appreciation is extended to Mr. W. R. Moore, Clerk of Circuit Court of Lunenburg County, and to Mrs. Grace T. Marshall, Deputy Clerk, for their courtesy and cooperation, and for their continued interest in the preservation of Lunenburg's records and history.

Emma R. Matheny

September 1967   Helen K. Yates

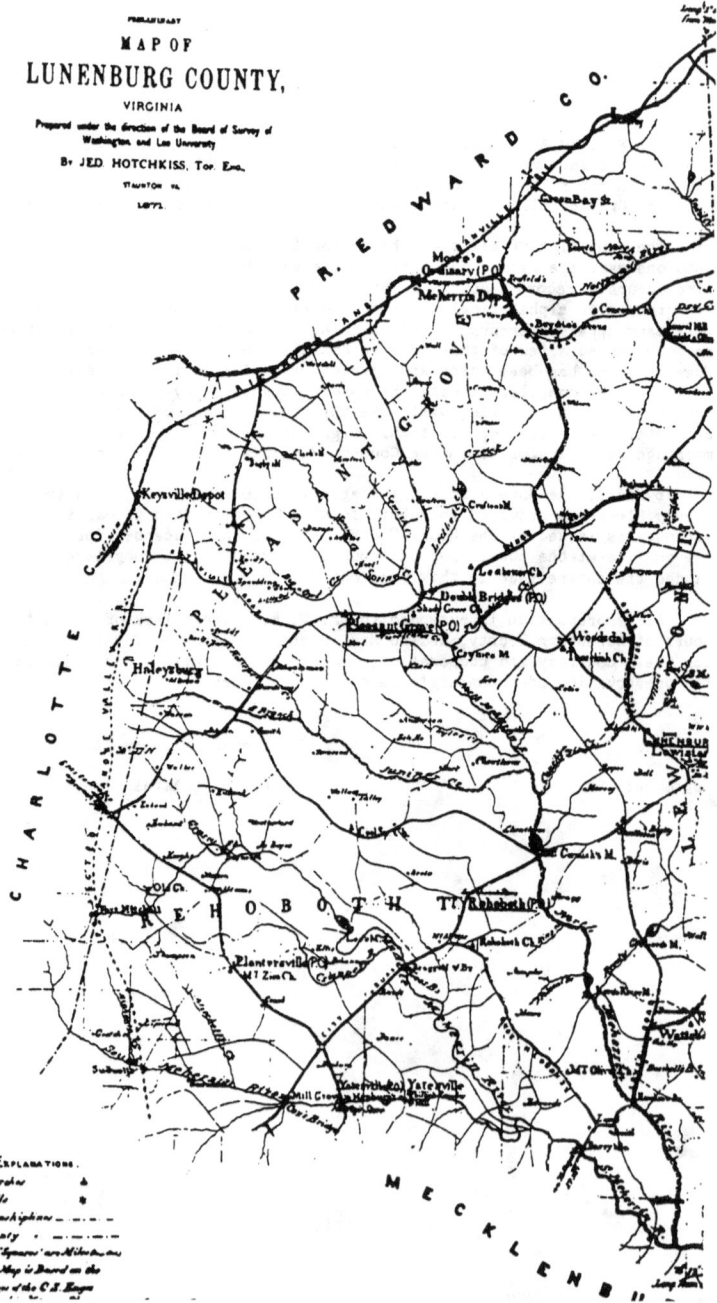

PRELIMINARY

MAP OF
LUNENBURG COUNTY,
VIRGINIA

Prepared under the direction of the Board of Survey of
Washington and Lee University

By JED. HOTCHKISS, Top. Eng.

STAUNTON VA.

1871.

PRINCE EDWARD CO.

CHARLOTTE CO.

MECKLENBURG

EXPLANATIONS.

Churches
Mills
Township lines
County
The "Squares" are Milestones
The Map is Based on the
Surveys of the C.S. Engrs

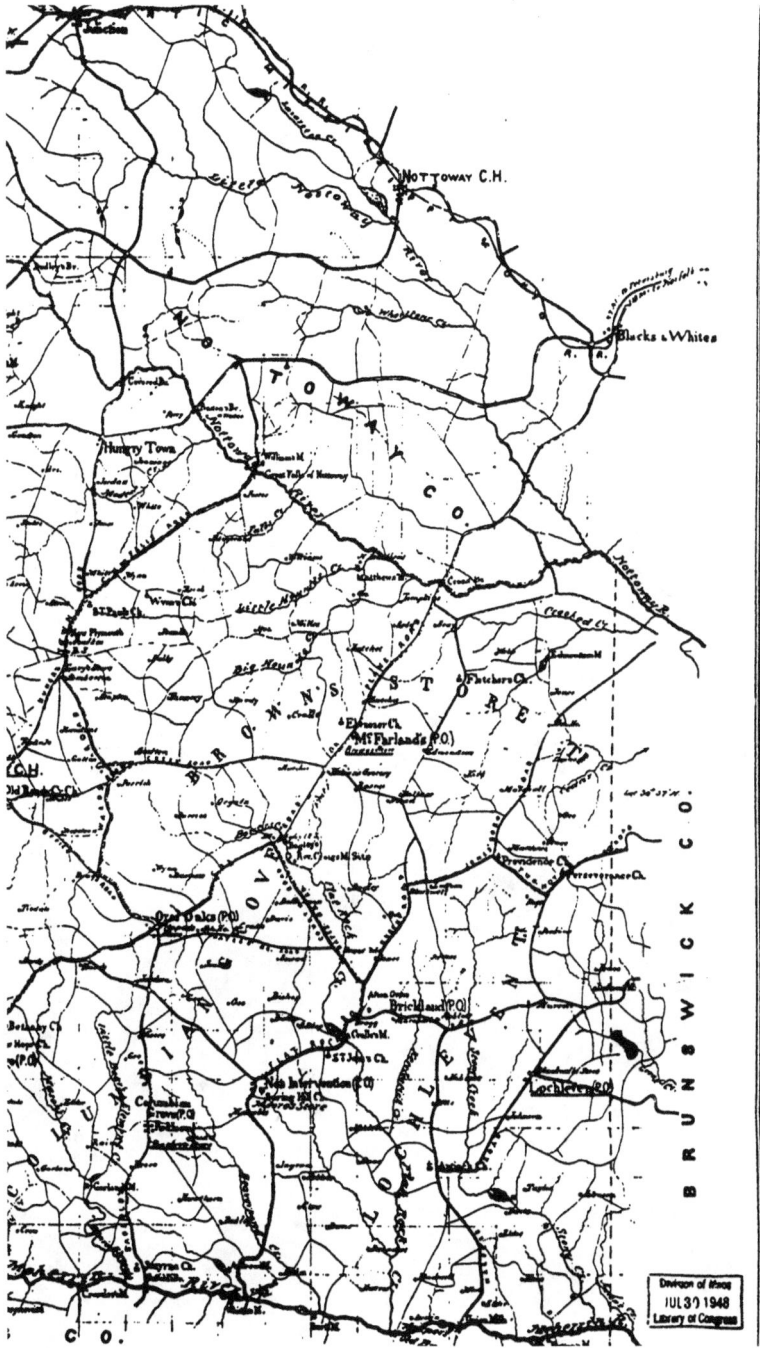

MARRIAGES
of
LUNENBURG COUNTY, VIRGINIA
1746 - 1853

ADAMS, James of Lunenburg, and Nancy Clarke, 22 February 1814. Sur. George
Clarke. Married 23 February 1814 by James Shelburne. p.29 and WB 7/110.

ADDAMS, John of Lunenburg County and Susannah Wood, spinster, daughter of
Richard Wood, dec'd, 22 _____ 1756. Sur. Richard Wilkins and
William Jones. p. 1.

ADAMS, William C. and Mary Ann Poultney, 23 November 1824. Sur. Thomas L.
Poultney. Married 25 November 1824 by Matthew M. Dance. p. 37 and
WB 8/479.

ADIN, John and Rebecca White. Married 11 November 1802 by James Shelburne.
WB 6/29.

AIKINS, John and Elizabeth A. White, 10 April 1848. Sur. John T. Dowdy.
Married 12 April 1848 by W. S. Wilson. p. 65 and WB 13/220.

AKIN, Jos. and Susan Crafton. Married 5 December 1805 by William Ellis.
WB 6/136.

ALDAY, Josiah of Lunenburg, and Anne Womack, daughter of Richard Womack,
14 January 1760. Sur. Richard Womack and Thomas Read. p. 3.

ALDERSON, John L. [or S.] and Sarah Estes. Married 15 January 1801 by
William Ellis. WB 5/67.

ALDERSON, Josiah and Alley Estes, 11 July 1803. Sur. Elisha Estes.
Married by Joel Johns 12 July 1803. p. 19 and WB 6/76.

ALDERSON, Richard and Elizabeth Crafton, 8 January 1807. Sur. Richard
Crafton, Sr. Married 27 January 1807 by William Ellis. p. 23 and
WB 6/187.

ALLEN, Charles and Betty Frith, widow, 8 February 1757. Sur. Thomas Nash
and Nath'l Terry. p. 1.

ALLEN, Charles and Lucy Bacon, spinster, daughter of Lyddal Bacon, Gent.,
7 September 1759. Sur. James Taylor and Thomas Read. p. 1.

ALLEN, James and Rebecca Allen, 26 November 1804. Sur. Jones Allen.
Married 28 November 1804 by Charles Ogburn. p. 19 and WB 10/181.

ALLEN, James of Brunswick County, and Polly Denton, 31 December 1811.
Sur. William Allen. Married 31 December 1811 by Thomas Adams.
p. 23 and WB 7/40.

ALLEN, Jno. J. and Emily C. Fowlkes, 30 November 1844. Sur. John R. Carter.
Married 18 December 1844 by William Wilson. p. 59 and WB 12/219.

ALLEN, Jones and Dorothy Gee, 21 November 1808. Sur. Jas. S. Gee.
Married November 1808 by Thomas Adams. p. 23 and WB 6/254.

ALLEN, Robert H. and Ann E. Bagley, 24 October 1836. Sur. George L.
Bagley. p. 49.

ALLING, John and Rebeckah Scott. Married 25 November 1794 by James
Shelburne. WB 4/107.

ALMOND, Austin and Nancy Sammons. Married 4 February 1805 by John
Robertson. WB 6/147.

ALMOND, David of Lunenburg, and Polly J. Williams, 8 December 1814.
Sur. John Knight. p. 27.

ALMOND, Elisha G. W. and Delia Barnes, 11 December 1843. Sur. Pleasant
Barnes. p. 57.

ALMOND, Phineas E. and Mary Susan Harding, daughter of John Harding,
8 September 1851. Elisha G. Almond, witness. p. 5.

ALMOND, Thomas and Elizabeth Wood, 28 February 1802. Sur. Benjamin G.
Tatom. Married 2 March 1802 by Edward Almond. p. 17 and WB 6/83.

AMBROSE, William and Elizabeth Parrish, 11 June 1804. Sur. Samuel Skinner.
Married 12 June 1804 by John Neblett. p. 19 and WB 6/124.

AMOS, George and Anny Bentley, 8 October 1807. Sur. James Hammack.
Married October 1807 by Thomas Adams. p. 21 and WB 6/254.

ANDERSON, Christopher and Polly Harding, 13 August 1812. Sur. John D.
Bayne. Married 19 August 1812 by James Shelburne. p. 25 and WB 7/124.

ANDERSON, Christopher and Eliner Couch, 11 January 1830. Sur. Thomas H.
Staples. Married 27 January 1830 by Silas Shelburne. p. 43 and WB 10/131.

ANDERSON, Garland and Nancy Hamlett. Married 10 October 1807 by William
Ellis. WB 6/207.

ANDERSON, Thomas and Sarah C. Davis. Married 3 October 1795 by Matthew
Dance. WB 4/146.

ANDREWS, A. and S. Gee. Married 28 November 1816 by Charles Ogburn.
WB 10/181A.

ANDREWS, Abraham and Nancy Waller, 1 December 1817. Sur. Lowry Andrews.
Married 16 December 1817 by Charles Ogburn who reported the marriage
on list of 1832. p. 31 and WB 10/181A.

ANDREWS, Elisha and Susan Waller, 13 March 1826. Sur. Daniel Hazlewood.
Married 14 March 1826 by Joshua Featherston. p. 41 and WB 8/572.

ANDREWS, George W. and Mary W. Morgan, 24 October 1844. Sur. Elisha
Andrews. On list returned to court 8 February 1847 by Daniel Petty,
but the exact date of marriage not shown. p. 59 and WB 13/14

ANDREWS, Jesse and Milly Andrews. Married 7 November 1795 by John Neblett.
WB 4/116A.

ANDREWS, JOHN and Rebecca Malone. Married 13 April 1785 by Thomas Crymes. WB 3/210.

ANDREWS, Lewis R. and Elizabeth G. Stone, 23 January 1821. Sur. David White. Married 23 January 1821 by Baxter Ragsdale. p.31 and WB 8/176.

ANDREWS, Peter and Amy Cooper. Married 12 November 1794 by John Neblett. WB 4/88.

ANDREWS, Richard J. and M. Cole. Married 31 October 1816 by Charles Ogburn. WB 10/181-A.

ANDREWS, William M. and Sarah E. Street, 7 June 1848. Sur. Peter Street. Married 7 June 1848 by Thomas Adams. p.65 and WB 13/232.

ANDREWS, William S. and Mary Jane Hawthorn, both of Lunenburg, 21 December 1852. On her certificate proved by oath of William A. Andrews, a witness thereto, who made oath that she was 21 years of age. Henry C. Hawthorn, Trustee. p. 11 and DB 35/350.

APPERSON, Jonathan and Elizabeth Moon, 12 February 1830. Sur. Mason Moore. Married 16 February 1830 by Joshua Featherston whose return states Elizabeth Moore. p. 43 and WB 10/101.

ARMS, Robert and Sarah Crafton, 13 February 1837. Sur. Richard Crafton. Married 23 February 1837 by Pleasant Barnes. p.53 and WB 11/281.

ARNOLD, James and Martha Reese. Married 19 October 1802 by John Neblett. WB 6/11-A.

ARNOLD, John J. and Elizabeth C. Tomlinson, 1 October 1823. Married 3 October 1823 by Charles Ogburn who reported the marriage in 1832. Sur. Thomas B. Tomlinson. p.35 and WB 10/181.

ARNOLD, Spencer and Sally H. Freeman. Married September 1820 by Thomas Adams. WB 8/151.

ARVIN, John and Catharine D. Johns, 3 January 1829. Sur. John A. Johns. p. 43.

ARVIN, Langston and Ellen [Elenor] Bayn, 12 February 1838. Sur. George L. Bayne. Married 28 February 1838 by James M. Jeter. p.53 and WB 11/328.

ARVIN, Thomas and Mary Jane Byng, 8 December 1834. Sur.Samuel Pettus. p.47.

ARVIN, William and Nancy J. Blackwell. Married 20 September 1832 by Silas Shelburne. WB 11/2.

ASHWORTH, Jonathan S. and Martha A. Wallace, 15 December 1851. On certificate of Susan J. Ashworth, his mother, proved by oath of Parks E. Ashworth, and on certificate of Martha A. Wallace the fact of her being 21 years of age, being proved by oath of said Parkes E. Ashworth, a witness thereto. p. 7.

ASHWORTH, William N. and Permelia Ann Bailey, 26 January 1849. Sur. Bryant
P. Franklin. Married 1 February 1849 by William S. Wilson. p.67 and
WB 13/353.

ATKINS, Abbie and Lucy Freeman, 14 September 1807. Sur. John Freeman.
Married by Thomas Adams __ September 1807, who gives the name
Abraham Atkins in his return. p.21 and WB 6/254.

ATKINS, Henry and Mary Davis. Married by James Shelburne whose return is
dated 5 May 1786 and states, "from October 1785 to May 1786." WB 3/25.

ATWELL, John B. and Martha F. Smithson, 14 November 1835. Sur. Benjamin
Thackston. Married 16.November 1835 by John Thompson. p.49 and
WB 11/173.

AVERETT, Chappell E. and Mary C. Neal, 10 April 1843. Sur. Alfred H. Hurt.
p. 57.

AVERETT, Henry W. and Sarah Hardy, 11 November 1822. Sur. Joshua Hardy.
Married 17 November 1822 by Silas Shelburne. p. 35 and WB 8/270.

AVERETT, Peter and Elizabeth Clay, daughter of Obed Clay, decd. Thomas
Clay, Trustee. Married 11 Mar. 1817 by James Robertson. DB 24/283
and WB 7/309.

AVERETT, Peter and Elizabeth Bennett. Married 9 March 1820 by James
Robertson. WB 8/99.

AVERETT, Rudd and Sally W. Pamplin, 30 December 1806. Sur. Lew Smithson.
Married 1 January 1807 by James Shelburne. p. 21 and WB 6/231.

AVERETT, Rudd and Harriet Peebles, 21 July 1836. Sur. Hatcher Clark. p.49.

AVORY, Peter and Polly Crymes. Married 7 September 1795 by William Ellis.
WB 4/123-A.

BACON, Edmund Parke and Martha Pettypool. Married 21 November 1782 by
Thomas Crymes. WB 3/131.

BACON, Edmund P. Jr. and Frances E. Winn. Married 17 December 1816 by
Joel Johns. WB 7/346.

BACON, Gillie M. and Elizabeth Rhodes. Married 26 February 1818 by Thomas
Adams. WB 8/67.

BACON, Gillie M. and Mary A. Jones, 13 July 1825. Sur. Jno. T. Street.
Married 14 July 1825 by William Hatchett. p. 39, WB 9/29 and
DB 27/31.

BACON, Lydal and Lucy A. Herring, 13 December 1810. Sur. Peter Stokes.
Married 17 December 1810 by Joel Johns. p. 23 and WB 7/60.

BACON, Richard C. and Mary E. Jordan, 21 January 1817. Sur. William H.
Taylor. Married 21 January 1817 by Stephen Jones. p.31 and WB 7/357.

BAGLEY, Anderson and Sarah C. Fowlkes. Married 20 April 1809 by William Ellis. WB 6/256.

BAGLEY, George L. and Cornelia Ann Elizabeth Adams. Married 11 May 1840 by Joshua Featherston. WB 12/7.

BAGLEY, James and Mary L. Lampkin. Married 23 December 1819 by Thomas Adams. WB 8/67.

BAGLEY, Robert and Lucy E. Garland. Married 26 December 1810 by Thomas Adams. WB 7/39.

BAGLEY, Robert S. and Susan Rives Stokes, 12 May 1851. Susan is daughter of Colin Stokes, "on certification of Colin Stokes, proved before me by oath of John S. Cralle, a witness thereto." p. 4.

BAGLEY, William and Elizabeth B. Hood. Married 29 January 1801 by William Ellis. WB 5/67.

BAGLEY, William M. and Ann M. Gauldin, 14 September 1847. Sur. John B. Gauldin. Married 14 September 1847 by Thomas Adams. p.63 and WB 13/105.

BAILEY, Abraham and Rebecca Cockerham. Married 22 June 1797 by William Ellis. WB 4/179-A.

BAILEY, Armestead W. and Ann K. Clark, 8 March 1847. Sur. Leonard T. Clark. Married 18 March 1847 by S. G. Mason. p. 63 and WB 13/245.

BAILEY, Edwin G. and Mary T. Wallace, 11 December 1851. Mary is daughter of Hugh Wallace, "on certification of her father proved by the oath of William J. Wallace, a witness thereto." p. 6.

BAILEY, German, and Martha J. Harding, 11 February 1835. Sur. Thomas J. Harding. p.47.

BAILEY, Henry and Phoebe Lester. Married 12 November 1796 by William Ellis. WB 4/168.

BAILEY, John and Jincey Hardwick, 13 August 1807. Sur. Joseph Rudd. Married 8 August 1807 by James Shelburne. p.21 and WB 6/231.

BAILEY, John Anderson and Fanny Overby, 29 July 1812. Sur. Edward Overby. Married 29 July 1811 by Thomas Adams. p. 25 and WB 7/40.

BAILEY, John D. and Elizabeth Ann Moore, 11 October 1830 [M.B. endorsement states 16 October 1830]. Sur. Henry Moore. Married by Silas Shelburne. p. 45 and WB 10/131.

BAILEY, Richard H. L. and Lucy Gee, 19 December 1834. Sur. William J. Gee. p. 47.

BAILEY, William H. and Narcissa Williams, 12 December 1842. Sur. Joel T. Collins. p. 55.

BAILEY, William G. and Mary E. Franklin. Married 16 August 1827 by Thomas
H. Jeffress. WB 9/212.

BAILEY, William J. and Nancy Wood. Married 31 October 1816 by James
Shelburne. WB 7/313.

BAKER, Allen E. and Serena C. Sterne, 12 December 1842. Sur. Eurebius
Stone. p.55.

BAKER, George and Amey Williams. Married 21 October 1807 by William Davis.
WB 6/199-A.

BANKS, Paschal and Nancy Daniel, 9 April 1825. Sur. Samuel U. Moore. p.39.

BANKS, William and Nancy Ann Lewis, 23 March 1846. Sur. John Thomas Holmes.
List returned 8 February 1847 by Daniel Petty, but exact date of
marriage not shown. p. 61 and WB 13/14.

BARNES, Asa G. and Missouri C. Bridgeforth, 27 September 1845. Sur. William
H. Maddux. Married 1 October 1845 by John C. Blackwell. p. 61 and
WB 12/286.

BARNES, Enos H. and Sally V. Hardy, 15 July 1850. "On certification of
Vincent Hardy, proved by Cornelius Hardy." p. 1.

BARNES, Francis G. and Eliza B. Weatherford, 20 August 1852. "On her certification proved by the oath of S. Gregory, a witness thereto, sub-
stantiated the fact of her being more than 21 years of age being proved
by the said Gregory." p. 9.

BARNES, George and Eliza Ellis, 14 July 1803. Sur. Richard Ellis, Jr.
Married 21 July 1803 by William Ellis. p. 17 and WB 6/76.

BARNES, John and Henrietta Floyd. Married 22 December 1796 by John Neblett.
WB 4/167-A.

BARNES, Joseph B. and Catharine P. Kelly, 23 October 1824. Sur. Benjamin
Barnes. Married 26 October 1824 by Joshua Featherston. p.37 and WB 8/431.

BARNES, Joshua Francis and Elizabeth Parish, 18 January 1841. Sur. James A.
Inge and Henry S. Parrish. p.55.

BARNES, Pleasant and Polly Shelton, 4 April 1814. Sur. Frederick N.
Robertson. Married 7 April 1814 by James Shelburne. p.29 and WB 7/82.

BARNES, William and Rebecca E. Clarke, 11 December 1837. Sur. Tyra Cooksey.
Married 20 December 1837 by W. S. Wilson. p. 51.

BARROW, Dennis and Nancy Moore, 26 December 1825. Sur. Edward W. Parker.
Married 27 December 1825 by John Doyle. p.39 and WB 8/550.

BARROW, Joseph L. [also shown as John] and Louisa Ann Peace, 25 April 1843.
Sur. Willis H. Peace. p.57.

BARROW, William J. and Virginia C. Hardy, 2 September 1837. Sur. Elisha Hardy. p.53.

BARRY, Josiah and Nancy Wells [or Wills]. Married 13 July 1797 by Matthew Dance. WB 4/233.

BARTLETT, Henry and Patsey Kelly, 26 November 1835. Sur. Nathan Holmes. p.49.

BASBECK, John and Elizabeth Farley. Married December 1788 by James Shelburne. W3 3/345.

BASS, Peter and Narcissa Fowlkes, 7 May 1834. Sur. Robert Fowlkes. p.47.

BATES, Abner and Polley Crafton. Married 23 December 1819 by James · Robertson. WB 8/99.

BATES, Jeremiah and Frances Crafton. Married 26 June 1818 by James Robertson. WB 8/1.

BATES, Pleasant and Rhoda Hood, 3 February 1824. Sur. Robert Hood. Married 4 January 1824 by Pleasant Barnes. [The marriage bond also states 3 February 1824.] p. 37 and WB 8/492.

BATES, William and Petronella W. Justice, daughter of Stephen Justis who was present and gave consent, 2 September 1850. Married 4 September 1850 by William Doswell. p.1 and WB 13/411.

BATTE, James and Tabitha Hamlin. Married by James Shelburne whose return was dated 5 May 1786 and stated marriages performed, "from October 1785 to May 1786. WB 3/252.

BAUGH, John A. and Lucinda Coleman, 7 June 1837. The M.B. states 1836, and the endorsement states 1837. Sur. James J. Jordan. p. 53.

BAYNE, John R. and Ann B. Keeton, 28 August 1844. Sur. Upton A. Edmundson. Married 28 August 1844 by Thomas E. Locke at Robert H. Allen's residence. p. 59 and WB 12/206.

BAYNE, William D. and Polly Coleman, 7 June 1837. Sur. James J. Jordan. p. 53.

BEACH, Branch B. and Mary A.C.S.Ellis, 8 January 1830 [bond states February]. Sur. John E. Overton. p.43.

BEACH, John B. and Judith P. W. Cooksey, 20 December 1824. Sur. Richard Owen. Married 21 December 1824 by James Robertson. p.37 and WB 8/534.

BEARICK, William and Mary George, Married 26 November 1789 by James Shelburne. WB 3/358.

BEARS, Zachariah and Phebe Perkerson [or Perkinson], 15 March 1803. Sur. William Perkinson. Married 16 Mar. 1803 by Joel Johns. p. 17 and WB 6/76.

BEASLEY, Robert of Lunenburg County, and Betty Winningham, spinster, 1 June 1762. Sur. Lodwick Farmer, Thomas Read, and Robert Breedlove. p.3.

BEASLEY, William and Nanny Mills. Married 10 December 1796 by James Shelburne. WB 4/159-A.

BEDFORD, Stephen, Jr. and Francis Walton Peerson, daughter of Charles Pearson, 15 May 1756. Sur. Thomas Bedford, G. Carrington, Jr. and Paul Carrington. p. 1.

BEEVERS, John of Lunenburg County and Francis Willson, 1 November 1790. Sur. Abraham Estes. p.11.

BELL, Adam and Sally M. Stokes. Married 20 March 1809 by Joel Johns. WB 6/264-A.

BELL, Adam and Eliza T. Stokes, 22 March 1836. Sur. John T. Street. p.49.

BELSHER, John and Fanny Willmut. Married by John Chappell whose list was returned to the June Court 1791. WB 4/7A.

BELCHER, Washington and Sally Hardy. Married 25 July 1805 by William Ellis. WB 6/135, 175.

BENNETT, Beriah and Martha Wilson. Married 21 November 1827 by Silas Shelburne. WB 9/480.

BENNETT, Griffin and Kitturah Stone. Married 15 September 1808 by Joel Johns. WB 6/244.

BENNETT, James of Lunenburg County, and Frances Brackett [Brachett in M.B.], 22 January 1811. Sur. Henry Harp. Married 22 January 1811 by Joel Johns. p.23 and WB 7/60.

BENNATT, Richard and Nancy Dagnal, 29 January 1836. Sur. John B. Davis. p.49.

BENTLY, Daniel V. and Sevilenda Saterfield, 16 December 1834. Sur. John C. Epes. Married 18 December 1834 by Pleasant Barnes. p. 47 and WB 11/281.

BENTLEY, Elisha and Martha Smith, 2 September 1818. Minister's name not shown on return to court April 8, 1819. WB 8/38.

BENTLEY, Robert and Catharine Haynes. Married 9 December 1802 by John Neblett. WB 6/11-A.

BENTLY, Robert H. and Clarassa Barnes, 9 January 1843. Sur. Henry LaFoon. Married 11 January 1843 by Willis H. Peace. p. 57 and WB 12/125.

BENTLEY, William and Jane Satterfield, 19 February 1838. Sur. James Satterfield. p.53.

BETHEL, William W. and Catharine Hardy, 5 October 1835. Sur. Charles Cox. Married 15 October 1835 by Joshua Featherston. p.49 and WB 11/156.

BETTS, Barbee and Judith Woodson Knight. Married 6 November 1789 by James Shelburne. WB 3/358.

BETTS, Charles and Martha C. Chambers, 30 December 1814. Sur. Edward Chambers. p.27.

BETTS, Roston and Elizabeth W. Neal. Married 4 August 1808 by James Shelburne. WB 7/3.

BEVIS, Zachariah and Phebe Perkerson, 15 March 1803. Sur. William Perkerson. M.B. 396.

BIASSE, Charles and Mary Estes, 10 August 1803. Sur. Elisha Estes. M.B. 374 and p.17.

BYASSE, John H. and Catharine Elvira Winfree. Married 27 September 1827 by Thomas H. Jeffress. WB 9/212.

BYESSEE, Thomas C. and Martha Jane Fowlkes, 12 March 1838. Sur. Joseph M. Fowlkes. Married 22 March 1838 by Matthew M. Dance. p. 53 and WB 11/336.

BIGGER, David J. and Mary E. Robertson, 18 January 1850. Sur. John S. Bayne. Married 23 January 1850 by William S. Wilson. p.67 and WB 13/353.

BING, George and Elizabeth Ann Robertson, 10 November 1817. Sur. Samuel Pettus. [M.B. shows name as BYNG]. p.31.

BIRCHETT, Edward H. and Pamelia C. Jordan, 18 December 1822. Sur. Richard C. Ellis. Married 19 December 1822 by Silas Shelburne. p.35 and WB 8/270.

BISHOP, Edmund Jr. and Salley Bowers. Sur. Philip H. Bowers. Married __ February 1823 by Thomas Adams. p.35 and WB 8/271.

BISHOP, Edmond and Mary A. Davis, 5 December 1837. Sur. Alfred Bishop. p.51.

BISHOP, Herman and Betsy Neblett. Married 14 March 1793 by John Neblett. WB 4/36-A.

BISHOP, James H. and Sarah F. T. Bowers, 10 March 1851 "on certification of her father, Francis Bowers, proven by the oath of C.C.Bishop." p.4.

BISHOP, Jeremiah and Rebecca Bishop, 24 December 1811. Sur. Edmund Bishop. Married 24 December 1811 by Jesse Brown. p.25 and WB 7/60.

BISHOP, John and Nancy Sydnor. Married 13 February 1799 by John Neblett. WB 5/2A.

BISHOP, Joseph S. and Frances Bowers, 23 December 1824. Sur. Samuel Ragsdale. Married 23 December 1824 by Baxter Ragsdale. p.37 and WB 8/454.

BISHOP, Matthew and Sarrah Singleton, 2 March 1814. Sur. Freeman Winn.
Married 2 March 1814 by Thomas Adams. p.27 and WB 7/248.

BISHOP, Thomas J. and Sally Ferguson, 12 October 1826. Sur. Henry Ferguson.
p.41.

BISHOP, William J. and Francis Leonard, 10 December 1825. Sur. Phillip H.
Bowers. Married 15 December 1825 by Baxter Ragsdale. p.39 and WB 8/572.

BLACK, Godrey and Polly Pollard. Married __ March 1789 by James Shelburne.
WB 3/345.

BLACKWELL, Chapman and Polly Hatchett, 13 March 1806. Sur. Joel Blackwell.
Married 2 April 1806 by William Ellis. p.21 and WB 6/175.

BLACKWELL, Chapman and Prudence R. Rutledge. Married 25 January 1809 by
William Ellis. WB 6/256.

BLACKWELL, Charles M. and Permelia Henry Hardy, daughter of Permelia Hardy,
31 August 1852, "on certification of her mother, proved by the oath of
Cornelius Hardy, a witness thereto." p.9.

BLACKWELL, James G. and Mary R. Williams, 29 November 1830. Sur. Lewis
Blackwell. p.45.

BLACKWELL, James J. and Mary B. Jeffress, 29 March 1836. Sur. Richard J.
Jeffress. p.49.

BLACKWELL, Joel and Sally B. Gunn. Married 24 March 1800 by John Neblett.
WB 5/35.

BLACKWELL, Joel and Martha F. Dance, 19 January 1821 [M.B. states 29 January].
Sur. Matthew M. Dance. p.31.

BLACKWELL, Joel, Jr. and Sally Gunn Blackwell, 24 May 1830. Sur. William
Williams. Married 2 June 1830 by Matthew M. Dance. p.43 and WB 10/130.

BLACKWELL, Joel, Jr. and Jane M. Cralle, 8 August 1836. Sur. William H.
Blackwell. p.49.

BLACKWELL, John and Polly Edmundson. Married 6 July 1796 by John Neblett.
WB 4/133.

BLACKWELL, Paul A. and Martha S. Jones, 10 June 1848. Sur. William Arvin, Jr.
p.65.

BLACKWELL, Robert and Polly Ann Abernathy. Married November 1818 by
Thomas Adams. WB 8/67.

BLACKWELL, Robert and Manerva E. Hardy, 13 December 1830. Sur. Elisha
Hardy. p.43.

BLACKWELL, Stephen J. and Maria W. Winn, 13 July 1829. Sur. Hezekiah
Freeman. p.43.

BLACKWELL, Thomas and Mary Bridgeforth, Married 5 September by John Jones. WB 4/116.

BLACKWELL, Thomas and Susanna Fisher. Married 4 June 1818 by Thomas Adams. WB 8/67.

BLACKWELL, Thomas and Polly A. M. Fisher. Married 23 December 1819 by Thomas Adams. WB 8/67.

BLACKWELL, Thomas and Martha A. Hardy, 9 August 1841. Sur. Robert Blackwell, Jr. Married 9 August 1841 by Joshua Featherston. p.55 and WB 12/54.

BLACKWELL, William Thweatt and Sally O. Penn, 11 July 1853. "Robert Blackwell, her guardian, being present and assenting thereto." p.13.

BLAGRAVE, Henry and Elizabeth Stokes, spinster, 22 July 1756. Sur. William Stokes, Charles Cupples and Clem. Read. p.1.

BLAKE, Edmund and Sarah W. Elmore, 22 May 1834. Sur. Matthew Russell. p.47.

BLANKENSHIP, Thomas and Elizabeth Stone. Married 10 June 1797 by Matthew Dance. WB 4/232-A.

BLUNT, William H. and Panthra A. Garland, 8 May 1843. Sur. Thomas Adams. Married 10 May 1843 by John G. C. Claiborne. p.57 and WB 12/133.

BOHANNAN, David and Elizabeth McLaughlin, 10 November 1803. Sur. Richard Stone. Married 17 November 1803 by William Ellis. p.17 and WB 6/76.

BOHANNON, Joseph and Patty [or Polly] Snead. Married 17 October 1799 by William Ellis. WB 5/22.

BOHANNON, Nathaniel and Sarah Hazlewood. Married 30 November 1797 by William Ellis. WB 4/244.

BOHANNON, Nathaniel and Elizabeth Russell. Married 21 September 1805 by James Shelburne. WB 6/146-A.

BOHANNON, William Anderson and Milly McLaughlin, 12 November 1803. Sur. Alex. Winn. Married 15 December 1803 by William Ellis. p.17 and WB 6/76.

BOHANNON, William N. and Ann J. Rash, 28 December 1847. Sur. William H. Brown. Married 30 December 1847 by Thomas Adams. p.63 and WB 13/232.

BOLLIN [Bolling], Robert and Nancy Blackwell. Married 22 December 1819 by Thomas Adams. WB 8/67.

BOLLING, Robert and Mary A. E. Stokes, 4 August 1829. Sur. James Baker. Married 6 August 1829 by Thomas H. Jeffress. p. 41 and WB 9/483.

BOLLING, Thomas of Lunenburg County and Eliza Williams, 14 February 1811.
Sur. Haynie Hatchett. p. 23.

BOOTH, John and Clarissa H. Lamb, 19 June 1826. Sur. Samuel Pettus.
Married 27 June 1826 by Silas Shelburne. p. 41 and WB 9/161.

BOOTHE, Nathaniel and Wineford Morgain. Married 4 April 1795 by John Neblett.
WB 4/88.

BOOTH, Patrick and Mary S. Saunders, 6 November 1824. Sur. William Frame.
Married 12 November 1824 by William Richards. p.37 and WB 8/550.

BOOTH, Robert and Susanna Tucker. Married 7 September 1819 by Baxter
Ragsdale. WB 8/96.

BOOTH, Thomas and Elizabeth Ragsdale, 13 December 1825. Sur. Mark Mize.
Married 20 December 1825 by Baxter Ragsdale. p.39 and WB 8/572.

BOSE, Hardy and Peggy Brooks, 25 December 1792. Sur. Minor Winn. p.13.

BOSWELL, Henry E. and Henryetta E. Yates, 14 October 1850. "On certification of her father, J. Murray Yates, Sr., proved by oath of William
T. Couch." p.2.

BOSWELL, John and Barbary Walker. Married 28 October 1797 by Matthew
Dance. WB 4/233.

BOSWELL, John J. and Nancy Coleman. Married 24 November 1818 by Matthew
Dance. WB 8/59.

BOSWELL, Joseph and Mary Jane Love, 11 November 1844. Sur. Jordan R.
Hardy. Married 23 November 1844 by Chester Bullard. p.59 and
WB 12/246.

BOULDIN, James of Lunenburg County, and Sarah Watkins, daughter of William
Watkins, 24 January 1761. Sur. William Watkins. p. 3.

BOULDIN, John and Patsey Brown Lampkin, 1 May 1805. Sur. Peter Lamkin.
Married 2 May 1805 by Rev. Dabbs. p. 21 and WB 6/193.

BOAEN [Bowen], Harrison and Mary Turner, 26 December 1821. Sur. Branch
Turner. p. 33

BOWEN, Irby S. and Susan Turner, 24 December 1833. Sur. David Harper. p.45.

BOWERS, Benjamin B. and Mary Seamore, 28 October 1845. Sur. Samuel W.
Snead. Married 29 October 1845 by William J. Norfleet. p.61 and
WB 12/310.

BOWERS, Francis and Angelina Bishop, 24 December 1829. Sur. Joseph Bishop.
Married 24 December 1829 by Baxter Ragsdale. p.43 and WB 10/71.

BOWERS, Giles and Ruthe Vaughan. Married 30 November 1797 by John Neblett.
WB 4/231-A.

BOWERS, John and Frances Dodd. Married 27 January 1816 by Thomas Adams. WB 7/249.

BOWERS, Philip H. and Permelia [or Pamela] Bishop, 5 November 1821. Sur. Joseph S. Bishop. Married November 1821 by Thomas Adams. p.33 and WB 8/209.

BRADSHAW, John and Mary Ann Elizabeth Barton. Married 11 July 1811 by Joel Johns. WB 7/60.

BRAGG, David B. and Sally G. Keeton. Married by Daniel Petty whose list is dated 8 June 1840. WB 11/415.

BRAGG, James and Lory Slaughter. Married 24 June 1815 by James Shelburne. WB 7/227.

BRAGG, Joel and Polly Ingram. Married 11 May 1797 by Matthew Dance. WB 4/181-A.

BRAGG, Robert W. and Minerva C. S. Orgain. Married 27 February 1828 by Littleberry Orgain. WB 9/240.

BRAGG, William and Unity Crenshaw, 19 December 1814. Sur. Richard Knott. p. 29.

BRAME, John J. and Martha J. M. Crenshaw, 12 June 1843. Sur. John A. H. Rutherford. Married 25 June 1843 by Chester Bullard. p.57 and WB 12/145.

BRANAGIN, John P. of Lunenburg and Lucy F. Branch, 14 December 1813. Sur. Cyrus Pond. Married 15 December 1813 by James Robertson. p. 27 and WB 7/124.

BRASEL, Charles and Mary Estes. Married 11 August 1803 by Joel Johns. WB 6/76.

BREEDLOVE, Benjamin and Mary Worsham, widow, 20 February 1762. Sur. Clement Read. p.3.

BRENT, John of Lunenburg County, and Margaret Caldwell, spinster, 2 June 1762. Sur. Paul Carrington, David Caldwell and Thomas Read. p.3.

BRIDE, Charles and Pamelia F. Staples. Married 19 April 1832 by Silas Shelburne. WB 11/2.

BRIDGEFORTH, George and Sallie A. Seay, daughter of George N. Seay, 19 November 1851. p.6.

BRIDGEFORTH, John and Elizabeth Christopher, 18 June 1821. Sur. Thomas Bridgeforth. Married 26 June 1821 by John Doyle. p.31 and WB 8/193.

BRIDGEFORTH, William L. and Frances W. Maddux, 29 August 1842. Sur. Enos H. Barnes. Married 1 September 1842 by John G. C. Claiborne. p.55 and WB 12/133.

BRIM, James and P. Russell. Married 21 August 1809 by Charles Ogburn. WB 10/181-A.

BRINTLE, James and Faithy Laffoon, __ December 1804. Sur. Matthew Lafoon. p. 19.

BRIZENTINE, Leroy and Lucy Barnes. Married 16 January 1789 by Thomas Crymes. WB 3/342.

BROOKS, Hurley and Jerusha Carreer. Married 17 December 1781 by Thomas Crymes. WB 3/104.

BROOKS, James R. and Elizabeth Chandler. Married 6 January 1810 by Hezekiah W. Lelland. WB 7/1A.

BROWDER, George E. and Judith R. Hawthorne, 17 September 1849. Sur. Edward Barrow. p.67.

BROWDER, Isham and Martha W. Burnett, 5 December 1836. Sur. Osborn Burnett. Married 8 December 1836 by Joshua Featherston. p. 49 and WB 11/182.

BROWDER, Urias and Susan M. Matthew. Married 10 December 1839 by Joshua Featherston. WB 12/7.

BROWN, Aaron J. J. and Caroline A. B. Edmondson, 28 October 1848. Sur. Reves Connally. p. 65.

BROWN, Alexander S. and Abigail C. Rash, daughter of Robert Rash, 22 November 1852, "on certification of her father, proved by the oath of P. H. Rainey, a witness thereto." p. 11.

BROWN, Daniel and Charlotte Conner. Married 9 February 1797 by John Neblett. WB 4/232A.

BROWN, George and Elizabeth Winn. Married 6 December 1792 by John Neblett. WB 4/36.

BROWN, James and P. Brown. Married 25 January 1808 by Charles Ogburn whose return was recorded in June 1832. WB 10/181.

BROWN, James S. and Nancy Brown, 6 December 1825. Sur. Daniel H. Robertson. p.39.

BROWN, John and Annie Willson, Married 8 September 1805 by James Shelburne. WB 6/146-A.

BROWN, Joseph C. and Martha N. Stephenson. Married 26 April 1827 by John Thompson. WB 9/292.

BROWN, Joshua C. and Sally C. Mallory, 9 April 1812. Sur. Aberry B. Ward. Married 10 April 1812 by Matthew Dance. p. 25 and WB 7/60.

BROWN, Noah and Mary M. Marable. Married 14 November 1815 by James Shelburne. WB 7/227.

BROWN, Paschal and Nancy Smith, 13 September 1824. Sur. Montfort S. Bacon. Married 15 September 1824 by Baxter Ragsdale. p.37 and WB 8/454.

BROWN, Robert and Ann Overby, 18 February 1823. Sur. George Overby. Married 18 February 1823 by Baxter Ragsdale. p.35 and WB 8/336.

BROWN, Shadarack of Lunenburg County, and Mary Nance, daughter of John Nance, 23 May 1761. Sur. William Nance. p.3.

BROWN, Thomas and Anna Jordan. Married 6 December 1800 by James Shelburne. WB 5/51.

BROWN, Thomas and Lucy Willson, 14 November 1804. Sur. Joshua Smith. Married 22 November 1804 by James Shelburne. p.19 and WB 6/147.

BROWN, Washington and Caroline Lester, 27 December 1847. Sur. Elijah J. Lester. Married 28 December 1847 by William S. Wilson. p.63 and WB 13/220.

BROWN, William of Lunenburg County and Sarah Wells, widow, 27 October 1762. Sur. Joel Towns and T. Read. p.3.

BROWN, William and Sarah Forlin Winn. Married 10 August 1797 by John Jones. WB 4/209.

BROWN, William and Ann Elizabeth Maddux. Married 4 February 1820 by Stephen Jones. WB 8/96.

BROWN, William and Delila Weatherford. Married 20 December 1827 by George Petty. WB 9/250.

BROWN, William W. and Jane Christopher, 11 December 1843. Sur. Washington Christopher. p.57.

BRUBB, Thomas and Patty Slaughter. Married 24 September 1809 by James Shelburne. WB 7/3.

BRUCE, Armistead and Susan P. Jeffress. Married 2 December 1818 by Joel Johns. WB 8/357.

BRUCE, Edward and Harriott Poultney, 30 January 1823. Sur. Thomas L. Poultney. p.35.

BRUCE, Robert L. and Diniaha (?) B. Johns, daughter of John A. Johns, 25 October 1853, "on certification of her father, proved by the oath of Martin Barnes, a witness thereto." p.14.

BRUCE, Samuel A. and Jamenia J. Bayn. Married 16 February 1831 by Silas Shelburne. WB 11/2.

BRUCE, Samuel B. and Mary E. Carter, 18 September 1826. Sur. John Fowlkes. Married 19 September 1826 by Silas Shelburne. p.41 and WB 9/161.

BRUCE, William and Elizabeth Ann Hayes, 11 January 1830. Sur. Robert Hayes. Married 12 March 1831 by Daniel Petty. p.43 and WB 10/119.

BRUMMER, John and Susanna Johns, 22 December 1817. Sur. Thomas B. Ellis.
    p. 31.

BRYANT, Stephen and Susan Webb. Married 26 December 1816 by Baxter
    Ragsdale. WB 7/383.

BRYANT, Tazewell and Narcissa J. Minor, 15 February 1836. Sur. Joel M.
    Parrish. Married by Daniel Petty whose list was dated 10 October
    1836. p. 49 and WB 11/179.

BRYDIE, Robert B. and Lucretia F. Maddux, daughter of Samuel Maddux,
    18 February 1852, "on certification of her father proved by the oath
    of Richard M. White a witness thereto." p. 8.

BUCKHANNON, Francis and Betsey Ann Pyle, 2 October 1821. Sur. George Pyle.
    Married 4 October 1821 by Thomas H. Jeffress. p.33 and WB 8/193.

BUCKNALL, John and Henrietta W. Brown, daughter of George Brown, 23 De-
    cember 1817. Sur. George Brown. Married 23 December 1817 by
    Stephen Jones. p.31 and WB 7/357.

BUCKNER, George W. and Mary S. Reese, 8 November 1851, "the fact of her
    being more than 21 years of age being proved by the oath of John G.
    Laffoon." p.6.

BUCKNER, James Hicks and Polly Kirk. Married __ December 1807 by Thomas
    Adams. WB 6/253A

BUCKNER, Matthew and Delphia Laffoon, 7 August 1823. Sur. William Lafoon.
    Married 9 August 1823 by John Doyle. p.37 and WB 8/316.

BUCKNER, William and Nancy Davis. Married 27 March 1796 by John Neblett.
    WB 4/127.

BUFORD, Edward and Margarett A. Tucker, Married 30 November 1831 by Joshua
    Featherston. WB 10/151A.

BUFORD, Gabriel and Susan Jackson, 14 May 1807. Sur. Drury A. Bacon.
    Married 18 July 1807 by William Ellis. p.21 and WB 6/208.

BUFORD, Larkin W. and Mary T. Bacon, 25 September 1843. Sur. William C.
    Snead. p.57.

BUFORD, William R. and Emma Jane Hardy, 4 October 1837. Sur. Elisha Hardy.
    p.51.

BUGG, Samuel and Ann Hix, spinster, 1 June 1757. Sur. Amos Hix and G.
    Carrington, Jr. p. 1.

BUGG, William S. and Amanda B. Piller [or Puller], 8 February 1847. Sur.
    John W. Piller. Married "about the middle of February 1847" by
    Thomas Adams. p.63 and WB 13/105.

BULLARD, Chester and Sophia A. Stone, 1 November 1842. Sur. William A.
    Stone. p.57.

BURGE, Tazewell T. and Rebeccah Tisdale, 9 July 1812. Sur. John Tisdale. Married 29 July 1812 by Matthew Dance. p.25 and WB 7/60.

BURK(E), Abner H. and Mary E. White, 20 May 1848. Sur. William M. White. Married 25 May 1848 by William S. Wilson. p.65 and WB 13/220.

BURK, Adolphus T. and Jane Crafton, daughter of Frederick Crafton, 27 September 1848. Sur. John E. Clark. Married 28 September 1848 by William Doswell. p.65 and WB 13/223.

BURNETT, Forester and Martha Andrews, 12 May 1814. Sur. Nevel Gee. Married 17 May 1814 by Charles Ogburn. p.27 and WB 10/181.

BURNETT, Jeremiah and Diana Davis, 19 December 1804. Sur. William Davis. Married 19 December 1804 by William Davis. p.19 and WB 6/135.

BURNETT, Joel and Sarah Flinn, 1 March 1834. Sur. George L. Rogers. p.47.

BURNETT, Joel and Margaret J. Elder, 18 December 1843. Sur. John Elder. p.57.

BURNETT, John and Mary H. Hurt, 22 November 1821. Sur. Allen Hurt. Married 27 November 1821 by Silas Shelburne. p.31 and WB 8/227.

BURNETTE, Lazarus L. and Elizabeth Edmunds. Married 26 November 1840 by Joshua Featherston. WB 12/7.

BURNETT, Leroy and Ann H. Keats. Married 12 February 1819 by Francis Smith. WB 8/96.

BURNETT, Nicholas B. and Mary Byassee, 1 December 1837. Sur. Leonard Goodwyn. Married 1 December 1837 by Baxter Ragsdale who states Nicholas E. Burnett. p.51 and WB 11/266.

BURNETTE, Osborn L. and Sarah A. E. Ussery, 30 July 1834. Sur. Thomas H. Vaughan. p.47.

BURNETTE, Robert and Cloe Maddux. Married 30 May 1800 by John Neblett. WB 5/35.

BURNETT, Samuel J. and Mary J. Garland, 9 September 1844. Sur. Peterson Goodwyne. p.59.

BURNETTE, William and Martha W. Hurt, 28 June 1822. Sur. Allen Hurt. Married 2 July 1822 by Silas Shelburne. p.33 and WB 8/270.

BURNETT, Zachariah D. and Mary R. Floyd, 21 April 1841. Sur. William D. Floyd. Married by Daniel Petty whose list was returned to Court dated 8 February 1847. p.55 and WB 13/14.

BURTON, Peter and Ann Mason, Married 14 November 1793 by James Shelburne. WB 4/45A.

BURTON, Peter and Petronella F. Craghead, 7 April 1821. Sur. William Craighead. Married 17 April 1821 by Silas Shelburne. p.31 and WB 8/140,227.

BUSH, George and Deliah Filboid. Married 7 May 1789 by Thomas Crymes. WB 3/342.

BUSTER, Josiah L. and Keziah F. Johnson, 24 February 1825. Sur. Robert Pewett. p.39.

CABINESS, Asa of Lunenburg County, and Sally Bacon of Lunenburg, 7 July 1788. Sur. Francis Bacon. p.9.

CABINESS, Asa of Lunenburg County and Eliza Bruce, 5 November 1814. Sur. William S. Clarke. p.27.

CABANESS, Charles and Nancy Hayes, 8 October 1803. Sur. William Taylor. p.17.

CABANESS, Sterling and Polly W. Ingram, 16 December 1817. Sur. Silvanius Ingram. Married __ December 1817 by Thomas Adams. p.29 and WB 7/356.

CABANISS, William and Rebecca Russell, 22 December 1817. Sur. Richard H. Gill. p.29.

CAIN, Alfred and Abbey Edmunds, 11 January 1837. Sur. Wilkins Edmunds. p.51.

CALIB, Benjamin Reives and Mary Pinnel, 21 July 1763. Sur. William Gee. p.3.

CALLIHAM, David of Lunenburg County and Katy Hightower, 9 November 1786. Sur. Richard Hightower. p.7.

CALLAHAM, Henry and Elizabeth Waller, 11 February 1824. Sur. John Callaham. Married 11 February 1824 by Joshua Featherston. p.37 and WB 8/431.

CALLIHAM, James and Susan Mayton. Married 9 November 1831 by Joshua Featherston. WB 10/151-A.

CALLIHAM, John of Lunenburg County, and Nancey Jarrett, 2 April 1792. Sur. Peter Jarrett. p.13.

CALLIHAM, John and Frances George, 8 January 1823. Sur. Thomas B. Green. p.37.

CALAHAM, John W. and Sarena Cole, 19 September 1850, "on certification of Josiah Cole, proved by William H. Cole a subscribing witness." Married 2 October 1850 by William Doswell. p. 1 and WB 13/411.

CALLAHAM, Matthew of Lunenburg County and Molly Callaham, 22 December 1797. Sur. John Ussery. Married 23 December 1797 by John Neblett. p.15 and WB 4/232.

CALLIHAN, Moses and P. Callihan. Married 1 January 1800 by Charles Ogburn whose return is recorded in 1832. WB 10/181-A.

CALLIHAM, Sherrard of Lunenburg County, and Mary Ussery, 3 October 1786. Sur. John Ussery. p. 7.

CALLIS, Abel and Martha Hudson. Married 3 January 1810 by Thomas Adams. WB 7/39.

CALLIS, John and Nancy Moore, 2 January 1804. Sur. James Sturdivant. p.19.

CALLIS, Richard and Barbara Morris. Married 8 May 1800 by John Neblett. W3 5/35.

CALLIS, Robert and Martha Steagall, daughter of Allen Steagall, 3 February 1813. Sur. Allen Stegall. Married 3 February 1813 by Thomas Adams. p.27 and WB 7/248.

CALLIS, Theoplilus and Salley Hudson, 8 December 1812. Sur. Robert Callis. Married 9 December 1812 by Thomas Adams. p.25 and WB 7/248.

CALLIS, Thomas of Lunenburg County, and Elizabeth W. Hite, 31 December 1810. Sur. William L. Hite. Married 1 January 1811 by Thomas Adams. p.23 and WB 7/40.

CAMERON, Ervin of Lunenburg County and Francis Buford, 14 December 1797. Sur. Duncan Cameron. p.15.

CAMP, John and Judith Wagstaff, relict of Francis Wagstaff, dec'd, 22 August 1766. Sur. Francis Sanders and Thomas Read. p.3 and DB 7/26.

CAMPBELL, George J. and Rainey Ames, 6 December 1814. Sur. Raleigh Hammons. Married 7 December 1814 by Thomas Adams. p.29 and WB 7/249.

CAMMEL, John of Lunenburg County, and Rebecca Hammons, 9 November 1796. Sur. Charles Fallin. Married 10 November 1796 by John Neblett. p.13 and WB 4/168.

CANTALOU, Lewis of Lunenburg County, and Alice Crymes, 8 April 1784. Sur. John Glenn. Married 8 April 1784 by James Shelburne. p. 7 and WB 3/169.

CARGILL, Cornelius of Lunenburg County and Judith Walker, widow and relict of Tandy Walker, dec'd, 24 October 1751. Sur. Thomas Nash and Clem Read, both of Lunenburg. p.1.

CARGILL, Cornelius and Hannah Blanks, widow of Thomas Blanks, dec'd, 3 April 1753. Sur. Thomas Nash, L. Claiborne, Jr., James Cary, Jr., James Claiborne, Paul Carrington, and Clem Read. p. 1.

CARGILL, Cornelius and Annie Carrol, 2 December 1761. Sur. Lyddal Bacon, C. Read, Thomas Read, and John Speed, Jr. p.3.

CARDEGILL, James of Lunenburg County and Mary Ann Johnson, 9 June 1785. Sur. Christopher Billups. Married 9 June 1785 by Thomas Crymes. p. 7 and WB 3/214.

CARRINGTON, Paul and Margaret Read, daughter of Clement Read, 25 September 1755. Sur. Thomas Nash and Clem Read. p.1.

CARTER, Francis and Martha Farmer. Married 9 January 1818 by Edward Almond. WB 8/357.

CARTER, Harrison of Lunenburg, and Sally Hatchett, 12 January 1797. Sur. Alexander Lester. Married 26 January 1797 by James Shelburne. p.17 and WB 4/160.

CARTER, John R. and Mary P. Farmer, daughter of Joseph W. Farmer who consents, 21 August 1851. p.5.

CARTER, Josephus and Martha Ann Stokes, 10 December 1838. Sur. John T. Street. p.53.

CARTER, Theodrick of Lunenburg and Sally Ealbank, 10 November 1763. Sur. Jacob Royster. p.3.

CARTER, Thomas and Judith K. Betts. Married 11 November 1819 by Silas Shelburne. WB 8/67.

CARTER, William of Lunenburg County, and Mary Scott, 10 June 1779. Sur. Robert Scott. p.5.

CAUDLE, Lewis of Lunenburg County, and Creesy Taylor, 30 December 1787. Sur. Benjamin Moore. p.9.

CAVENDER, James of Lunenburg County, and Betsy Sammons, 14 March 1793. Sur. James Sammons. Married 14 March 1793 by James Shelburne. p.13 and WB 4/46.

CARVER, W. and R. Russell. Married 25 December 1818 by Charles Ogburn. WB 10/181-A.

CAYCE, Pleasant and Prudence Ellis, 9 October 1829. Sur. Montfort J. Hurt. Married 29 October 1829 by Thomas H. Jeffress. p.41 and WB 9/483.

CHAMBERS, Edward Osborn of Lunenburg County, and Ann Hurt, 8 January 1796. Sur. William White. Married 8 January 1796 by John Neblett. p.15 and WB 4/124.

CHAMBERS, John W. and Nancy C. Poultney, 27 December 1834. Sur. John C. Stokes. Married 29 January 1835 by Mathew M. Dance. p.45 and WB 11/336.

CHANDLER, Manson and Nancy Cheatham, 8 May 1812. Sur. John Cheatham. p.25.

CHANDLER, Martin and Nancy Swinney [or Sweeney], 2 March 1804. Sur. Reuben Skinner. Married 3 March 1804 by Joel Johns. p.19 and WB 6/128.

CHANDLER, Sterling and Lucy Moore. Married 14 December 1809 by Matthew Dance. WB 7/1A.

CHANDLER, Thomas of Lunenburg County, and Sarah Fallin, 21 December 1796. Sur. John Skinner. Married 22 December 1796 by John Neblett. p.15 and WB 4/168.

CHAPPELL, John of Lunenburg and Martha Cross, 4 August 1788. Sur. Peter Lampkin, Jr. p. 9.

CHAPPELL, John C. and Milly Thompson Sandys, 29 July 1812. Sur. David Parrish. p.25.

CHAPPELL, Robert and Salley Garland. Married __ July 1808 by Thomas Adams. WB 6/253-A.

CHAPPELL, Robert, Jr. and Julia A. Jefferson, 23 April 1817. Sur. William G. Pettus. Married __ April 1817 by Thomas Adams. p.31 and WB 7/356.

CHAVERS, James and Sally Valentine, 26 January 1836. Sur. Henry Ragsdale. p.49.

CHAVES, Charles and Lucy Chapman. Married 20 December 1810 by Thomas Adams. WB 7/39.

CHEANY, John L. and Phebe Elam, 3 August 1833. Sur. Willie Ward. p.45.

CHANEY, Jonas and Sarah Harding. Married 30 July 1828 by Thomas H. Jeffress. WB 9/483.

CHEANEY, Philip and Charlotte Lester. Married 27 July 1809 by Edward Almond. WB 7/1.

CHEATHAN, Eleazer and Permelia J. Smithson, 19 August 1836. Sur. Clement Smithson. p.51.

CHEATHAM, James and Barsheba Wood. Married 10.April 1828 by Silas Shelburne. WB 9/480.

CHEATHAM, James and Mary Cheatham, 7 December 1823. Sur. Thomas Cheatham. Married 18 December 1823 by Silas Shelburne. p.35 and WB 8/340.

CHEATHAM, John M. and Elizabeth Overton, 1 June 1829. Sur. Nathaniel Pennington. [In the M.B. the name is shown John W. Cheatham, but the signature is John M. Cheatham.] p. 43.

CHEATHAM, Phineas and Martha W. Smithson, 27 October 1826. Sur. Nicholas Smithson. Married 2 November 1826 by Silas Shelburne. p.41 and WB 9/161.

CHEATHAM, Robert D. and Jane Cheatham, 17 December 1823. Sur. Thomas Cheatham. Married 18 December 1823 by Silas Shelburne. p.35 and WB 8/340.

CHEATHAM, Thomas of Lunenburg County and Polly Rowlett, 21 November 1797. Sur. Field Clark. p.17.

CHEATHAM, Thomas and Mary (Polly) Jordan, 31 January 1825. Sur. Walker Pettus. Married 2 February 1825 by Silas Shelburne. p.39 and WB 8/492.

CHEATHAM, Thomas and Nancy [Mary in Will Book] Cheatham, 15 December 1830. Sur. Thomas Cheatham. Married 15 December 1830 by Silas Shelburne. p. 43 and WB 10/131.

CHEATHAM, William and Elizabeth Epes, 22 December 1834. Sur. Henry Ragsdale. p.47.

CHISLOM, John and Elizabeth Mize, 2 February 1772. Sur. William Chislom.
p.5.

CHITTON, James and Mary E. Johns. Married 5 September 1832 by Silas
Shelburne. WB 11/2.

CHRISTIAN, Thomas and Lucy N. Williams. Married 18 January 1816 by
Thomas Adams. WB 7/249.

CHRISTOPHER, John of Lunenburg County, and Nancey Ussery, 19 December 1787.
Sur. Samuel Ussery. p. 9.

CHRISTOPHER, John and Elizabeth Winn, 19 December 1821. Sur. William
Snead. p.31.

CHRISTOPHER, John M. and Sally Wilkes. Married __ December 1818 by
Thomas Adams. WB 8/67.

CHRISTOPHER, Theodorick L. and Frances Ann Ellett Walker, 11 December 1833.
Sur. Garner Webb. p.45.

CHRISTOPHER, Thomas and Dolly White, 30 August 1814. Sur. Benjamin
Wallace. Married 30 August 1814 by Thomas Adams. p.29 and WB 7/249.

CHUMLEY, James and Lucretia Pully. Married 18 December 1818 by Silas
Shelburne. WB 8/67.

CHUMNEY, Robert B. and Ermin W. Keeton, daughter of Thomas Keeton, 31 January
1852; "on certification of her father and the fact of her being over
21 years of age known by me. --T.W. Winn, Clerk." p.8.

CHUMNEY, Robert B. and Martha L. Keeton, daughter of Thomas Keeton, 13 December 1853. p.15.

CLADWELL, George of Lunenburg County and Isbell Davis, daughter of Joseph
Davis, 23 January 1760. Sur. Robert Woods. M.B. #42.

CLAIBORNE, Richard of Lunenburg County and Mary Cook, 4 July 1786. Sur.
Henry Cooke. Married 9 August 1786 by Thomas Crymes. p.7 and WB 3/263.

CLARDY, James and Nancy Clardy. Married 23 November 1782 by Thomas Crymes.
WB 3/131.

CLARKE, Benjamin and Elizabeth Grear, 26 January 1807. Sur. Philip
Dedman. Married 28 January 1807 by Matthew Dance. p.21 and WB 6/181.

CLARKE, Ellison and Elizabeth W. M. Crymes, 10 November 1823. Sur. C.C.M.
Marable. Married 18 November 1823 by William Hatchett. p.37 and
WB 8/336.

CLARKE, Field and Nancy Keeton. Married 21 March 1816 by James Shelburne.
WB 7/313.

CLARK, George and Amey Smith. Married 2 February 1782 by Thomas Crymes.
WB 3/104.

CLARKE, George and Elizabeth Tisdale, 13 December 1804. Sur. John
Tisdale. Married 16 December 1804 by James Shelburne. p. 19 and
WB 6/147.

CLARK, George W. and Jane Shelton. Married November 1819 by Thomas Adams.
WB 8/67.

CLARKE, Godfrey of Lunenburg and Mary Pollard, 12 March 1789. Sur. James
Harris. p. 11.

CLARK, James H. and Martha J. Crafton, 11 March 1850. Sur. William Townsend and William Keeton. Married 20 March 1850 by William Doswell.
p. 67 and WB 13/375.

CLARKE, Jesse C. and Jane S. Gee, 9 March 1829. Sur. Drury Gee. Married
25 March 1829 by James Smith. p. 43 and WB 10/119.

CLARKE, John of Lunenburg County, and Sally Evans, 19 March 1781. Sur.
William Evans. p. 5.

CLARKE, Joshua and Lucretia Ellis, 3 November 1803. Sur. John Ellis.
Married 3 November 1803 by William Ellis. p. 17 and WB 6/76.

CLARKE, Shaderick of Lunenburg County, and Rebecca Crymes, 11 December
1788. Sur. Thomas Crymes. Married by James Shelburne whose list
was recorded 9 July 1789. p. 9 and WB 3/345.

CLARKE, Shadrack and Polly Johnson. Married 12 April 1810 by James
Shelburne. WB 7/15.

CLARKE, Thomas C. and Susanna Jordan, 9 July 1812. Sur. Field Clark, Jr.
Married 22 July 1812 by James Shelburne. p. 23 and WB 7/124.

CLARKE, Tyree J. and Martha W. Brown, 11 January 1841. Sur. Jesse Brown.
p. 55.

CLAUGHTON, George and Frances Harding, daughter of Thomas Harding, Sr.,
12 June 1817. Sur. Samuel Crawley. p. 31.

CLAYTON, James of Lunenburg, and Milley Murrell, 30 March 1792. Sur. Bailey
George. Married 5 April 1792 by William Ellis. p. 13 and WB 4/28.

CLAYTON [Claughton], Lindsey and Elizabeth Anderson. Married 20 March
1800 by Matthew Dance. WB 5/16-A.

CLEMENTS, Claiborne and Caroline E. Smith, 7 December 1836. Sur. George
S. Smith. Married 21 December 1836 by M. M. Dance. p. 49 and
WB 11/336.

CLEUVERIUS, R. Coleman and Susan G. Lanier, 11 January 1825. Sur. George
Jefferson. Married 18 January 1825 by Silas Shelburne. p. 39 and
WB 8/492.

COCKE, Abraham and Agness May, 11 April 1767. Sur. Thomas Chambers. p. 3.

COCKERHAM, Littlebury of Lunenburg, and Polly Wilks, 11 June 1789. Sur. Phillip Snead. Married by James Shelburne whose list was dated 9 July 1789, exact date of marriage not shown. p. 11 and WB 3/345

COCKERHAM, William Winn of Lunenburg, and Nancy Estes, 20 June 1793. Sur. Matthew Estes. p. 13.

COLE, George of Lunenburg and Mary Singleton Crafton, 9 November 1797. Sur. John Crafton. p. 17.

COLE, James of Lunenburg, and Mary Clarke, 8 June 1781. Sur. Benjamin Edmundson. p. 5.

COLE, James and Martha J. E. Barnes, daughter of Pleasant Barnes, "proved by affirmation of Mastin Barnes," 10 November 1851. p. 6.

COLE, Josiah and Elizabeth Harrison. Married 8 August 1799 by James Shelburne. WB 5/51.

COLE, Nunn and Martha Wood. Married 3 July 1828 by Silas Shelburne. WB 9/480.

COLE, Theodrick N. and Martha Cole, 8 October 1838. Sur. Jonah Cole. p. 53.

COLEMAN, Abel of Lunenburg, and Nancy Priest, 24 April 1787. Sur. Cornelius Priest. Married 26 April 1787 by Thomas Crymes. p. 9 and WB 3/309.

COLEMAN, John L. and Mary Ann Fellia Almond, 11 December 1837. Sur. Thomas F. Hawthorne. p. 51.

COLEMAN, Joshua and Sally P. Estes, 17 October 1826. Sur. Lew A. Tucker. Married 18 October 1826 by Thomas H. Jeffress. p. 41 and WB 9/116.

COLEMAN, Peter W. and Martha C. Almond, 10 September 1838. Sur. John S. Coleman. Married 12 January 1839 by B. R. DuVal. p. 55 and WB 11/354.

COLEMAN, Stephen of Lunenburg, and Sarah Watson, daughter of Matthew Watson, 13 November 1761. Sur. Dudley Barksdale and Thomas Read. p. 3.

COLEMAN, William of Lunenburg, and Martha Allen, 20 February 1797. Sur. Wiltshire G. Pettypool. Married 24 February 1797 by John Neblett. p.15.

COLEMAN, William G. and Cicily J. Ragsdale, 25 November 1826. Sur. Washington Maddux. Married 5 December 1826 by Silas Shelburne. p. 41 and WB 9/161.

COLLIER, Henry of Lunenburg, and Mary Cocke, 11 August 1796. Sur. Michael McKee. Married 17 August 1796 by John Neblett. p. 15 and WB 4/133.

COLLIER, Henry and Jane Parrish. Married 18 October 1798 by John Neblett. WB 5/2.

COLLINS, John and Tabitha Weatherford, 31 Mar. 1830 [M.B. says May and the endorsement says Mar.] Sur. Hillery Weatherford. Married 17 June 1830 by Silas Shelburne. p. 43 and WB 10/131.

COLTER, Samuel and Fanny Buck. Married 23 June 1793 by James Shelburne.
WB 4/46.

COMBS, William of Lunenburg County, and Sally Nance, 10 November 1791.
Sur. William Johnson. Returned to court February 1792 by John
Chappell, but exact date of marriage not shown. p.11 and WB 4/17.

COMER, Moses and Letty Cole. Married 10 March 1810 by James Shelburne.
WB 7/15.

CONNER, Alfred and Elizabeth Birton, daughter of Itha G. Birton, 6 September 1852, "on certification of her mother proved by the oath of
Benja. W. Hines, a witness thereto." p. 10.

CONNER, John of Lunenburg County, and Charlotte Cabiness, 10 November 1788.
Sur. Asa Cabaniss. p. 9.

COOK, John of Lunenburg, and Elizabeth Cousins, 13 March 1777. Sur.
Jeremiah Glenn and D. C. Stokes. p. 5.

COOK, Shem of Lunenburg County, and Nancy Moss, 17 March 1788. Sur. John
Hawkins. p. 9.

COOKSEY, Hartwell P. and Evelina Royall, 17 January 1844. Sur. Albert
Royall. Married 10 January 1844 by Samuel G. Mason, Charlotte C.H.
p. 59 and WB 12/205.

COOKSEY, Miles H. and Martha Cheatham. Married 30 November 1831 by Silas
Shelburne. WB 11/2.

COOPER, William of Lunenburg County, and Rainey Andrews, 26 August 1785.
Sur. Sterling Cooper. p. 7.

CORDLE, Sterling and Mary A. Roberson, 16 December 1844. Sur. John Cordle.
Married 18 December 1844 by Joshua Featherston. p.59 and WB 12/238.

CORNNELL [Connell], Francis Pace of Lunenburg County, and Elizabeth Russell,
11 January 1786. Sur. Richard Russell. p. 7.

COTTER, Samuel of Lunenburg County, and Fanny Bush, 19 June 1793. Sur.
William Bush. Married 23 June 1793 by James Shelburne. p.13 and WB 4/46.

COUCH, Thomas and Elizabeth Dunn, 14 August 1826. Sur. Lew Smithson.
Married 24 August 1826 by Silas Shelburne, who shows the bride's
name as Frances Dunn. p. 41 and WB 9/161.

COUSINS, Henry and Susan Ragsdale, 19 June 1844. Sur. George W. Ragsdale.
p. 59.

COVINGTON, John of Lunenburg County, and Polly Williams, 26 January 1779.
Sur. Abraham Cocke. p. 5.

COWAN, William and Mary Billups, 9 December 1773. Sur. Christopher
Billups and Lyddal Bacon. p. 5.

COX, Charles and Mary Ann Tucker, 21 November 1837. Sur. George Cox.
p. 53.

COX, George and Julia A. Hardy, 1 November 1837. Sur. Charlie Cox.
p. 51.

COX, John, Jr. and Francinie Bouldin, spinster, 19 July 1758. Sur.
Thomas Bouldin. p. 1.

COX, Josiah B. and Mary N. Thackston, daughter of Josiah Watson, and sister
of Nelson Watson, 11 June 1834. Sur. James Anderson. Married
18 June 1834 by M. M. Dance. p. 45, WB 11/336, and DB 30/112.

COX, William H. and Anna B. Hawthorn, 24 December 1850. Anna certifies
she is over 21 years of age and proved by oath of P. H. Rainey, a
witness thereto. p. 3.

COX, William J. [or F.] and Amanda F. Robertson, daughter of Frederick
N. Robertson, 13 March 1851, "on certification of her father, proved
by the oath of Thomas W. Cox, a witness thereto." p. 4.

CRAFTON, Bennett and Elizabeth Russell, 9 February 1829. Sur. Thomas M.
Smith. p. 43.

CRAFTON, Bobb and Sary Shelborn. Married 20 December 1786 by Thomas
Crymes. WB 3/268.

CRAFTON, Daniel A. and Mary Virginia Winn, 25 December 1848. Sur. James
E. Jeter. Married 26 December 1848 by Thomas Adams. p. 65 and
WB 13/232.

CRAFTON, Ebenzer and Martha Ann Barnes. Married 30 June 1831 by Pleasant
Barnes. WB 11/281.

CRAFTON, Ebenezer and Catharine E. Ellis, 12 February 1838. Sur. Robert
Armes. Married 15 February 1838 by Pleasant Barnes. p. 53 and
WB 11/281.

CRAFTON, Elisha and Elizabeth Bates, 26 November 1821. Sur. Pleasant
Bates. Married 29 November 1821 by James Robertson. p. 33 and
WB 8/230.

CRAFTON, Frederick and Mourning Crafton, 25 December 1846. Sur. Josephus
Crafton. p. 61.

CRAFTON, George W. and Mary Barnes, daughter of Pleasant Barnes, 1 May 1852,
"on certification of the said Pleasant Barnes, proved by oath of
Martin Barnes, a witness thereto." p. 9.

CRAFTON, James of Lunenburg and Francis Staples, 10 December 1778. Sur. John Crafton and N. Hobson. p.5.

CRAFTON, John and Elizabeth Hardwick, 13 November 1817. Sur. Pleasant Barnes. Married 13 November 1817 by James Robertson. p.29 and WB 8/1.

CRAFTON, John of Lunenburg County, and Sally Staples, 1 February 1787. Sur. Thomas Staples. Married 15 February 1787 by Thomas Crymes. p.9 and WB 3/269.

CRAFTON, John D. and Celia Young, 18 September 1817. Sur. William Young. Married 23 September 1817 by Joel Johns. p.31 and WB 7/346.

CRAFTON, John and Louisa Ellis. Married 23 June 1828 by Silas Shelburne. WB 9/480.

CRAFTON, Joseph of Lunenburg County, and Patsey Stembridge, 10 November 1785. Sur. William Stembridge. Married by James Shelburne whose return included marriages between October 1785 and May 1786, but the exact date of marriage not shown. p.7 and WB 3/252.

CRAFTON, Richard and Nancy Martin. Married 26 September 1799 by Garner McConnico. WB 4/261-A.

CRAFTON, Richard and Sally A. Rutledge, 14 October 1844. Sur. Joseph M. Rowlett. p.59.

CRAFTON, Richard, Sr. and Leanner O. W. Cooksey, 15 August 1836. Sur. John T. Keeling. p.49.

CRAFTON, Staples and Elizabeth D. Alderson. Married 4 January 1800 by James Shelburne. WB 5/51.

CRAFTON, Thomas of Lunenburg County, and Mary Sammons, 10 February 1785. Sur. James Sammons. Married by James Shelburne who did not show exact date of marriage. p.7 and WB 3/212.

CRAFTON, Thomas and Sally Powers, 13 March 1826. Sur. George Tucker. Married 14 March 1826 by Silas Shelburne. p.41 and WB 9/161.

CRAFTON, Thomas H. and Sarah Ann Tunstill, 8 January 1849. Sur. Josiah W. Foster. Married 10 January 1849 by William Doswell. p.65 and WB 13/232.

CRAFTON, William and Mary Newbill. Married 28 April 1802 by Matthew Dance. WB 6/29.

CRAFTON, William and Polly Nance, 11 June 1807. Sur. Thomas Staples. Married 8 July 1807 by William Ellis. p.21 and WB 6/208.

CRAFTON, William and Wealthy Haley. Married 8 June 1819 by James Robertson. WB 8/52.

CRAIG, Edward C. and Ann T. Jones, 3 July 1837. Sur. John A. Smith. p.51.

CRAIGHEAD, William Jr. and Fanney Glenn, 3 October 1791. Sur. William Craghead, Sr. p. 11.

CRALLE, Alexander B. and Mary E. Chappell, 9 February 1829. Sur. Charles Smith. p.43.

CRALLE, Alfred and Patty Ingram. Married 20 November 1800 by James Shelburne. WB 5/51.

CRALLE, Rainer [or Rumer] and Nancy Hatchett. Married 25 February 1801 by William Ellis. WB 5/67.

CRALLE, Richard Kennon of Lunenburg County and Sarah Jones, 1 November 1795. Sur. Branch Jones. p.15.

CRAWLEY, Samuel and Lucy Harding, 16 July 1817. Sur. George Claughton. p.31.

CRALLE, Thomas and Polly Farley. Married 14 February 1801 by William Ellis. WB 5/67.

CRAWLEY, Thomas G. and Sarah Overton, 8 July 1844. Sur. Edward Overton. Married in 1844 by William Wilson, the exact date not shown. p.59 and WB 12/220.

CRAVEN, Oran C. and Malvina F. Johnson, 25 January 1849. Sur. Joel Parrish. p.65.

CREATH, James W. and Rebecca J. Cox, 9 June 1845. Sur. James H. Marable. Married __ June 1845 by William Norfleet. p.61 and WB 12/310.

CREATHE, William R. and Elizabeth L. Gee, 8 December 1823. Sur. William S. Gee. Married by James McAden whose return was recorded 16 March 1825, the exact date of marriage not shown. p.35 and WB 8/470.

CRENSHAW, Abner and Philadelphia Fowlkes. Married 15 March 1806 by Richard Dabbs. WB 6/193.

CRENSHAW, Daniel of Lunenburg County, and Nancy Jennings, 19 June 1789. Sur. James Jennings. Married 2 July 1789 by David Ellington. p.9 and WB 3/344.

CRENSHAW, Jesse and Jane C. Blanton. Married 14 January 1805 by Joel Johns. WB 6/128.

CRENSHAW, Matthew of Lunenburg County, and Polly Fears, 10 August 1792. Sur. James Griffin. p.13.

CRENSHAW, Nathan and Suckey Jones. Married 11 April 1782 by James Shelburne. WB 3/118.

CRENSHAW, Nathaniel and Unity Pamplin. Married 1 January 1783 by Thomas Crymes. WB 3/131.

CRENSHAW, Pleasant and Eliza Mayes. Married 22 April 1805 by Joel Johns.
WB 6/128.

CRENSHAW, Thomas of Lunenburg County, and Sarah Pettus of Lunenburg,
10 August 1786. Sur. Jona Patterson. p.7.

CRENSHAW, William and Molley Haney, 14 May 1767. Sur. Elisha Betts and
N. Hobson. p.3.

CRENSHAW, William and Rebecca Jackson. Married 16 November 1820 by Joel
Johns. WB 8/357.

CRENSHAW, William and Jane Hurt, 2 March 1822. Sur. John C. North.
Married 7 March by Silas Shelburne. p.33 and WB 8/227.

CROSS, Charles and Phebe Tomlinson, 8 November 1770. Sur. Michael McKee
[signed Michael MacKey]. p. 5.

CROSS, Richard of Lunenburg and Sally Chambers, 18 February 1797. Sur.
Edward Chambers. p.15.

CROW, John and P. Townsend. Married 1 November 1832 by Silas Shelburne.
WB 11/2.

CROW, John W. and Martha F. Rux, daughter of Susan A. Rux, 18 December 1852,
proved by the oath of Edmunds Webb, a witness thereto. p.11.

CROWE, Nathaniel and N. Johnson. Married 6 December 1818 by Charles Ogburn.
WB 10/181-A.

CROW, Thomas and Nancy Cabiness. Married 10 July 1810 by Thomas Adams.
WB 7/39.

CROW, Upton S. and Jenicy Townsend, 20 December 1830. Sur. Daniel Townsend.
Married 23 December 1830 by Silas Shelburne. p.45 and WB 10/131.

CROWDER, Anderson M. and Harriet Fisher, 25 March 1822. Sur. William F.
Abernathy. Married __ March 1822 by Richard Dabbs. p.33 and WB 8/271.

CROWDER, Boling and Polly Munday, daughter of John Munday, dec'd, 31 March
1813. Sur. Thomas Stokes. Married 1 April 1813 by James Robertson.
p.25 and WB 7/59.

CROWDER, George and Sally Thompson, 19 December 1803. Sur. Harris
Tomlinson. p.17.

CROWDER, George and Martha H. Freeman, both of Lunenburg, between 27 August
1840 and 14 December 1840. DB 32/59-61.

CROWDER, James T. and M. C. Harris. Married 1 December 1830 by Charles
Ogburn. WB 10/181A.

CROWDER, Richard and Polly Eastham. Married 15 December 1800 by James
Shelburne. WB 5/51.

CROWDER, Stephen and Malissa B. Eastes [or Estes], 22 July 1834. Sur. James A. W. Green. Married 4 July 1834 by Pleasant Barnes. p. 47 and WB 11/281.

CRYMES, George and Louisa Johns, 14 December 1846. Sur. John Crymes. Married 16 December 1846 by Samuel G. Mason, Charlotte C.H. p.61 and WB 13/10.

CRYMES, John and Lauretta S. Johns, 13 December 1833. Sur. Thomas A. Johns. Married 18 December 1833 by Pleasant Barnes. p.45 and WB 11/281.

CRYMES, Robert and Martha N. Gee, 11 January 1836. Sur. Jesse H. Gee. p.51.

CRYMES, William and Kiziah Dozer, 11 December 1769. Sur. Leonard Dozer. p.5.

CULLY, Robert and Martha Ann Redmon, 6 November 1843. Sur. Allen Duffer. p.57.

CUMBY, Major and Nancy Morgan, 13 October 1835. Sur. Thomas Hutcheson. Married by Daniel Petty whose return was dated 10 October 1836. p.49 and WB 11/179.

CUNNINGHAM, John and Mary Hill Pettipool, 2 December 1771. Sur. Edmd. Jordan. p.5.

CURETON, John, Jr. of Lunenburg and Sarah Moon, 19 December 1778. Sur. Jeffrey Murrell and William Taylor. p.5.

CURETON, John and Hannah Davies [in ink on bond is Hannah Dawes], 14 March 1783. Sur. William Taylor. p.7.

CURETON, Nathaniel of Lunenburg, and Elizabeth Eastham, 4 May 1795. Sur. James Farmer. Married by James Shelburne, no date given. p.15 and WB 4/107

DACUS, Nathaniel and Mary Arvin. Married by James Shelburne who gave no specific date, but list stated, "between February 1785 and June 1785." WB 3/212. [See Nathaniel Davis on page 32.]

DACUS, Nathaniel of Lunenburg County, and Elizabeth Thackston, 13 February 1796. Sur. Anthony Fullilove. M.B. #343.

DABBS, B. B. and Ann Vaden. Married 28 August 1844 by Thomas E. Locke at the Rectory. St. John's Church Register.

DABBS, John W. and Sarah A. Vaden, 19 September 1844. Sur. Beverly R. White. p.59.

DABBS, Richard of Lunenburg County, and Elizabeth Mitchell, 14 February 1793. Sur. Abel Jackson. p.13.

DABBS, Silas and Martha Smith, 8 September 1823. Sur. John Key. Married 10 September 1823 by William Hatchett. p. 37 and WB 8/336.

DALTON, Richard and Elizabeth White, 6 December 1835. Sur. David W. Fowlkes. p.47.

DALTON, Walker of Lunenburg County, and Mary Winn, 2 September 1793. Sur. John Conner. Married 3 September 1793 by William Ellis. p.13. and WB 4/43.

DALTON, William T. and Sally Ann Winn, 17 December 1838. Sur. Thomas Winn. p.53.

DALY, Daniel and Polly Fisher, 11 February 1811. Sur. David Garland. Married 13 February 1811 by Thomas Adams. p.25 and WB 7/40. [See Dayley, page 33]

DANCE, Stephen and Martha Willson, 19 April 1814. Sur. Joseph W. Rudd. Married A[pril] 19, 1814 by Charles Ogburn. p.29 and WB 10/181.

DANIEL, John of Lunenburg and Rhody Dickson, 6 May 1813. Sur. Nathan Potts. p.27.

DANIEL, Joseph and Letty Laffoon, 24 May 1824. Sur. Samuel Moore. Married 24 May 1824 by John Doyle. p.39 and WB 8/402.

DANIEL, Joseph and Elizabeth Hammonds, 16 October 1850. Sterling Craulle made oath that Elizabeth was over 21 years of age. p.2.

DANIEL, Mobray and Rebecca Laffoon. Married 29 August 1805 by John Neblett. WB 6/147.

DANIEL, Richard T. and Susan A. R. Matthews, 21 December 21, 1841. Sur. James Dixon. p.55.

DANIEL, Thomas W. and Tabitha W. Winn. Married 7 March 1833 by Pleasant Barnes. WB 11/281.

DARDIN, Charnal of Lunenburg, and Rebecca Gill, 24 December 1791. Sur. Benjamin Andrews. M.B. #258. p. 11.

DAVIDSON, William B. [also shown William R.] and Ann E. Johns, 12 July 1847. Sur. John F. Lee. p.63.

DAVIS, ARPHAROD L. and Almedia J. Bowers, 9 March 1847. Sur. Chatten C. Bishop. Married "about the middle of March 1847" by Thomas Adams. p.63 and WB 13/105.

DAVIS, Asa C. and Mary C. Ship, 10 December 1834. Sur. John T. Dowdy. p.45.

DAVIS, Ashley of Lunenburg County and Mary Cross, 17 December 1785. Sur. James Scott. p.7.

DAVIS, Copeland of Lunenburg, and Polly Garland, 21 November 1791. Sur. William T. Garland. p.11.

DAVIS, Cornelius Washington and Nancy E. Bowers, 12 March 1849. Sur. Robert L. Bishop. Married 15 March 1849 by T. E. Locke at Philip H. Bowers'residence. p.65 and St. John's Church Register.

DAVIS, David and Mary Overby. Married 7 July 1815 by Baxter Ragsdale.
WB 7/246.

DAVIS, Henry and Nancy Fullilove [also shown Fullerlove], 11 December
1788. Sur. Samuel Ward. Married 16 December 1788 by Thomas Crymes.
p.9 and WB 3/342.

DAVIS, Hezekiah of Lunenburg, and Milley Johnson, 29 October 1789. Sur.
James Wallace. p.11.

DAVIS, Jacob of Lunenburg and Mary Ann Neal, 10 December 1789. Sur. Johnathan
Booker. Married 26 December 1789 by James Shelburne. p. 11 and WB 3/358.

DAVIS, James and Agnes Puckett. Married 14 November 1806 by Joel Johns.
WB 6/197.

DAVIS, John of Lunenburg, and Sophiah Barnes, 13 December 1787. Sur.
Richard Claughtin. p.9.

DAVIS, John and Phoebe Wallace. Married 16 December 1819 by Thomas
Adams. WB 8/67.

DAVIS, John B. and Mary Overton, 14 December 1838. Sur. Nathaniel
Pennington. p.53.

DAVIS, Matthew of Lunenburg, and Mary Davis, 20 December 1790. Sur. John
Elmore. p.11.

DAVIS, Nathaniel of Lunenburg, and __[omitted]__, 12 March 1785. Sur.
David Stokes. M.B. #149. See Nathaniel Dacus on page 30.

DAVIS, Nicholas E. and Eliza L. P. Lamkin, 29 May 1826. Sur. John Beath.
p. 41.

DAVIS, Pascal and Nancy Toone, daughter of Lewis Toone, 4 November 1812.
Sur. William Johnson. Married 5 November 1812 by James Shelburne.
p. 25 and WB 7/124.

DAVES, Peter and Henrietta Maria Washington Winn, 1 October 1814. Sur.
Thomas Gregory. Married 4 October 1814 by Charles Ogburn. p.27
and WB 10/181.

DAVIS, Robert H. and Rebecca Ann Crow, 17 July 1844. Sur. Sterling L.
Crow. Married __ July 1844 by Robert Michaels. p. 59 and
WB 12/245.

DAVIS, [DAVIES], Samuel D.[1] and Mary R. Stout,[2] 1 December 1810. Sur.
John H. Street [probably Stout]. p.23.

DAVIS, Samuel S. and Frances W. Hines, 30 December 1847. Sur. Benjamin
W. Hines. Married 11 January 1848 by Richard E. G. Adams. p.63
and WB 13/191.

DAVIS, William and Elenor Howard, daughter of Francis Howard, dec'd,
3 March 1756. Sur. George Farrow, Thomas Stith, and George Carrington, Jr. p.1.

DAVIS, William and Jane Hopkins, 2 December 1760. Sur. Edmond Taylor. p.1.

DAVIS, William and Anna Burnett, 10 October 1804. Sur. Robert Burnett.
Married 11 October 1804 by Mathew Dance. p.19 and WB 6/100.

DAVIS, William and Sarah Connell. Married __ December 1808 by Thomas
Adams. WB 6/253-A.

DAVIS, William and Temperance Gill, 14 February 1825. Sur. Matthew C.
Gill. p.41.

DAY, Henry and Kezia W. Crymes. Married 15 February 1833 by Pleasant
Barnes. WB 11/281.

DAY, John F. and Mary Farmer, 28 December 1836. Sur. Simeon Shelburne.
Married 4 January 1837 by M. M. Dance. p.51 and WB 11/336.

DAYLEY, Benjamin of Lunenburg, and Sally Mize, 22 January 1787. Sur.
John Mize.
[See DALY, page 31.]

DEDMAN, Francis and Temple Crafton. Married 12 January 1809 by Joel
Johns. WB 6/264-A.

DEDMAN, Philip and Polly Hawkins. Married 20 October 1800 by James
Shelburne. WB 5/51.

---

1 - Additional information on Samuel D. Davies and Mary R. Stout is found in a Bible at the Virginia
Historical Society (Mss6:4, D2894:1) as follows: Samuel David Davies was b. Aug. 6, 1787,
Chesterfield Co., Va. and d. Nov. 6, 1839, Chesterfield Co., Va. He was the son of Samuel
David Davies and Amelia Holt. Samuel David Davies, Sr. was b. 28 Sept. 1750, Hanover Co.,
Va. married 4 Sept. 1774 and died 9 Oct. 1804. He was the son of Samuel Davies (Pres. New Jer-
sey College, now Princeton) b. Nov. 3, 1723, Newcastle, Chester, Pa. and his wife Jane Holt.
They were married Oct. 4, 1748. Amelia Holt was b. Apr. 9, 1753 and died Dec. 11, 1836.

2 - Mary R. Stout was b. Oct. 4, 1795 Lunenburg County, Va. and d. March 12, 1860, Lunenburg Co.,
Va., daughter of John Hoff Stout (b. Jan. 20, 1767, Quakertown, N. J. and son of Joseph &
Theodocia Stout). He was married June 25, 1792 in Lunenburg Co., Va. to Ann Beasley, and d.
Sept. 17, 1814. Ann Beasely was b. May 13, 1772 in Nottoway County, Va. daughter of William
and his wife Ann (Hurt) Beasley.

DeGRAFFENREIDT, Metcalf of Lunenburg and Mary Ann Maury, 2 June 1783. Sur. Matthew F. Maury. p.7.

DeGRAFFENREIDT, Tscharner of Lunenburg, and Elizabeth Embry, 10 February 1763. Sur. David Garland, Benjamin Whitehead and John Hanna. p.3.

DeGRAFFENREIDT, Tscharner and Lucretia Robertson, 14 December 1780. Sur. William Taylor. p.5.

DeGRAFFENREID, William and Sophia Winn, daughter of Horatio Winn, 30 October 1817. Sur. William G. Pettus. p.29.

DeGRAFFENREIDT, William and Elizabeth Robertson, __ December 1772. Sur. Joseph Jeter and N. Hobson. p.5.

DeGRAFFENREID, William and Nancy Tomlinson, 21 December 1824. Sur. James Smith, Jr. Married 23 December 1824 by Charles Ogburn. p.37 and WB 10/181-A.

DENKENS, John of Lunenburg, and Cealah Hoomes, 12 December 1797. Sur. Joshua Evans. p.15.

DENTON, Augustin and Sally Turner, 19 December 1791. Sur. John Thompson. p.11.

DENTON, Theophilus F. and Elizabeth G. Blackwell, 14 March 1825. Sur. James Blackwell. p.41.

DENTON, Thomas G. and Nancy Ussery. Married October 1816 by Thomas Adams. WB 7/356.

DENTON, Wyatt and Elizabeth Deminan. Married 8 December 1805 by John Neblett. WB 6/147.

DESHAZOR, John J. and Permelia A. Snead, 24 January 1827. Sur. James Snead. p.41.

DICKS, Edward and Elizabeth Turner, 9 November 1835. Sur. James S. Turner. Married 18 November 1835 by Joshua Featherston. p.49 and WB 11/156.

DICKS, Tandy and Sally Sturdivant. Married 16 May 1800 by John Neblett who shows the name as Tandy Decker on return. WB 5/35.

DICKS, William of Lunenburg and Jerusha Farguson, 22 January 1787. Sur. Carrington Garrett. p.9.

DICKS, William and Fanny Scarbrough. Married 28 March 1813 by Thomas Adams. WB 7/248.

DICKS, William and Sally Ussery. Married 29 May 1816 by Thomas Adams. WB 7/248.

DILLINGHAM, Vachel and Elizabeth Evans, 24 January 1807. Sur. John Evans. Married 29 January 1807 by Matthew Dance. p.21 and WB 6/181.

DIXON, Henry and Mary A. Parrish. Married 2 January 1841 by Joshua Featherston. WB 12/7.

DIXON, James and Martha Laffoon, 11 November 1812. Sur. Sterling Parrish. p.25 and M.B.

DIXON, James and Mary A. Laffoon, 22 December 1843. Sur. Thomas G. Moore. p.57.

DIXON, John and Mary Brintle, 9 March 1846. Sur. James Dixon. p.63.

DIXON, Robert and Ame Bacon, 30 September 1764. Sur. Bartlett Anderson. p.3.

DIXON, William J. and Sarah Frances Hurt, 23 May 1848. Sur. M. E. Hurt. p.65.

DIZMANG, James and Sally Huling, 25 September 1794. Sur. Parsons Wright. Note: The M.B. gives the name William Dizmang in the instrument itself and in the signature. The M.B. endorsement and the marriage register gives the name James.

DIZMANG, James of Lunenburg, and Dolly Wright, 2 January 1790. Sur. Parsons Wright. p.11.

DIZMANG, John of Lunenburg, and Sidny Moore, 29 October 1790. Sur. Parsons Wright. p. 11.

DIZMANG, William. See James Dizmang and Sally Huling above.

DOAK [or DOKE], Robert and Hannah Armstrong, daughter of Rebecca Armstrong, 6 May 1761. Sur. John M'Nees [McKneese] p.3.

DOBBYNS, Boller and Nancy Newbill. Married 25 November 1807 by Matthew Dance. WB 6/230-A.

DOBBINS, Daniel of Lunenburg, and Rebecca Dunn, 24 December 1795. Sur. Benjamin Dunn. p.15.

DOBBIN, James H. and Mrs. Emma Alston. Married 30 December 1851 by Thomas E. Locke at Mrs. Alston's residence, Nottoway County. St. John's Church Register.

DOBBYNS, John A. and Narcissa Moon [or Moor]. Married 16 March 1820 by Silas Shelburne. WB 8/140.

DODD, James W. and Mary F. Bayne, daughter of Griffin Bayne, 29 June 1852, "proved by the oath of James H. Bishop, a witness thereto." p.9.

DODD, Walker of Lunenburg, and Mary Webb, 8 September 1814. Sur. Matthew Dance and married 23 September 1814 by Matthew Dance. p.27 and WB 7/124.

DODD, Walker and Amy Ann Goodwin, 3 January 1825. Sur. Green W. Webb. p.39.

DUDSON [DODSON], E. C. and May L. Jordan. Married 29 May 1832 by Silas Shelburne. WB 11/2.

DODSON, Joel and Nancy G. Clark, 7 October 1822. Sur. Thomas C. Clark. Married 20 November 1822 by Silas Shelburne. p.35 and WB 8/270.

DOGGETT, Benjamin and Mary Clark. Married 21 February 1816 by James Shelburne. WB 7/313.

DOWDY, John T. and Martha W. Roach, 23 May 1836. Sur. Richard J. Epes. p.51.

DOWDY, Martin S. and Jane McLaughlin. Married 27 November 1816 by Joel Johns. WB 7/280.

DOZIER, Richard M. of Lunenburg County, and Mary Gayle, 9 September 1789. Sur. William Dozier. p.11.

DOZER, Thomas of Lunenburg, and Catey Pryor, 17 June 1775. Sur. John Barry. p.5.

DOZER, William of Lunenburg, and Elizabeth Stokes, 14 May 1775. Sur. William Hunley. p.5.

DRAKE, John D. and Mary P. Foster. Married 28 June 1827 by Thomas H. Jeffress. WB 9/212.

DRAKE, Samuel and Terely Barnes. Married 2 May 1810 by Joel Johns. WB 7/9.

DRESKILL, Daniel of Campbell County, and Agness Hawkins, 9 September 1788. Sur. Claiborn Johnson of Lunenburg County. Married by James Shelburne whose list was returned to court 9 July 1789. p.9 and WB 3/345.

DUDLEY, William of Lunenburg and Rachel Knight, 12 August 1784. Sur. Woodson Knight. Married 19 August 1784 by Thomas Crymes. p. 11 and WB 3/185.

DUNMAN, John and Sukey Moore, 1 February 1804. Sur. William Moore. Married 3 February 1804 by John Neblett. p.21 and WB 6/123.

DUNMAN, Joseph, Jr. of Lunenburg, and Jamina Sturdivant, 7 November 1789. Sur. Drury Ragsdale. p.9.

DUNN, Billington and Fanny Smith. Married 17 October 1815 by James Shelburne. WB 7/227.

DUNN, David of Lunenburg, and Obedience Weatherford, 1 January 1793. Sur. John Robertson. p.13.

DUNN, Gray and Eliza Davis, 1 January 1812. Sur. Clement Mitchell. Married 1 January 1812 by Thomas Adams. p.25 and WB 7/40.

DUNN, John F. and Perlina B. Davis, 12 November 1849. Sur. Edmond Bishop. p.65.

DUNN, Richard and Polly Lambert, 30 December 1812. Sur. John Russell. Married 31 December 1812 by Baxter Ragsdale. p.25 and WB 7/82.

DUNNAVANT, Joseph C. and Jane Moore, 7 October 1830. Sur. William Moore. Married 13 September by Silas Shelburne. p.45 and WB 10/131.

DUNEVANT, Will and Porch P. Pulliam. Married 1 December 1831 by Silas Shelburne. WB 11/2.

DUPREE, Daniel of Lunenburg County, and Sally Ellington, 30 November 1789. Sur. David Street. p.9.

DUPREE, James R. and Lucinda H. Edmondson, 11 June 1838. Sur. Daniel W. Parsons. p.53.

DUPREE, William S. and Sarah H. E. Williams, 18 July 1846. Sur. William H. H. Williams. p.63.

EAGLES, William H. and Elizabeth L. Cumby, 13 March 1815. Sur. Warner Pollard. p.29.

EAST, William and Laura Ann Robertson, daughter of John J. Robertson who consents, 25 January 1851. p.3.

EASTHAM, James and Anne Farmer, 14 April 1768. Sur. Richard Claiborn. p.5.

ECKLES, Alpheus W. and Ann Fitzwilson, 7 October 1848. Sur. Job Savill. Married 8 October 1848 by Thomas E. Locke at Job Saville's residence. p.65 and St. John's Church Register.

ECHOLS, John of Lunenburg and Lucy Annah Moore, daughter of William Moore, 6 September 1760. Sur. George Walton. p. 1.

EDDINGS, Joseph of Lunenburg County and Elizabeth Kirk, 16 November 1790. Sur. James Kirk. p.11.

EDMONDSON, Coleman of Lunenburg County and Francis Bowers, 8 September 1790. Sur. Sanford Bowers. p.11.

EDMONDSON, Benjamin of Lunenburg County, and Martha Tomlinson, 12 May 1791. Sur. Benjamin Orgain. p.11.

EDMUNDS, Alfred and Martha S. Taylor, 2 October 1848. Sur. James W. Taylor. Married 4 October 1848 by Richard E. G. Adams. p.65 and WB 13/213.

EDMUNDS, Bartlett and _____ Steagall [no other name shown]. Married 7 June 1819 by Thomas Adams. WB 8/67.

EDMUNDS, Cain and Tabitha Steward. Married __ November 1807 by Thomas Adams. WB 6/253A.

EDMONDS, John and Martha S. Crow. Married 1 April 1844 by Thomas E. Locke at James Edmunds' residence. St. John's Church Register.

EDMONDS, Laban and Nancey Laffoon, 30 December 1823. Sur. William Thomason. p.35.

EDMUNDS, Nicholas and Lucretia J. Parish, 8 October 1847. Sur. Lazarus L. Burnett. p.63.

EDMUNDS, Richard and Mourning Laffoon, 29 December 1830. Sur. Daniel Laffoon. Married 6 January 1831 by Joshua Featherston. p.45 and WB 10/152.

EDMUNDS, Washington and Ann Taylor, 22 January 1849. Sur. Peterson G. Taylor. Married 30 January 1849 by Richard E. G. Adams. p.67 and WB 13/334.

EDMUNDS, Wilkins and Polly Steward. Married 5 June 1815 by Thomas Adams. WB 7/248.

EDMUNDSON, Upton and Frances Bagley, 16 August 1817. Sur. Anderson Bagley. Married 21 August 1817 by Thomas Adams. p.31 and WB 7/356.

EDWARDS, Nicholas M. and Lucy W. Boswell, 1 November 1824. Sur. William C. Boswell. Married 2 November 1824 by James Smith. p.37 and WB 8/473.

EDWARDS, Peter of Lunenburg County and Patsey M. Fisher, 18 July 1797. Sur. Thomas Edwards. Married 18 July 1797 by John Neblett. p.15 and WB 4/232.

EDWARDS, William and Elizabeth Barksdale, spinster, 19 February 1762. Sur. John Barksdale. p.3.

EGGLESTON, Gravet A. and Elizabeth Frances Smith, 17 February 1845. Sur. William Townsend, Jr. p.61.

EGGLESTON, Joseph E. and Lucy Jane Smith, 17 February 1845. Sur. William Townsend. p.61.

EGLETON [EGGLESTON], Thomas of Lunenburg, and Anne Watson, 10 September 1763. Sur. Richard Wilton. p. 3.

ELAM, Edward of Lunenburg County, and Jinney Pamplin, 12 May 1791. Sur. John Pamplin. p.11.

ELAM, Martin of Lunenburg and Mary Philips, 9 June 1775. Sur. Edward Waller. p.5.

ELDER, Brooken and Elizabeth G. Hawthorne, 14 December 1829. Sur. Thomas D. Fisher. p.43.

ELDER, Harrison and Nancy A. Collier, 11 October 1817. Sur. William Parrott, Jr. p.31.

ELDOR, Travers of Lunenburg and Sally Skinner, 22 December 1790. Sur. Charles Gee. p.11.

ELDRIDGE, Thomas and Elizabeth C. Niblett. Married 5 October 1809 by Thomas Adams. WB 7/39.

ELLET, Samuel and Elizabeth Ward, 6 March 1837. Sur. William A. Ward. Married 23 February 1837 by Pleasant Barnes who gives the bride's name as Elizabeth Moore. p. 51 and WB 11/281.

ELLINGTON, Creed W. and Martha Yarbrough, 18 October 1821. Sur. John J. Wells. Married 19 October 1821 by Joel Johns. p.33 and WB 8/357.

ELLINGTON, Simeon and Elizabeth W. Pettus. Married 4 April 1802 by Edward Almond. WB 6/83.

ELLINGTON, William and Rebecca W. Yarbrough, 7 March 1846. Sur. John W. Yarbrough. Married 10 March 1846 by John Thompson. p.61 and WB 13/24.

ELLIOTT, Richard and Kitturah Winn. Married 31 April 1801 by William Ellis. WB 5/67.

ELLIOTT, Thomas P. and Elizabeth W. Cheatham, 23 February 1824. Sur. Thomas Cheatham [signed E. Cheatham]. Married 26 February 1824 by Silas Shelburne. p. 37 and WB 8/340.

ELLIS, Ambrose of Lunenburg and Sicily Stokes, 12 October 1769. Sur. Henry Stokes. p.5.

ELLIS, Ambrose, Jr. and Elizabeth Herring. Married 18 March 1800 by William Ellis. WB 5/22.

ELLIS, Ellison W. and Louisa Jane Fowlkes. Married 9 May 1839 by Charles F. Burnley. WB 11/370.

ELLIS, Fielding and Elizabeth A. Betts. Married 21 January 1801 by William Ellis. WB 5/67.

ELLIS, John T. and Nancy I. Hendrick, 17 March 1823. Sur. Paschall Hendrick. Married 18 March by James Robertson. p. 35 and WB 8/309.

ELLIS, Joseph F. and Charlotte Jane Ellis, 20 November 1830. Sur. Adamson T. Cox. Married 1 December 1830 by John Wesley Childs. Wit: Ellison W. Ellis and William E. Elmore as reported by the minister. p.45 and WB 10/124.

ELLIS, Littleberry of Lunenburg County [minister's return says "of Amelia County"] and Mary Barnes of Lunenburg, 26 January 1784. Sur. Jonathan Zachary. Married 4 February 1785 by Thomas Crymes. p.7 and WB 3/210.

ELLIS, Richard and Sarah G. Aiken, 6 April 1826. Sur. Ebenezer Crafton. Married 6 April 1826 by James Robertson. p.41 and WB 9/127.

ELLIS, William of Lunenburg and Sarah Briggs Chappell, 1 February 1780. Sur. Obed Clay. p.5.

ELLIS, William T. and Edity A. Elizabeth Nance, daughter of Johnson T. Nance, 14 December 1853. Sur. John H. Leigh. p.16.

ELMORE, John and Jane E. Wilkes, 1 December 1834. Sur. John Winn. p.47.

EMBRY, Henry of Lunenburg and Ann Porteson, 31 March 1780. Sur. John
Ragsdale. [The M.R. says Ann Peterson.] p.5.

EPPES, Edward of Lunenburg and Elizabeth Cobb, 8 October 1787. Sur. John
Robertson. p.9.

EPES, Francis W. and Mrs. Frances Susan Beverley. Married 10 September 1839
by Thomas E. Locke, at St. Paul's Church. St. John's Church Register.

EPES, Isaac Oliver and Maria Rosalie Beverley. Married 23 July 1850 by
Thomas E. Locke, at F. W. Epes' residence, Nottoway. St. John's Church
Register.

EPES, James and Milley Stewart, 28 March 1804. Sur. Buckner Valentine. p.19.

EPES, John and Elizabeth Cuttaloe, 25 March 1803. Sur. Freeman Epes. p.19.

EPES, John C. and Sarah A. Smith, 10 October 1825. Sur. Gillie M. Bacon.
p.39.

EPES, Peter and Mary T. Sale, 21 July 1821. Sur. W.M.R. Fontaine. Married
__ July 1821 by Thomas Adams. p.31 and WB 8/209.

EPES, Peter, Jr. of Lunenburg and Peggy Baker Cowan, 9 May 1793. Sur.
Philip W. Jackson. p.13.

EPES, Thomas W. and Emily G. Williams, 28 September 1835. Sur. William
Fitzgerald. p.47.

EPPERSON, David and Patsey Moore. Married 26 January 1816 by Thomas Adams.
WB 7/248.

EPPERSON, David and Eve Laffoon, 12 September 1842. Sur. Edmund F. Taylor.
p.55.

EPPERSON, James and Polly Moore. Married 31 March 1813 by Thomas Adams.
WB 7/248.

EPPERSON, Jonathan of Lunenburg, and Sarah Parrish, 28 December 1789. Sur.
William Parrish. p.11.

ERAMBERT, Augustus A. and Missouri F. Lester, 29 April 1848. Sur. Thomas
G. Crawley. p.65.

ERSKINE, Patrick A. and Sarah A. Williams, 16 December 1826. Sur. Joseph
F. Ellis. Married 21 December 1826 by Silas Shelburne. p.41 and
WB 9/161.

ESTES, Bartlett and Susanna Estes, 13 January 1791. Sur. Thomas Estes. p.11.

ESTES, Benjamin, Jr. of Lunenburg and Jeane Hawkins, 22 January 1796. Sur.
John Wrenn. Married 25 January 1796 by James Shelburne. p.15 and
WB 4/160.

ESTES, Edmund and Martha Gee Ragsdale, 9 November 1814. Sur. Drury Gee. Married 9 November 1814 by Matthew Dance. p. 27 and WB 7/124.

ESTES, Edmund and Sally Walker, 30 June 1822. Sur. William Parrott, Jr. Married 7 "J." 1822 by Charles Ogburn who states Sally Waller. p.33 WB 10/182.

ESTES, Elijah J. and Mary A. Hudson, 24 October 1838. Sur. James E. Hazlewood. p.53.

ESTES, Elisha and Lucy Blankenship, 29 November 1806. Sur. William Gee. Married 3 December 1806 by Matthew Dance. p.21 and WB 6/181.

ESTES, Henson and Martha Blankenship. Married 26 December 1799 by James Shelburne. WB 5/51.

ESTES, John of Lunenburg and Mary Estes, 23 January 1778. Sur. John White. p.5.

ESTES, John and Elizabeth Pamplin, 9 March 1804. Sur. Robert Pamplin. p.19.

ESTES, John and Patsey Locke, 7 October 1806. Sur. George Locke. Married 16 October 1806 by Joel Johns. p.21 and WB 6/197.

ESTES, Lyddal B. of Lunenburg and Nancy A. Winn, 10 March 1814. Sur. Elisha Estes. Married 10 March 1814 by Matthew Dance. p.27 and WB 7/124.

ESTES, Matthew of Lunenburg and Martha Hawkins, 19 October 1795. Sur. William Wrenn, Jr. p.15.

ESTES, Thomas of Lunenburg, and Ann Buford, 25 June 1791. Sur. William Ragsdale. p. 11.

ESTES, Thomas of Lunenburg and Anne Wilson, 13 December 1792. Sur. Benjamin Estes. p.13.

ESTES, William and Mary Jane Pilkinton, 24 January 1837. Sur. Martin Phillips. p.53.

ESTES, William H. and Martha T. Floyd, 12 April 1847. Sur. William D. Floyd. p.63.

EUBANK, James of Lunenburg and Sally Thompson, 14 December 1797. Sur. Johnson Wood. p.15.

EUBANK, Philip G. and Elizabeth F. Gregory, 11 May 1835. Sur. Huse [Hughes?] W. Knight. p.47.

EVANS, Benjamin of Lunenburg and Elizabeth Weatherford, 9 August 1791. Sur. Joseph Weatherford. p.11.

EVANS, Charles J. and Lucretia Parrish. Married 3 February 1802 by John Jones. WB 6/14-A.

EVANS, Hansel and Elizabeth Johnson, 15 January 1821. Sur. Claiborn P. Johnson. p.31.

EVANS, Joshua and Judah Harris. Married 16 December 1797 by John Neblett. WB 4/232.

EVANS, Joseph D. and Abigail C. Barnes, 28 July 1835. Sur. William M. Gill. p.49.

EVENS, J. P. and M. Evens. Married 16 December 1828 by Charles Ogburn. WB 10/181-A.

EVANS, Lewis of Lunenburg, and Ann Calliham, 11 June 1788. Sur. Nicholas Calliham. p.9.

EVANS, Mark of Lunenburg and Winifred Andrews, 12 December 1795. Sur. Peter Andrews. Married 13 December 1795 by Charles Ogburn. p.15 and WB 4/147. [This marriage reported again in list of June 1832]

EVANS, Robert and Lucy Andrews, 6 March 1803. Sur. Drury Andrews. Married 19 March 1803 by Charles Ogburn [Recorded 1832]. WB 10/181 and p.17.

EVANS, Robert and Martha Johnson. Married 31 July 1815 by Baxter Ragsdale. WB 7/246.

EVANS, Thomas and Delphia Kelly, 25 December 1830. Sur. Henry Ragsdale. Married 28 December 1830 by Thomas D. Garrott. p.45 and WB 10/115.

EVANS, J. Daniel William and Lucy Thompson. Sur. Francis Gill. Married 1 December 1830 by J. W. Fowler. p.45 and WB 10/95.

FALCON, John and Elizabeth Moore, 21 February 1804. Sur. Jesse Moore. p.19.

FARGUSON, Horatio of Lunenburg and Rebecca Dickes, 20 December 1785. Sur. William Dicks. p.7.

FARGUSON, Jacob and Sarah Mason, Married 13 May 1784 by Thomas Crymes. WB 3/162.

FARGUSON, James of Lunenburg and Mary Parrish, 17 December 1792. Sur. William Parrish. p.13.

FARGUSON, Thomas of Lunenburg and Hannah Brinkle, 12 March 1787. Sur. Dn'l Taylor. p.9.

FARGUSON, William and Dolly Garrett, 17 December 1795. Sur. William Garrett. Married 24 December 1795 by John Neblett. p.15 and WB 4/124.

FARGUSON, William and J'ncy Hudson. Married 9 January 1806 by John Neblett. WB 6/147.

FARLEY, Edward and Polly Lester. Married 4 January 1800 by James Shelburne. WB 5/51.

FARLEY, Henry and Elizabeth Penick. Married 16 April 1816 by Joel Johns. WB 7/280.

FARLEY, John and Nancy Crafton. Married 8 October 1802 by James Shelburne. WB 6/28-A. [In WB 6/147 James Shelburne duplicates this marriage, but gives the date as 15 October 1802.]

FARLEY, Joseph H. and Sarah A. Walthall, 19 September 1845. Sur. Chatten C. Bishop. Married 1 September 1845 by Richard E. G. Adams. p.59 and WB 13/14.

FARLEY, Mackerness and Salley Crafton, 13 November 1806. Sur. Thomas Crafton. Married 5 December 1806 by William Ellis. p.21 and WB 6/187.

FARLEY, Robert A. and Mary M. Wood. Married 16 December 1828 by Silas Shelburne. WB 9/480.

FARLEY, Seth of Lunenburg and Sarah Crafton, 30 February 1778. Sur. William Crafton. p.5.

FARLEY, William and Martha Farley [M.R. says Martha Bailey], 9 November 1780. Sur. William Rucks. p.5.

FARLEY, William and Judah Crafton, 8 December 1803. Sur. Thomas Crafton. Married 16 December 1803 by Joel Johns. p. 17 and WB 6/76.

FARMER - See also PARMER and PALMER

FARMER, Benjamin Jr. and Peranna Farmer, 9 January 1813. Sur. Benny Harding. Married 14 January 1813 by James Shelburne. p.27 and WB 7/124.

FARMER, Elam of Lunenburg and Polly Hardying, 10 September 1795. Sur. Robert Harding. Married 27 September 1795 by James Shelburne. p.15 and WB 4/159-A.

FARMER, George of Lunenburg and Nancey Farmer, 8 May 1794. Sur. James Farmer. Married 15 May 1794 by James Shelburne, who states Nancey Harding. p. 13 and WB 4/107.

FARMER, Henry A. and Martha H. Walton, 5 July 1824. Sur. Champ C. M. Marable. Married 6 July 1824 by William Hatchett. p.37 and WB 8/470.

FARMER, James of Lunenburg and Elizabeth Harding, 15 April 1794. Sur. George Farmer. Married 19 April 1794 by William Ellis. p.13 and WB 4/75.

FARMER, Jeremiah of Lunenburg, and Polly Knight, 16 August 1788. Sur. John Knight. Married 23 August 1788 by Thomas Crymes. p.9 and WB 3/342.

FARMER, John of Lunenburg and Nancy Crymes, 14 September 1797. Sur. Leonard Crymes. p.15.

FARMER, John and Elizabeth Shelburn. Married 18 July 1799 by James Shelburne. WB 5/51.

FARMER, Joseph W. and Eliza L. Williams. Married 10 December 1828 by Silas Shelburne. WB 9/480.

FARMER, Lodwick Jr. of Lunenburg and Elizabeth Herring, 27 October 1779.
Sur. Benjamin Farmer and William Taylor. p.5.

FARMER, Lodowick of Lunenburg and Bettsy Knight, 11 October 1787. Sur.
William Taylor. p.9.

FARMER, Theodrick and Elizabeth Moon, 9 November 1829. Sur. Thomas Farmer.
p.43.

FARRISS, James J. and Mary Jane Hamblin. Married 21 August 1831 by
Shelburne. WB 11/2.

FEARS, Thomas and Elizabeth Toombs, both of Lunenburg, 11 March 1784. Sur.
Philip Rowlett. Married 13 March 1784 by Thomas Crymes. p.7 and
WB 3/162.

FEARS, Thomas and Sally Powel, 22 September 1815. Sur. James Smith. p.29.

FEATHERSTON, Joshua and Ann Wilkinson, 16 October 1821. Sur. Stephen
Brown. Married __ October 1821 by Thomas Adams. p.31 and WB 8/209.

FEATHERSTON, Lewis and Sally Hurt. Married 20 December 1810 by James
Shelburne. WB 7/3.

FERRELL, William and Elizabeth J. Redmond, 22 January 1844. Sur. Allin
Duffer. p.59.

FIGG, Alfred H. and Sarah Jane Fowlkes, ward of William J. Fowlkes who
consents, 13 September 1852. p.10.

FILBERT, Alexander Josiah and Judith Staples. Married 6 January 1800 by
James Shelburne. WB 5/51.

PHILBERD, Archibald of Lunenburg and Susanna Nance, 9 September 1796. Sur.
Hezekeiah Philberd. Married 9 September 1796 by James Shelburne, who
spells the name Filberd. The marriage bond is signed Archibald
Filberd. p.15 and WB 4/160.

FILBIRD, John and Polly A. Rutledge. Married 21 December 1808 by William
Ellis. WB 6/256.

FISHER, Thomas D. and Martha E. Blackwell, 9 March 1829. Sur. Turner
Abernathy. p.43.

FLINN, John and Lucy Parrish, 21 _____ 1803. Sur. Matthew Hubbard. p.17.

FLINN, William and Drucella Depreist, 3 February 1834. Sur. David Farley.
p.47.

FLOURNOY, Gideon of Powhatan County, and Gracy Tarry, 2 December 1786.
Sur. Samuel Tarry. p.7.

FLOYD, Allen and Jincey Singleton. Married 7 January 1820 by Thomas Adams.
WB 8/67.

FLOYD, Freeman M. and Lucy Taylor, 20 September 1824. Sur. William
Matthews. p.37.

FLOYD, Robert J. and Milly Wright. Married 6 November 1802 by John
Neblett. WB 6/11-A.

FLOYD, William D. and Eliza Thompson. Married 23 October 1816 by James
Shelburne. WB 7/313.

FORD, James P. - See James P. HAINES, page 55.

FORD, John and Sukey Slaughter, 11 March 1803. Sur. William Townsend.
Married 11 March 1803 by James Shelburne. p. 17 and WB 6/29.

FOSTER, Andrew W. and Tabitha Gunn. Married 11 September 1839 by
Samuel G. Mason. WB 12/22.

FOSTER, Burwell W. and Wealthy T. Robertson, 20 May 1823. Sur. Nathaniel
B. G. T. Robertson. Married 20 May 1823 by James Robertson. p.35
and WB 8/309.

FOSTER, Claiborne and Patsy Griffin. Married 21 October 1784 by Thomas
Crymes. WB 3/200.

FOSTER, James A. and Martha Anderson. Married 15 June 1831 by Silas
Shelburne. WB 11/2.

FOSTER, James, batchellar,and Susanna Wells, spinster. No date shown on
marriage bond #1510. Sur. Barttelot Anderson.

FOSTER, J. and A. W. Watts. Married 3 November 1815 by Charles Ogburn.
WB 10/181-A.

FOSTER, Josiah of Lunenburg, and Elizabeth Johnson, daughter of Joseph
Johnson, deceased, 29 November 1762. Sur. James Foster. p.3.

FOSTER, William and Milley Bohannon, 13 February 1837. Sur. William
Bohannon. p.51.

FOWLKES, Asa and Sarah C. Farmer. Married 18 September 1805 by William
Ellis. WB 6/175 and 136.

FOWLKES, Dabney G. and Laura A. Lester, ward of John D. Bailey who
consents, 25 November 1853. p.15.

FOWLKES, David W. and Tabitha Ann Jeffress, 18 June 1830. Sur. Thomas
H. Jeffress. p.43.

FOWLKES, Henry and Mary Crenshaw. Married 15 November 1802 by Joel
Johns. WB 6/11.

FOWLKES, James and Polly Jeffress. Married 15 March 1797 by William
Ellis. WB 4/244.

FOWLKES, Jennings and Eliza Jane Jeffress, 29 August 1829. Sur. Thomas
H. Jeffress. Married 1 September 1829 by Joel Johns. p.43 and
WB 9/483.

FOWLKES, John and Nancy Newby, 13 September 1787. Sur. John Newby.
Married 18 September 1787 by James Shelburne. p.9 and WB 3/309

FOWLKES, John and Mary Vaughan, 5 January 1813. Sur. William J. Bailey.
Married 14 January 1813 by James Shelburne. p. 27 and WB 7/124.

FOWLKES, John and Lucy B. Burks [or Bucks], 18 September 1826. Sur.
Samuel B. Bruce. Married 19 September 1826 by Silas Shelburne.
p.41 and WB 9/161.

FOWLKES, John J. and L. J. Fowlkes. Married 27 September 1832 by Silas
Shelburne. WB 11/2.

FOWLKES, Liberty B. and Harriet Bruce, 11 July 1825. Sur. Sm'l A. Bruce.
Married 21 July 1825 by Silas Shelburne. p.39 and WB 8/490.

FOWLKES, Robert and Emily F. Knight, 11 December 1837. Sur. William
Doswell. p.53.

FOWLKES, Thomas and Elizabeth Slaughter. Married 8 August 1821 by Silas
Shelburne. WB 8/227. [See Thomas Williams]

FOWLKES, Thomas H. and Emily L. Hurt, 18 November 1829. Sur. Richard C.
Mills. p. 43.

FOWLKES, Thomas P. and Clarky Cheatham, 12 September 1842. Sur. Madison
Cheatham. Married 21 September 1842 by James P. Arvin. p.55 and
WB 12/104.

FOWLKES, William A. and Eliza B. Ellis, 12 July 1824. Sur. John F. Ellis.
Married 21 July 1824 by William Hatchett. p.37 and WB 8/470.

FOWLKES, William E. and Ann P. Fowlkes. Married 13 July 1820 by Silas
Shelburne. WB 8/140.

FOWLKES, William J. and Mary G. Jordan, 29 November 1825. Sur. Miles
Jordan, Jr. Married 8 December 1825 by Thomas H. Jeffress. p.39
and WB 8/529.

FOWLKES, William S. and Narcissa Willson, 12 December 1836. Sur. James
Willson. Married 22 October 1836 by James M. Jeter whose return
was headed Brunswick County. p.51 and WB 11/272.

FRANKLIN, Bryant P. and Elizabeth D. Wood, 23 March 1849. Sur. Ira
Warner. Married 29 March 1849 by Samuel G. Mason. p.65 and WB 13/349.

FRANKLIN, Burrell W. and Martha Tunstill, 12 November 1821. Sur. Robert
Tunstill. Married 15 November 1821 by Thomas H. Jeffress. p.31 and WB 8/193.

FRANKLIN, Thomas and Polley Coleman, 10 February 1817. Sur. Laban
Coleman. Married 27 February 1817 by James Shelburne. p.31 and
WB 7/313.

FREEMAN, Arthur and Elizabeth Winn, 31 March 1830. Sur. John C. Freeman.
p.43.

FREEMAN, Calthrop and Letty Washband. Married 25 December 1782 by David Ellington. WB 3/132.

FREEMAN, Edward and Martha Cabaness. Married 29 April 1801 by John Neblett. WB 5/68.

FREEMAN, Edward R. and Christianna Watkins. Married 31 August 1819 by Thomas Adams. WB 8/67.

FREEMAN, Hamlin of Lunenburg, and Lucy Hazlewood, 27 March 1797. Sur. Samuel Ussery. Married 23 March 1797 by Charles Ogburn. p. 15 and WB 10/181.

FREEMAN, Henry and Sally A. Harris, 25 November 1842. Sur. James E. Hazelwood. Married 29 November 1842 by Thomas E. Locke at Miss Molly Bishop's residence. p.55, WB 12/97 and St. John's Church Register.

FREEMAN, John C. and Eliza A. Hurt, 19 October 1830. Sur. Hartwell Freeman. Married 19 October 1830 by Charles Ogburn. p.43 and W3 10/181.

FREEMAN, Thomas A. and Precilla Francis Toombs, 5 October 1843. Sur. Allen Duffer. Married by Daniel Petty whose list was returned to court 8 February 1847. p.57 and WB 13/14.

FREEMAN, Thrower and Jincy Cabaniss, 7 November 1797. Sur. Hamlin Freeman. Married 14 November 1797 by John Neblett. p.15 and WB 4/232.

FREEMAN, Thrower and Amey Gill, 18 September 1826. Sur. Webster Gill. Married 17 October 1826 by Charles Ogburn. p.41 and WB 10/181.

FROST, Beverly and Ann E. Rash, 30 December 1847. Sur. James Winn. Married 30 December 1847 by Thomas Adams. p.63 and WB 13/232.

FULLILOVE, Anthony of Lunenburg, and Nancey Thaxton, 12 January 1788. Sur. William Thaxton. p.9.

FUQUA, Isaiah and Emily Saterfield, 16 November 1846. Sur. Albert Royall. p.63.

FUQUA, Samuel and Susan White, 31 March 1836. Sur. Martin Phillips. p.51.

GAINES, S. and Susanna Harwood. Married 23 "M." 1816 by Charles Ogburn, whose list was returned June 1832. WB 10/181.

GALLION, Hail T. and Armentia D. White, 27 December 1843. Sur. Robert Phillips. Married by Robert Michaels whose return was dated October 25, 1844. p. 57 and WB 12/215.

GANDY, Samuel and Sarah Litina Barry. Married __ November 1790 by James Shelburne. WB 4/11A.

GARLAND, David of Lunenburg and Lucy Sturdivant, 24 March 1792. Sur. John Moody. p.13.

GARLAND, Peter of Lunenburg, and Martha Garland, 12 March 1767 [the M.R. says 10 March]. Sur. Sm'l Garland. p. 3.

GARLAND, Robert and Nancy Skinner, 17 February 1826. Sur. Edward R. Chambers. Married 18 February 1826 by Baxter Ragsdale. p.41 and WB 8/572.

GARLAND, Robert C. and Mary Jefferson, 20 September 1821. Sur. John Gee. Married 22 September 1821 by John Doyle. p.33 and WB 8/193.

GARLAND, William Terrel of Lunenburg and Martha Broadnax, 29 December 1786. Sur. Edward Broadnax. p.7.

GARNER, Samuel and Susanna Hazlewood, 23 March 1815. Sur. W. Williamson. p.29.

GARRETT, James and Nancy Rudder, 8 November 1803. Sur. Stephen Browne. p.17.

GARROTT, James of Lunenburg and Polly Johnson, 8 September 1796. Sur. Carril Jackson. p.15.

GARRETT, Nathaniel and Eleanor Hight, 20 March 1770. Sur. David Garland, Bartt: Anderson, and Samuel Overton, Jr. p.5.

GARRETT, William of Lunenburg and Nancy Talley, 3 January 1797. Sur. William Farguson. Married 5 January 1797 by John Neblett. p.15 and W3 4/168.

GARY, Henry R. and Elizabeth Keeton. Married by Daniel Petty who does not show the exact date of marriage. The return is dated 13 July 1835. WB 11/124.

GARY, Henry R. and Louisa Rose, 15 January 1844. Sur. David B. Bragg. Married by Daniel Petty whose list was returned to court dated 8 February 1847. p.59 and WB 13/14.

GARY, Henry R. and Mary F. Rose, both of Lunenburg, 24 January 1853. Mary is daughter of Archibald and Elizabeth Rose, both deceased, and is 21 years of age as proved by William T. Gary, a witness. Bros. & Sisters: Thomas A. Rose, Rebecca E. Rose, William Grigg and Elisa, his wife. p.12 and DB 35/340-341.

GASQUET, William A. and Martha J. Vaughan, 22 September 1823. Sur. Philip Poindexter. p.35.

GAULDIN, Drury E. and Virginia A. Hurt, 8 January 1844. Sur. Hartwell P. Cooksey. p.59.

GEE, A. L. and Susan L. Tisdale. Married 15 December 1824 by Charles Ogburn. WB 10/181A.

GEE, Benjamin and Bridgett Gee, 20 February 1793. Sur. Nathan Gee. p.13.

GEE, Charles of Lunenburg, and Sally Wilson, 12 March 1787. Sur. Jesse Gee. p.9.

GEE, Charles of Lunenburg and Kizzia Skinner, 15 September 1789. Sur.
Samuel Skinner. p.11.

GEE, Charles and Rebecca Gee. Married 29 December 1810 by Thomas Adams.
WB 7/39.

GEE, Edward W. and Rebecca C. Gee, 12 January 1829. Married 27 March
1828 by Thomas H. Jeffress who shows the name as Everard W. Gee.
p. 99 and WB 9/349.

GEE, Everard W. Gee and Martha B. Marable, 20 December 1844. Sur. James
F. Marable. Married 23 December 1844 by John C. Blackwell. p.59
and WB 12/286.

GEE, George L. and S. G. Shelor. Married 30 March 1819 by Charles Ogburn.
WB 10/181A.

GEE, Hartwell and Hannah P. Gee, 8 December 1823. Sur. Edward B. Gee. p.37.

GEE, James and Fanny W. Williams. Married 30 November 1809 by Thomas
Adams. WB 7/39.

GEE, James S. and Martha J. Crowder, 18 January 1836. Sur. Robert A.
Raney. Married by Daniel Petty whose list was returned 10 October
1836. p.51 and WB 11/179.

GEE, Jesse and Jincey Moore, 15 December 1806. Sur. John Ussery. Married
18 December 1806 by Matthew Dance. p.21 and WB 6/181.

GEE, John and Elizabeth Ragsdale. Married 4 February 1815 by Thomas Adams.
WB 7/249.

GEE, Joshua and Patsy Crymes. Married 25 December 1800 by William Ellis.
WB 5/67.

GEE, Matthew C. and Nancy Johnson. Married 11 November 1822 by Silas
Shelburne. WB 8/270.

GEE, Nathan and Ann McCraw. Married 9 August 1832 by Pleasant Barnes.
WB 11/281.

GEE, Nelson W. and Catharine Byars, 14 December 1811. Sur. Thomas Morgan.
Married 15 December 1811 by Thomas Adams. p.23 and WB 7/40.

GEE, Reuben and Jane Gee. Married 1 January 1801 by Charles Ogburn whose
return was dated June 1832. WB 10/181A.

GEE, Thomas and Mourning Crymes, 26 December 1806. Sur. Drury Gee. p.21.

GEE, Thomas N. and Mary E. Gee, 23 February 1847. Sur. Nathan Gee.
Married "about 24th February 1847" by Thomas Adams. p.63 and WB 13/105.

GEE, William and Elizabeth Gee. Married 20 December 1801 by John Neblett.
WB 5/67A.

GEE, William and Salley Moody. Married 12 September 1805 by Matthew Dance. WB 6/138.

GEE, Wilson P. and Ann W. Rainey. Married by Daniel Petty whose list was returned to court dated 8 February 1847. WB 13/14.

GEE, William S. and Mary R. Tisdale, 3 January 1824. Sur. James A. Smithson. Married 13 January 1824 by Charles Ogburn. p.37 and WB 10/181A.

GEE, William O. and Nancy Knott, 10 December 1821. Sur. Charles Smithson. p.31.

GEERS, William R. of Lunenburg, and Sarah Moon, 15 November 1813. Sur. Cornelius Crenshaw. Married 11 November 1813 by James Shelburne. p.27 and WB 7/110.

GEORGE, Herbert and Scelah Hill, 21 December 1785. Sur. Thomas Taylor. p.7.

GEORGE, Jeremiah of Lunenburg and Sarah Calliham, 22 September 1787. Sur. John Ritchie. p.9.

GEORGE, Thomas of Lunenburg and Betty Wrenn, 27 February 1783. Sur. David Abernathy. p.7.

GERNEY [or GURNEY], Daniel and Jerusha Winn. Married 16 November 1786 by Thomas Crymes. WB 3/268.

GILL, Francis and Nancy Allen Andrews, 17 October 1836. Sur. Elisha Andrews. p.51.

GILL, Hamlin and Elizabeth Russell. Married 16 October 1805 by James Shelburne. WB 6/146A.

GILL, Matthew C. and Nancy Johnson, 11 November 1822. Sur. George L. Bayne. Married 11 November 1822 by Silas Shelburne. p.33 and WB 8/270.

GILL, Philip, Jr. and Eliza A. Graham, 12 December 1825. Sur. Daniel Daly. Married 22 December 1825 by Sterling W. Fowler. p.39 and WB 8/544.

GILL, Richard H. and Martha Maddux, 30 November 1833. Sur. William H. Taylor. p.45.

GILL, W. D. and Temperance Gill. Married 17 February 1824 by Charles Ogburn. WB 10/181A.

GILL, William M. and Nancy F. Hardy, 20 September 1834. Sur. Joel Blackwell, Jr. p.45.

GILLET, Peter and Patsey Elmore, both of colour. Married 6 January 1818 by Francis Smith. WB 8/28.

GILLIUM, Hail T. and Ariamentia D. White, granddaughter of Carter White, between December 28, 1843 and November 28, 1844. DB 33/242.

GILLIAM, James and Martha Isbell, 1 December 1761. Sur. Henry Isbell.
  p. 3.

GLASSON, William and Louisa Edmonds, 3 September 1851. Louisa being
  21 years of age as proved by Henry Dinkins. p. 5.

GLEN, Jeremiah of Lunenburg and [Anne] Blagrave, 28 January 1765. Sur.
  Edwin Jordan, Jr., Samuel Garland, David Garland, and Peter Garland.
  [The bride's first name was left blank on marriage bond, but Bell
  gives it as Anne] p.3

GLEN, John and Sarah Bacon, 12 July 1770. Sur. William Taylor and A.
  Johnston, Jr. p. 5.

GLENN, Nathaniel P. and Eliz. A. Stephenson, 20 September 1830. Sur.
  Henry W. Stephenson. Married 21 September 1830 by Silas Shelburne.
  p. 43 and WB 10/131.

GLEN, Tyree of Cumberland Parish, Lunenburg County, and Mary Roe, 5 April
  1751. Sur. John Cox and Clem Read. p. 1.

GLENN, Tyree and Rachel Moon, 12 May 1785. Sur. William Glenn. Married
  31 May 1785. p. 7 and WB 3/214.

GOBER, William of Lunenburg and Lucy Campbell, 18 April 1785. Sur. George
  Campbell. p. 7.

GOIN, John and Olive May Robertson. Married 13 November 1802 by James
  Shelburne. WB 6/29.

GOODE, Phillip and Anne Jones, 14 February 1766. Sur. Grey Smith. p. 3.

GOODWIN, James and Nancy H. Ragsdale. Married __ December 1818 by
  Thomas Adams. WB 8/67.

GOODWIN, John Sr. and Martha Jackson, 16 November 1808. Sur. Stith Hardy.
  p. 23.

GOODWIN, John and Matilda Burnett. Married __ April 1819 by Thomas Adams.
  WB 8/67.

GOODWYN, John William and Henrietta Barnes, 18 October 1838. Sur. John L.
  Morgan. p.53.

GOODWYNE, Peterson E. and Evelina V. Davis 13 December _____*. Sur. John
  A. Bishop. *On marriage bond #1506 the date reads 1861 and states,
  "... bound unto John Rutherford, acting governor..." He was Acting
  Governor March 31, 1841 - March 31, 1842, therefore the compilers
  believe this date should be 1841.

GORDON, James S. of Lunenburg and Nancey M. Johnson, 24 April 1813. Sur.
  Joseph Keeton. Married 24 April 1813 by Baxter Ragsdale. p.27 and
  WB 7/82.

GORDON, Roderick of Lunenburg, and Susanna Stokes Ellis, 21 December 1787. Sur. Jonathan Zachary. Married 25 December 1787 by Thomas Crymes. p. 9 and WB 3/309.

GORDON, William and Elizabeth Bacon, spinster, 22 May 1754 [the marriage bond states 1756]. Sur. Nathaniel Bacon. p. 1.

GORDON, William T. and Patsy Winn, 29 August 1811. Sur. Jesse Laffoon. Married 29 August 1811 by Thomas Adams. p. 23 and WB 7/40.

GOSEE, James and Rebecca Bowers, Married 20 January 1800 by John Neblett. WB 5/35.

GOSEE, John of Lunenburg, and Elizabeth Tucker, 16 February 1796. Sur. Robert Davis. Married 18 February 1796 by John Neblett. p.15 and WB 4/127.

GRAHAM, Robert and Eliza Lockhead, 21 September 1803. Sur. James MacFarland. p. 17.

GRANGER, John of Lunenburg, and Agness Roberts, 21 February 1781. Sur. Henry Gill. p. 5.

GRANGER, Moses and Patty Phillips. Married 28 March 1799 by John Jones. WB 5/6A.

GRANT, Elisha and Elizabeth Meanly. Married 18 July 1805 by John Jones "of Nottoway". WB 6/147.

GRANT, William and Elizabeth M. Reese, 27 October 1838. Sur. Irwin Hammock. Married 30 October 1838 by Joshua Featherston. p. 53 and WB 12/7.

GRAY, Frederick and Martha Williams, 19 December 1803. Sur. William Weaver. Married 21 December 1803 by John Rogers. p.17 and WB 6/82.

GRAY, Jo: and Elizabeth deGraffenreid. Married 31 January 1805 by William Ellis. WB 6/135 and 175.

GREEN - See also GUNN.

GREEN, Abraham Keen and Martha F. Jordan. Married 7 October 1828 by Silas Shelburne. WB 9/480.

GREEN, Albert and Narcissa B. Estes. Married 18 September 1832 by Pleasant Barnes. WB 11/281.

GREEN, Cannon Jones of Lunenburg, and Elizabeth Goodwin Blackwell, 15 August 1796. Sur. Joel Blackwell. Married 17 August 1796 by John Neblett. WB 4/133 and p. 15.

GREEN, Charles and Phebe B. Buck. Married 2 November 1807 by Joel Johns. WB 6/244.

GREENE, Coleman and Nancey Crymes, 14 June 1792. Sur. D. Green. Married 14 June 1792 by William Ellis. p.13 and WB 4/28.

GREEN, Croxson and Sarah Crymes. Married 19 February 1801 by William Ellis. WB 5/67.

GREEN, Everett and Sophia A. Winn, 26 December 1836. Sur. Thomas E. Winn. p.51.

GREEN, John C. and Eliza Ann Jordan. Married 24 April 1827 by Silas Shelburne. WB 9/161.

GREEN, Matthew of Lunenburg and Ann Dowsing, 3 July 1775. Sur. William Dowsing. p.5.

GREEN, Thomas B. and Ann E. Neblett. Married __ December 1820 by Thomas Adams. WB 8/151.

GREGG, William F. and Eliza Rose, daughter of Elizabeth Rose, 15 September 1847. Sur. Elizabeth Rose. Married "about 15 September 1847" by Thomas Adams. p.63 and WB 13/105.

GREGORY, Edmund of Lunenburg and Fanny Boswell, 13 October 1785. Sur. William Boswell. Married by Arch^d McRoberts in 1785. p. 7 and WB 3/252.

GREGORY, George E. and Caroline Anderson, 11 November 1844. Sur. Garner Webb. p.59.

GREGORY, Joseph, Jr. of Lunenburg and Peggy Evans, 8 May 1788. Sur. Joseph Gregory, Sr. p.9.

GREGORY, Joseph and Alice Davis. Married 11 December 1828 by Silas Shelburne. WB 9/480.

GREGORY, Joseph and Mary B. Lee. Married 27 January 1831 by Silas Shelburne. WB 11/2.

GREGORY, Richard C. and Martha A. Hamlin, 9 November 1835. Sur. William Williams. p.47.

GREGORY, Roderick and Cinthy Couch, daughter of Thomas Couch, 29 April 1817. Sur. Thomas Couch. Married 1 May 1817 by James Shelburne. p.29 and WB 7/313.

GREGORY, Roger and Francis Loury, 30 March 1776. Sur. Drury M. Daniel and Martha Taylor. p.5.

GREGORY, Thomas and Patsey [or Martha] Parsons, 11 October 1804. Sur. Thomas Parsons. Married 5 November 1804 by James Shelburne. p. 19 and WB 6/147.

GREGORY, Thomas and Keturah Rowlett Winn, 24 February 1809. Sur. William Taylor. p.23.

GREGORY, Thomas N. and Betsy Ann Williams. Married 7 November 1816 by William Richards. WB 7/307.

GREGORY, Thomas N. and Martha A. Eubank. Married 1 January 1829 by Silas Shelburne. WB 9/480.

GREGORY, Wright of Lunenburg, and Margaret Bragg, 13 November 1794. Sur. John Bragg. Married 27 November 1794 by John Williams. p. 13 and WB 4/88.

GRIFFIN, Anthony of County of Halifax, and Susannah Crenshaw, 14 January 1793. Sur. Jeremiah Terry. Married 15 January 1793 by James Shelburne. p. 13 and WB 4/46.

GRIFFIN, James of Lunenburg, and Christian Crenshaw, 4 January 1785. Sur. Daniel Crenshaw. Married 6 January 1785 by Thomas Crymes. p. 7 and WB 3/200.

GRIFFIN, William and Deanna L. Morgan, 30 October 1824. Sur. Hugh Wallace. p. 37.

GRIMES, William and Sarah Dizmang, 21 August 1806. Sur.Joel Moore. p. 21.

GRISHAM, Asa of Lunenburg, and Elizabeth Hudson, 3 November 1785. Sur. William Hudson. p. 7.

GRISHAM, Asa and Elizabeth Lacey, 2 February 1804. Sur. William Garrett. p. 19.

GUATNEY, Paraham and Martha Crow, 6 March 1822. Sur. Phillip Russell. Married 7 March 1822 by Silas Shelburne. p. 33 and WB 8/227.

GWATNEY, Benjamin and Sally Sire. Married 10 November 1815 by Matthew Dance. WB 7/219.

GUNN - See also GREEN.

GUNN, Daniel, Jr. of Lunenburg, and Jerusha Winn, 9 November 1786. Sur. Philip Snead. Married 16 November 1786 by Thomas Crymes. p. 7.

GUNN, Daniel E. and Tabitha Jane Lee, 14 November 1842. Sur. Ed. Lee. Married 23 November 1842 by Samuel G. Mason. p. 55 and WB 12/170.

GUNN, Gabriel and Martha Lambert, 13 December 1803. Sur. Lewis Lambert. p. 17.

GUNN, James of Lunenburg, and Morning Winn, 24 December 1789. Sur. Samuel Winn. p. 11.

GUNN, James and Tabitha Edmundson. Married May 1808 by Thomas Adams. WB 6/253.

GUNN, James H. and Emily C. Saunders. Married 20 June 1832 by Silas Shelburne. WB 11/2.

GUNN, James H. and Mary A. Hawkins, 12 August 1850. Samuel E. Lee made oath that Mary is more than 21 years of age. p. 1.

GUNN, William S. and Harriet S. Wyatt, 17 October 1825. Sur. William P.
Penn. p.39.

GWIN, David and Dorothy Jones, spinster, __ June 1757. Sur. Godfrey
Jones and G. Carrington, Jr. p. 1.

HAINES, James P. and Martha Haines, 24 November 1834. Sur. Thomas E.
Byassee. [The signature on the marriage bond reads Jas. P. Ford,
and the endorsement also reads Ford.] p. 45.

HAINES, John of Nottoway County, and Martha Walker of Lunenburg County.
Married 8 December 1791 by John Jones of Nottoway. WB 4/20.

HAILEY, Ambrose and Mary Woodard. Married 24 December 1782 by David
Ellington. WB 3/132.

HALY, Ambrose and Nancy P. Smithson, 8 December 1823. Sur. Francis
Radford. Married 11 December 1823 by Silas Shelburne. p.35 and WB 8/340.

HAILEY, John and Susanna Tatum. Married 11 March 1784 by Thomas Crymes.
WB 3/156.

HALEY, Henry B. and Casandra Smithson, 30 November 1830. Sur. Henry A.
Fowlkes. Married 1 December 1830 by Silas Shelburne. The signature
of Vivalai Harper appears on the marriage bond. p.45 and WB 10/131.

HALEY, William and Olive Winn. Married 2 April 1795 by John Neblett.
WB 4/87A.

HAMLETT, John and Elizabeth Simmons, 11 May 1835. Sur. Fred^k Lester. p.47.

HAMLETT, Stephen B. of Lunenburg, and Mary Johns, 10 August 1813. Sur.
John Leigh. p. 25.

HAMLETT, Turner and Susanna Farguson, 29 September 1817. Sur. Benjamin
Wilkinson. Married __ September 1817 by Thomas Adams. p.29 and
WB 7/356.

HAMLIN, John and Ann Elizabeth White, 26 January 1836. Sur. Richard C.
Gregory. p.51.

HAMLIN, Thomas and Mary Ligon Stainback, 28 April 1807. Sur. Thomas
Blackwell. Married 5 May 1807 by John Jones. p.21 and WB 6/187.

HAMLIN, William B. and Mary D. Yates. Married 5 October 1810 by James
Shelburne. WB 7/15.

HAMMOCK, Hugh and Lucy M. Peace, 14 November 1825. Sur. John Peace.
Married 22 November 1825 by J. R. Foster. p.39 and WB 8/572.

HAMMOCK, James of Lunenburg and Elizabeth Amos, 17 Jan. [or June], 1805. Sur.
James Amos. Married 20 June 1805 by John Jones of Nottoway. p.21
and WB 6/147.

HAMMOCK, John and Caty Hanks. Married 6 August 1791 by John Rogers.
WB 4/19.

HAMMOCK, John and Elizabeth Amos, 9 March 1815. Sur. James Hammock.
Married 25 March 1815 by Stephen Jones. p.29 and WB 7/276.

HAMMOCK, Lewis and Elizabeth S. Freeman, 4 October 1852. John T. Hammock
made oath that Elizabeth is more than 21 years of age. p. 10.

HAMMONDS, Anderson and Eliza Dicks, 27 September 1836. Sur. James Dicks.
Married 27 September 1836 by Joshua Featherston. p.49 and WB 11/182.

HAMMONS, Richard and Dolly Calliham, 17 September 1823. Sur. Henry
Calliham. p. 35.

HAMMONS, Robert and Sally Singleton, 4 December 1804. Sur. William
Hammons. Married 5 December 1804 by John Neblett. p. 19 and WB 6/124.

HAMMOND, Rolly and Lucy Ambrose. Married __ November 1808 by Thomas
Adams. WB 6/253A.

HAMMONDS, Wells and Susan Edmunds, 12 October 1835. Sur. Wilkins Edmunds.
Married 12 October 1835 by Joshua Featherston. p.49 and WB 11/156.

HAMMONDS, Washington and Rebecca Waller, 18 January 1849. Sur. Mortimor
Laffoon. p.67.

HAMMOND, William and Elizabeth Rudder. Married 25 March 1800 by John Neblett.
WB 5/35.

HAMMONS, William and Clary Smith. Married 19 September 1819 by Stephen
Jones. WB 8/96.

HAMMONS, Wyatt and Rebecca Stewart, 13 November 1833. Sur. Wilkins
Edmunds. Married 14 November 1833 by Joshua Featherston. p. 45 and
WB 11/54.

HAMPTON, Zachariah and Dicy Homles [Hanks or Hawks?], 26 December 1803.
Sur. Norman Hawks. Married 27 December 1803 by John Rogers who
shows name as Dicey Hanks. p. 17 and WB 6/82.

HANKIN, Moses and Katy Ann Ford. Married 27 February 1804 by Matthew
Dance. WB 6/78. [See Moses Hawkins on page 60.]

HANKINS, Thomas and Elizabeth E. Marable, daughter of Hartwell Marable,
14 November 1853. Thomas J. Lockett, witness. p.15.

HANKS, Thomas and Nancy Hammock. Married 31 March 1791 by John Rogers.
WB 4/7A.

HANN, Uriah and Polly Shelborn. Married __ November 1790 by James
Shelburne. WB 4/11A.

HANSBROUGH, James and Eliza Robins, 23 August 1830. Sur. Josiah Roberts
and Solomon Robins. Married 25 August 1830 by Joshua Featherston.
p. 45 and WB 10/101.

HARDING, Edward and Phebe Hudson. Married 14 December 1793 by James
Shelburne. WB 4/46.

HARDING, James H. and Emily S. Harding, 9 November 1846. Sur. John
Harding. Married 25 November 1846 by Samuel G. Mason whose list
is headed, "Charlotte C.H." p.63 and WB 13/10.

HARDING, Robert and Sarah Crafton, 17 August 1835. Sur. Felix Crafton.
Married 26 August 1835 by M. M. Dance. p.47 and WB 11/336.

HARDING, William and Susan Moore, 23 March 1843. Sur. John T. Dowdy.
p.57.

HARDIE, Christopher and Polly Palmore. Married 25 September 1805 by
Matthew Dance. WB 6/138.

HARDY, George Edward and Mary Ellen Irby, daughter of William Irby who
signs certificate, 27 October 1853. Samuel Hardy, witness. p.14.

HARDY, George W. and Paulina C. Rowlett, 10 December 1851. Joseph G.
Hardy made oath that Paulina is over 21 years of age. p.6.

HARDY, Griffin O. and Lucy R. Bridgeforth, 8 January 1849. Sur. George
H. Hardy. Married 10 January 1849 by Thomas Adams. p.65 and
WB 13/232.

HARDY, Henry and Mary S. Neblett, 11 June 1812. Sur. Charles Hardy.
Married 12 June 1812 by Thomas Adams. p.25 and WB 7/40.

HARDY, Henry and Pamelia Betts, 13 December 1824. Sur. Larkin Hardy. p.37.

HARDY, Henry G. and S. [or L.] Gee. Married by Daniel Petty whose list
is dated 7 December 1833, the exact date not shown. WB 11/32.

HARDY, J. Covington and Sarah A. Boswell, 9 September 1844. Sur. Henry
G. Hardy. Married by Daniel Petty whose list was returned to court
dated 8 February 1847. p.59 and WB 13/14.

HARDY, John and Sally Betts. Married 5 February 1801 by William Ellis.
WB 5/67.

HARDY, Jordan R. and Ann Eliza Love, 15 March 1841. Sur. Henry G. Hardy.
p. 55.

HARDY, Joshua and Elizabeth Gee. Married 26 October 1808 by Richard Dabbs.
WB 7/9.

HARDY, Joshua and Mary A. Yarbrough. Married 27 December 1820 by
Joel Johns. WB 8/357.

HARDY, Miles and Hannah Pettus, 22 November 1803. Sur. John C. Hardy.
Married 24 November 1803 by Matthew Dance. p.17 and WB 6/73.

HARDY, Miles and Tabitha Lambert, 21 October 1830. Sur. Daniel H.
Robertson. p. 45.

HARDY, Vincent and Mary A. Betts, Married 5 June 1802 by W. M. Ellis.
WB 6/11.

HARDY, William H. and Petronella S. Hardy, 16 December 1845. Sur.
William F. Blackwell. Married 23 December 1845 by Richard E. G.
Adams. p.61 and WB 13/14.

HARDWICK, Joseph and Elizabeth Toone. Married 30 April 1807 by James
Shelburne. WB 6/230A.

HARDWICK, Leonard and Ermer Ragsdale. Married 8 November 1810 by
Matthew Dance. WB 7/10A.

HARDRICK, Moses and Nelly Overby. Married 12 March 1796 by John Neblett.
W3 4/127.

HARPER, Daniel and Rhody Morris. Married 13 October 1791 by William
Ellis. WB 4/14.

HARPER, V. and Mary A. Fuqua. Married 18 December 1832 by Silas Shelburne.
WB 11/2.

HARRIS, Benjamin and Rebecca Dance. Married 15 December 1802 by Matthew
Dance. WB 6/29.

HARRIS, Giles and Caroline Ellis. Married 1 September 1831 by Silas
Shelburne. WB 11/2.

HARRIS, John A. and Ann C. Gee, 26 August 1835. Sur. William J. Gee.
p.49.

HARRIS, Samuel and Mary Davis. Married 3 June 1816 by Thomas Adams.
WB 7/249.

HARRIS, Thomas and Sarah A. R. Ellis, 14 February 1825. Sur. Ellison
Ellis. p. 39.

HARRIS, W. and P. G. Ballard. Married 9 February 1820 by Charles
Ogburn. WB 10/181A.

HARRISON, James and Ella Shelton. Married 14 November 1799 by James
Shelburne. WB 5/51.

HARRISON, James P. and Salley Landrum. Married 10 September 1807 by
William Ellis. Sur. Arthur Landrum. WB 6/207A.

HARSING, Robert and Sarah Crafton. Married 26 August 1835 by M. M.
Dance. WB 11/336.

HARVEY, John P. and Drusilah E. W. Pennington, 27 January 1851. Robert
Roberts proves she is over 21 years of age. p. 3.

HARWOOD, Warner R. and Elizabeth H. Pettus. Married 24 December 1828 by Silas Shelburne. WB 9/480.

HARDWOOD, John J. and L. G. Crowder. Married 23 December 1828 by Charles Ogburn. WB 10/181A.

HASKINS, Christopher C. and Martha H. Blackwell, 10 May 1841. Sur. William L. Bridgforth. p.55.

HASTIN, John and Cloa Boze. Married 8 April 1793 by William Ellis. WB 4/43.

HASTINGS, William A. and Eliza Johnson. Married 5 December 1816 by Joel Johns. WB 7/280.

HATCHETT, Daniel F. and Jane Brown. Married 19 February 1828 by Abner Watkins. WB 9/396.

HATCHETT, Edward and Mary Newsteys Blagrove. Married 18 December 1781 by Thomas Crymes. WB 3/104.

HATCHETT, Hanie and Francis Jones. Married 23 April 1816 by James Shelburne. WB 7/313.

HATCHETT [HATCHELL in bond], James L. and Susan Edmonds, 29 November 1847. Sur. James Edmonds. p. 63.

HATCHITT, John A. and Narcissa W. Jeffress, 14 October 1822. Sur. Achillis J. Norment. Married 29 October 1822 by Thomas H. Jeffress. p. 35 and WB 8/263.

HATCHETT, John Smith and Phebe Bailey, 8 August 1811. Sur. Richard Alderson. Married 17 August 1811 by Joel Johns. p. 23 and WB 7/60.

HATCHETT, William and Elizabeth Farmer, 10 December 1804. Sur. James Farmer, Jr. Married 13 December 1804 by William Ellis. p. 19 and WB 6/175.

HATCHETT, William H. and Virginia A. M. Epes, 6 October 1841. Sur. James P. Street. Married 14 October 1841 by Thomas G. Locke at Mrs. Rebecca Epes' residence. p.55, WB 12/97 and St. John's Church Register.

HATCHET, William H. and Martha A. Beverly. Married 26 November 1844 by T. E. Locke at F. W. Epes' residence, Nottoway Co. St. John's Church Register.

HAWKES, John A. and Martha Butler, 16 December 1817. Sur. Anderson Vaughan. Married 3 December 1817 by Caleb N. Bell. p. 29 and WB 7/365.

HAWKINS, Isaiah and Polly Farmer. Married 30 September 1801 by W. M. Ellis. WB 6/11.

HAWKINS, John and Jenny Johnson. Married 30 December 1789 by James
    Shelburne. WB 3/358.

HAWKINS, John and Elizabeth Hix. Married November 1790 by James
    Shelburne. WB 4/11A.

HAWKINS, Joshua and Suckey Johnson. Married 29 March 1782 by James
    Shelburne. WB 3/118.

HAWKINS, Laban and Eady Jane Foster. Married 2 August 1827 by Thomas
    H. Jeffress. WB 9/212.

HAWKINS, Moses and Katy Ann Ford, 25 February 1804. Sur. William
    Richards. Married 27 February 1804 by Matthew Dance.
    [See Moses Hankin on page 56.] p. 19 and WB 6/78.

HAWKINS, Thomas and Mary Howard, 29 January 1753. Sur. Pinkethman
    Hawkins, Paul Carrington and Thomas Nash. p. 1.

HAWTHORNE, James and Rebecca A. Freeman. Married by Daniel Petty whose
    list is returned to court dated 8 February 1847. WB 13/14.

HAWTHORNE, Peter W. and Phebe Reese, 30 May 1825. Sur. Daniel Reese.
    p. 39.

HAWTHORNE, Peter W. and Pamela J. Peace, 2 November 1835. Sur. Willis
    H. Peace. p.49.

HAWTHORNE, Peter W., Jr. and Lucy A. M. Featherstun, 31 October 1842.
    Sur. Samuel A. Peace. p. 57.

HAWTHORN, Robert M. and Sarah M. Manson, daughter of Susan H. Manson,
    20 August 1852, proved by oath of W. Thweatt Blackwell. p.9.

HAYS, George L. and Sarah Munford Jones. Married 10 September 1839 at
    Mrs. Branch Jones' residence. The name F. H. McGuire also appears
    on this marriage but no connection stated. St. John's Church
    Register.

HAYES, James and Camilla M. Smith, 25 December 1843. Sur. John Henry
    Smith. p. 57.

HAYES, James and Henrietta A. Smith, daughter of Anthony W. Smith who
    consents, 13 June 1853. p. 13.

HAYES, Robert and Sarah B. Winn. Married 20 November 1800 by John
    Neblett. WB 5/35.

HAYS, Thomas W. and Dorothy B. Smith, daughter of Drury A. Smith who
    consents, 18 December 1850. p. 3.

HAYMORE, Daniel and Polly Chickley. Married 24 January 1799 by William
    Ellis.

HAIMOUR [HAYMORE], John and Polly Callis. Married 26 March 1795 by John
Neblett. WB 4/88.

HAZELWOOD, Green and Polly Ann Cooper, 28 December 1841. Sur. Joseph
Dyson. p. 55.

HAZELWOOD, James E. and Martha H. Jones, 6 May 1850. Sur. R. H. Allen.
p. 67.

HAZELWOOD, James E. and Roberta J. Tucker, 5 August 1850, "on certification
of William Tucker proved by George C. Robertson." p. 1.

HAZLEWOOD, John and Nancy Bohannon. Married 23 September 1799 by William
Ellis, Sr. WB 5/22.

HAZELWOOD, John and Dicey M. Bohannon, 14 August 1843. Sur. Philip H.
Bohannon. p.57.

HAZLEWOOD, John, Sr. and Nancy Cole, 13 September 1803. Sur. Josiah
Alderson. Married 17 September 1803 by Joel Johns. p. 17 and
WB 6/76.

HAZLEWOOD, Larkin and Lucy Kelly, 5 October 1824. Sur. Anderson Stewart.
Married 6 October 1824 by Baxter Ragsdale. p. 37 and WB 8/454.

HAZLEWOOD, Reuben and Elizabeth Bohannon. Married 20 September 1797 by
William Ellis. WB 4/244.

HAZLEWOOD, Richard and Eliza G. Brown. Married 19 March 1819. Included
on list returned to court 8 April 1819 but the minister's name not
shown. WB 8/38.

HENDRICK, Moses and Nelly Overby. Married 12 March 1796 by John Neblett.
WB 4/127.

HENDRICK, Obediah and Polly Haley. Married 18 December 1800 by Edward
Almond. WB 6/81A.

HENRY, Robert, Clerk, and Jane Cladwell [Caldwell?], widow, 11 February
1754. Sur. David Caldwell and P. Carrington. p. 1.

HERRING, Stephen and Dorothy Johns. Married 24 December 1801 by Joel
Johns. WB 6/11.

HERRING, William and Betsy Flipping. Married 22 March 1796 by William
Ellis. WB 4/168.

HICKS, Balaam and Elizabeth J. Gee, 17 December 1833. Sur. E. W. Gee.
Married by Daniel Petty whose list was dated 13 July 1835. p.45
and WB 11/124.

HIGHTOWER, John and Elizabeth Locke. Married 14 September 1781 by James
Shelburne. WB 3/92.

HIGHTOWER, Juden and Cushy Hazlewood. Married 22 January 1800 by
Charles Ogburn whose list was recorded June 1832. WB 10/181A.

HIGHTOWER, William and S. Andrews. Married 27 March 1810 by Charles
Ogburn whose list was recorded June 1832. WB 10/181A.

HILL, William E. and Ellen C. Bacon, 13 June 1848. Sur. Gillie M.
Bacon. Married 14 June 1848 by Richard E. G. Adams. p. 65 and
W3 13/191.

HILTON, William and Betsey Taylor, 4 October 1822. Sur. Joseph Winn.
p. 35.

HINES, Millington and Nancy L. Hite. Married 2 August 1805 by John
Neblett. WB 6/147.

HINES, Samuel T. and Emily Frances Anderson. Married 26 March 1840
by Samuel G. Mason. WB 12/22.

HINES, Thomas and Martha J. Walker, 10 August 1850, "on certification
given by herself proved by oath of Turner S. Hines." p. 1.

HINES, Washington S. and Mary A. Turner, 16 January 1852. George
Thompson made oath that Mary is 21 years of age. p. 7.

HINES, William A. and Mary D. Hite, 16 November 1829. Sur. Julius Hite.
Married 27 November 1829 by Joshua Featherston. p. 41 and WB 10/1.

HINES, William A. and Martha S. Pennington, 4 November 1846. Sur. James
L. Hite. Married 5 November 1846 by John C. Blackwell. p. 63 and
WB 13/11.

HINES, William T. and Sarah Ann Watson, 11 November 1844. Sur. Elisha
M. Watson. Married 28 November 1844 by John Thompson. p. 59 and
WB 12/286.

HITCHENS, Jesse and Martha Richardson. Married 30 March 1825 by Baxter
Ragsdale. WB 8/572.

HITE, Benjamin W. and Jane Marie Hatchett, 13 June 1836. Sur. Haynie
Hatchett. p. 51.

HITE, Benjamin W. of Lunenburg County, and Sarah Moore, 9 October 1800.
Sur. Edmund F. Taylor. Married 20 October 1806 by Matthew Dance.
p. 17 and WB 6/181.

HOBSON, John and Ermina B. DeGraffenreidt, _____ 1812. Sur. William
B. DeGraffenreidt. Married 24 February 1812 by Joel Johns. p. 25
and WB 7/120.

HOLMES, Curtis R. and Sarah P. Yarbrough, 8 January 1821. Sur. Joshua
Hardy. p. 31.

HOLMES, Isaac and Henrietta Willson, 9 April 1814. Sur. Joseph W.
Rudd. Married "A." 1814 by Charles Ogburn. p. 27 and WB 10/182.

HOLMES, Isaac E. and Rebecca E. Dance, 16 August 1850. M. M. Dance
certifies that Rebecca is of age. p. 1.

HOLMES, Joseph and Polly H. Holmes, 10 November 1845. Sur. John
Holmes. p.61.

HOLMES, Nathan and Susan Hitchens, 26 November 1835. Sur. Edward
Holmes. p.49.

HOOMES [HOLMES], William H. and Mary Jane [or Jones] Hitchins, 1 September 1842. Sur. Edward Hoomes. Married by Daniel Petty whose
list was returned to court dated 8 February 1847. p. 57 and
W3 13/14.

HOLMES, William T. M. and Martha Augustine Gee, 12 December 1836. Sur.
Wilson Harris. p. 51.

HOOD, Robert and Rebecca Bates, 4 January 1823. Sur. Pleasant Bates.
Married 4 January 1823 by James Robertson. p. 37 and WB 8/309.

HOOD, Royal and Biddy Pully, 21 August 1836. Sur. William Harding.
Married 25 August 1836 by Pleasant Barnes. p. 49 and WB 11/281.

HOOD, William and Nancy Landrom. Married 21 January 1795 by James
Shelburne. WB 4/107.

HOLT, Thomas J. and Rebeccah Rowlett, 26 September 1836. Sur. William
W. Moring. p. 49.

HOLT, William and Rachel Jones, 25 April 1750. Sur. Godfrey Jones and
Thomas Nash. p. 1.

HOPKINS, Arthur and Judith Jefferson, spinster, 7 September 1762. Sur.
Edmund Taylor and Robert Munford. p. 3.

HOWARD, Henry and Priscilla Farrar, spinster, 4 May 1762. Sur. John
Potter. p. 3.

HUBBARD, H. G. and Mary Laurella Tisdale, daughter of John D. Tisdale,
12 January 1852. John D. Tisdale present and consents. p. 7.

HUDDLESTONE, Thomas and Usille Moore, spinster, 2 December 1758. Sur.
William Moore. p. 1.

HUDGIN, Aaron and Martha Dobbins. Married 1 June 1797 by John Neblett.
WB 4/231A.

HUDGINS, John J. and Bidsey N. Steagall, 31 August 1822. Sur. George
Steagall. p. 33.

HUDSON, Ambrose and Hannah Willson. Married 16 December 1804 by James
Shelburne. WB 6/147.

HUDSON, E. and Amanda Jane Poultney. Married 7 September 1831 by M. M. Dance. WB 11/19.

HUDSON, ETHELBERT J. and Susan W. Yarbrough, 26 May 1836. Sur. Elijah D. Hardy. Married 1 June 1836 by John Thompson, who gives the first name of the bride as Luciann. p. 49 and WB 11/173.

HUDSON, Freeman and Elizabeth Callis, 5 August 1817. Sur. John Singleton. Married __ August 1817 by Thomas Adams. p. 31 and WB 7/356.

HUDSON, Irby and Nancy B. McConnico, 30 October 1808. Sur. Charles Betts. Married 3 November 1808 by William Ellis. p. 23 and WB 6/256.

HUDSON, James and Nancy Harris. Married 5 May 1781 by James Shelburne. WB 3/252.

HUDSON, James M. and Martha B. Marable, 28 October 1844. Sur. Joseph F. Ellis. p. 59.

HUDSON, James W. and Martha Eliza Rogers, 15 February 1836. Sur. Reuben Rogers. p. 49.

HUDSON, John and Mary Beasley. Married by Thomas Crymes whose list was dated 16 October 1781. WB 3/104.

HUDSON, Peter and Mary Murrill. Married 24 November 1789 by James Shelburne. WB 3/358.

HUDSON, Robert and Zillah Jackson, 23 November 1808. Sur. John Christian. Married __ November 1808 by Thomas Adams. p.23 and WB 6/254.

HUDSON, Rowland and Doshe Harding. Married 14 January 1806 by William Ellis. WB 6/175.

HUDSON, Ward and Anna Threatt. Married 1 March 1787 by Thomas Crymes. WB 3/269.

HUDSON, Ward and Martha Ann Estes, 29 August 1838. Sur. Elijah J. Estes. p.53.

HUGHES, William and Polly Winn. Married 30 June 1802 by W. M. Ellis. WB 6/11

HUGHES, William and Mariah Winn. Married 7 May 1816 by James Shelburne. WB 7/313.

HULL, Green and Patsey Dailey, 11 September 1804. Sur. Allen Steagall. Married 12 September 1804 by John Neblett. p. 19 and WB 6/124.

HUNDLEY, William and Mary Stone. Married 3 December 1805 by William Ellis. WB 6/136.

HUNNICUT, James W. and Martha F. Smith, 13 June 1835 [endorsement on bond states 1836] Sur. Samuel Jefferson. p.49.

HURT, Alfred H. and Louisa E. Rowlett, 9 January 1843. Sur. William H. Taylor and Thomas Arvin. Married 2 February 1843 by Chester Bullard. p. 57 and WB 12/145.

HURT, Alfred H. and Jane T. Jeffress, 9 August 1846. Sur. Joel P. Bragg. p. 63.

HURT, Alfred H. and Sarah E. Farmer, daughter of Joseph W. Farmer, 13 May 1850. Sur. Joseph W. Farmer. p.67.

HURT, Dudley and Mary Ann Evans. Married 2 December 1802 by Edward Almond. WB 6/82A.

HURT, Macom and Nancy Gunn. Married 14 June 1800 by John Neblett. WB 5/35.

HURT, Munfort and Denitia Johns, 12 December 1825. Sur. Henry N. Watkins. Married 22 December 1825 by Thomas H. Jeffress. p.39 and WB 8/551.

HURT, Munford A., Jr., son of Patrick H. Hurt, and Ann E. Neal, daughter of James Neal, 8 March 1852. Thomas D. Johnson, witness. p. 8.

HURT, Patrick H. and Maria Louisa Rutherford. Married 28 February 1828 by Silas Shelburne. WB 9/480.

HURT, William R. and Rhody Clarke. Married 9 December 1810 by James Shelburne. WB 7/15.

HUTCHERSON, Aaron and Nancy Blagrave. Married 27 December 1781 by Thomas Crymes. WB 3/104.

HUTCHERSON, Ambrose and Hannah Willson, 13 December 1804. Sur. Robert Jones. Married 16 December 1804 by James Shelburne. p. 19.

HUTCHINSON, Joseph and Rebecca Neblett. Married 19 November 1800 by John Neblett. WB 5/35.

HUTCHERSON, Thomas and Nancy Hurt, 13 March 1815. Sur. John Brown. Married "M" 13, 1815 by Charles Ogburn. p. 29 and WB 10/181.

INGE, Archer B. and Sarah Perkinson. Married 7 March 1827 by Joshua Featherston. WB 9/127.

INGE, Charles B. and Sarah Inge. Married 17 February 1831 by Joshua Featherston. WB 10/151A.

INGE, Charles W. and Lucy A. Pease, 14 July 1851. George W. Buckner made affidavit that Lucy was more than 21 years of age. p.4.

INGE, Edward and Mary N. L. Burnett, 30 October 1843. Sur. Sam J. Burnett. p. 57.

INGE, George and Susanah E. Hawthorn, 28 July 1837. Sur. James Inge. p.51.

INGE, James and Polly Chandler. Married 29 March 1800 by William Ellis.
WB 5/22.

INGE, James and Elizabeth S. Chandler, 15 December 1835. Sur. John Inge.
Married 15 December 1835 by James M. Jeter. p. 49 and WB 11/169.

INGE, James and Elizabeth Laffoon, 12 July 1845. Sur. William B. Moore. p.61.

INGE, James E. and Martha A. Inge, 1 May 1841. Sur. James Inge. p.55.

INGE, John and Nancy Skinner. Married 23 November 1802 by John Neblett.
WB 6/11A.

INGE, John and Martha Moore, 24 November 1836. Sur. George Inge. Married
29 November 1836 by Joshua Featherston. p. 51 and WB 11/182.

INGE, Spencer and Permelia Ann Hammock, 11 August 1845. Sur. John Inge. p.61.

INGE, Thomas C. and Elizabeth Skinner, Married 29 August 1832 by Joshua
Featherston. WB 11/8A.

INGE, Thomas S. and Martha J. Ragsdale, daughter of Thomas M. Ragsdale,
6 January 1851. Wit. Charles W. Inge. p. 3.

INGE, Vincent and Martha A. Garratt, 15 December 1845. Sur. Robert C.
Garland. Married 18 December 1845 by Joshua Featherston. p.59 and
WB 13/5.

INGE, William and Polly Fallin. Married 14 December 1792 by John Neblett.
WB 4/36.

INGE, Willis and Elizabeth C. Inge, 11 January 1836. Sur. John B. Inge.
Married 11 January 1836 by Joshua Featherston. p.51 and WB 11/156.

INGRAM, Samuel H. and Ann H. Davis, 16 February 1847. Sur. C. C. Bishop.
p. 63.

INGRAM, Sylvanus and Sally Gill. Married 18 August 1799 by John Neblett.
WB 5/2A.

INGRAM, Silvanus and Francis H. Taylor, 11 March 1822. Sur. Thomas Taylor.
Married ___ March 1822 by Thomas Adams. p. 33 and WB 8/271.

INGRAM, Thomas and Fanny Pettypool. Married 6 October 1797 by Charles
Ogburn, whose list was recorded in 1832. WB 10/181A.

INGRAM, William and Priscilla Ragsdale. Married 14 January 1802 by John
Neblett. WB 6/11A.

INNES, William T. and Julia A. Minor, 30 October 1849. Sur. Algernon S.
Williams. p. 67.

INSCO, William and Nancy Andrews, 21 April 1812. Sur. Samuel G. Insco.
p. 25.

IRBY, Edmund and Cordelia A. Williams, 25 September 1847. Sur. Fayette
W. Williams. [Marriage bond is signed Fayette C. Williams.] p. 63.

IRBY, John L. and Frances Williams. Married 23 October 1840 by Freeman
Fitzgerald. WB 12/7.

IRBY, John W. and Martha Taylor. 24 November 1843. Sur. William H. Taylor.
p. 57.

IRVINE, William and Peggy Harding. Married 26 December 1807 by William
Ellis. WB 6/207A.

JACKSON, Andrew and Frances E. Winn, 22 December 1845. Sur. P. H. Raney.
Married 24 December 1845 by Richard E. G. Adams. p. 61 and
WB 13/14.

JACKSON, Benjamin and Lucy Smith. Married 18 December 1810 by James
Shelburne. WB 7/15.

JACKSON, Burwell W. [Bennett on bond] and Sopha A. Parrish, 21 September
1843. Sur. Lazarus L. Burnett. Married 21 September 1843 by Joshua
Featherston. p.57 and WB 12/160.

JACKSON, Carter of Lunenburg, and Dolly W. Westbrook, 10 September 1805.
Sur. Stewart Jackson. Married 19 September 1805 by William Ellis.
p. 21 and WB 6/136.

JACKSON, Clement and Rebecca Gee, 23 July 1817. Sur. Nelson W. Gee.
Married 24 July 1817 by Stephen Jones. p. 29. and WB 7/357.

JACKSON, Dabney and Rebecca M. Winn. Married 22 October 1818 by Joel
Johns. WB 8/357.

JACKSON, Elisha B. and Sarah Jane Stokes, 14 December 1847. Sur. Drury
H. Lett. Married 14 December 1847 by Thomas Adams. p. 63 and WB 13/232.

JACKSON, Francis T. and Dorothy Stanback, daughter of Peter Stanback, all
of Lunenburg, 21 January 1831. Sur. Jacob White. p. 45 and DB 29/153.

JACKSON, Green and Ann A. Neblett. Married 18 September 1827 by James
Smith. WB 9/267.

JACKSON, Isaac and Caty Bird. Married 22 September 1797 by William Ellis.
WB 4/244.

JACKSON, Jordan and Nancy Rigigett (?). Married 8 November 1791 by
Aaron Brown. WB 4/32A.

JACKSON, Peter and Rebecca Edmunds, 29 November 1822. Sur. John Taylor. p.35.

JACKSON, Stewart and Salley White, 22 October 1803. Sur. Henry Buford. p.17.

JAMESON, William H. and Sally S. Street, 5 May 1823. Sur. David Street.
Married 6 May 1823 by Joel Johns. p. 35 and WB 8/357.

JARROTT, David of Lunenburg and Judy Mizes, 18 December 1786. Sur. Drury
Allen. p.7.

JARROTT, John J. and Emily J. Simmons, 17 February 1834. Sur. Edward J.
Jones. Married by Daniel Petty whose list was dated 13 July 1835.
p. 47 and WB 11/124.

JEFFERSON, Field and Mary Allen, widow, 31 October 1753. Sur. Robert Wooding,
Paul Carrington, George Baskerville, and John Hopson. p. 1.

JEFFERSON, Peter and Martha Russell, 5 May 1804. Sur. John Woods ["Woods"
was typed on the marriage bond, then scratched through, and "Moody"
written above it.] Married 7 May 1804 by Charles Ogburn. p. 19 and
WB 10/181.

JEFFERSON, Samuel G. and Mary E. Smith. Married 31 March 1840 by James W.
Hunnicut. WB 12/7.

JEFFRESS, Edward T. and Dicy Fowlkes. Married 3 August 1815 by James
Shelburne. WB 7/227.

JEFFRESS, James G. and Jane M. Crymes, 12 December 1842. Sur. Leonard
Crymes. p.57.

JEFFRESS, James G. and Mary B. Carter, 26 February 1844. Sur. Philip H.
Bohannon. p.59.

JEFFRESS, John C. and Sally B. Knight, 14 June 1824. Sur. Jordan W.
Jeffress. Married 22 June 1824 by Thomas H. Jeffress. p.37 and
WB 8/431.

JEFFRESS, Joseph M. and Sarah Harding, 12 December 1842. Sur. Philip H.
Bohannon. Married 22 December 1842 by John C. Blackwell. p. 57 and
WB 12/177.

JEFFRESS, Richard J. and Martha C. Hurt, 13 January 1834. Sur. Albert J.
Hurt. Married 28 January 1834 by M. M. Dance. p.45 and WB 11/336.

JEFFRESS, Richard J. and Emily F. Jeffress, 26 November 1838. Sur. William
A. Borum. p. 53.

JEFFRESS, Robert T. and Eliza T. Staples, 22 November 1841. Sur. Thomas A.
Johns. p. 55.

JEFFRESS, Thomas B. and Polly Haney Carter, 11 August 1824. Sur. Richard
Jeffress. Married 18 August 1824 by M. M. Dance. [Bride's name
omitted on marriage bond. The minister's return gave the information.]
p. 37 and WB 8/479.

JEFFRESS, Thomas H. and Christianna Blackwell. Married 12 June 1816 by
Thomas Adams. WB 7/249.

JENKINS, Daniel Y. and Jane E. Rash, 14 November 1838. Sur. Elijah J. Estes. p. 53.

JENKINS, Joel W. and Sarah T. Overton, daughter of John E. Overton, 13 December 1852, Matthew Barnes, witness. p. 11.

JENNINGS, James of Lunenburg and Prudence Herring, daughter of Stephen Herring, who is Surety, 13 January 1814. p. 27.

JENNINGS, Joseph and Dicey E. Fowlkes, 22 May 1844. Sur. John L. Bruce. p. 59.

JETER, James A. and Mary L. Jeter, 7 April 1846. Sur. Thomas Taylor. Married 8 April 1846 by W. S. Wilson. p. 63 and WB 13/46.

JETER, James E. and Sarah Jane Tucker, 24 February 1852, on certification of George Tucker, her father, proved by Thomas Crafton a witness. p. 8.

JETER, John and Susanna M. de Graffenreid. Married 17 October 1805 by William Ellis. WB 6/136.

JETER, John H. and Lucy B. Jeter, 8 September 1817. Sur. Jesse D. Abernathy. p. 29.

JETER, Philip and Barbara Wrenn, 19 September 1811. Sur. James Wrenn. Married 18 September 1811 by James Shelburne. p. 23 and WB 7/32.

JETER, Philip T. and Eliza M. Bragg. Married 20 December 1827 by Silas Shelburne. WB 9/480.

JETER, William J. and Sarah Harding. Married 8 June 1845 [bond]. Sur. John Hazelwood. [Marriage register states 1846.] p. 63.

JETER, William W. and Mary T. Russell, 15 November 1825. Sur. William T. Abernathy. Married 21 July 1825 by Silas Shelburne. p. 39 and WB 9/161.

JOHNS, Robert and Mary Tucker. Married 25 December 1787 by Thomas Crymes. WB 3/309.

JOHNSON, Alvin J. and Lucia H. Warner, both more than 21 years of age. Married 17 May 1851 by T. E. Locke at Mrs. Sarah G. Jones' residence, Lunenburg C.H. p. 4 and St. John's Church Register.

JOHNSON, Amos S. and Susanna Hazelwood, 7 April 1812. Sur. David White. Married 29 April 1812 by James Shelburne. p. 25 and WB 7/124.

JOHNSON, Amos S. and Rittah Cockerham, 9 April 1812. Sur. Allen Garrett Cockerham. p. 25.

JOHNSON, Anson and Elizabeth T. Freeman. Married 14 December 1827 by George Petty. WB 9/250.

JOHNSON, Bemis [or Binns] and Judy Ambrose. Married 22 March 1792 by John Neblett. WB 4/19A.

JOHNSON, Claiborn and Mary Hawkins. Married 5 May 1786 by James
Shelburn. WB 3/252.

JOHNSON, Claibourne B. and Nancy Thomas, 12 September 1821. Sur.
Leonard Gill. Married __ September 1821 by Thomas Adams. p. 33
and WB 8/209.

JOHNSON, Cornelius and Ritter Townsend, 27 October 1806. Sur. Daniel
Townsend. Married 30 October 1806 by Edward Almond. p.21 and
WB 7/1.

JOHNSON, Henry and Martha Singleton. Married 7 February 1815 by Thomas
Adams. WB 7/249

JOHNSON, Jesse and Polly Johns. Married by James Shelburne whose list
was returned to court 9 July 1789. WB 3/345.

JOHNSON, Jesse [Jossee on marriage bond] and Elizabeth Cockerham, 28 May
1307. Sur. Anderson Cockerham. Married 5 June 1807 by William
Ellis. p. 21 and WB 6/187.

JOHNSON, James and Sarah Edmunds. Married 2 September 1831 by Joshua
Featherston. WB 10/151A.

JOHNSON, John and Rhoday Beasley. Married 15 April 1791 by David
Ellington. WB 4/12A.

JOHNSON, John and Ermin Lester, 9 October 1806. Sur. Edmund Lester.
Married 4 November 1806 by Joel Johns. p. 21 and WB 6/197.

JOHNSON, John and Ritter Hitchens. Married 31 July 1815 by Baxter
Ragsdale. WB 7/246.

JOHNSON, Julius and Polly Walker. Married 2 December 1790 by Henry
Ogburn. WB 4/7.

JOHNSON, Lewis W. and Rebecca Hudson. Married 26 January 1815 by Thomas
Adams. WB 7/248.

JOHNSON, Reuben and Patsey Vaughan VanDyke, 1 February 1803. Sur. Asa
Johnson. p.19.

JOHNSTON, Samuel and Sally Smithson, 1 April 1812. Sur. John Wood. p.25.

JOHNSON, Thomas and Sarah E. Featherstun, 23 October 1848. Sur. John
Hawthorn. p.65.

JOHNSON, Thomas D. and Mary Susan Hurt, daughter of Patrick H. Hurt,
13 October 1851. Meintford A.Hurt, witness. p.5.

JOHNSON, William and Ann Sturdivant. Married 9 December 1798 by John
Neblett. WB 5/2.

JONES, Algerson S. and Mary Jane Overton, 7 February 1837. Sur. Tsch. Woodson. p. 51.

JONES, Armstead. and Jean Smithson. Married 26 December 1799 by James Shelburne. WB 5/51.

JONES, Edward and Susanna Walker, 21 January 1812. Sur. Robert D. Parrish. Married 21 January 1812 by Matthew Dance. p.25 and WB 7/60.

JONES, Edward W. and Martha B. Cole, 21 September 1843. Sur. Green W. Crowder. Married by Daniel Petty whose list was returned to court 8 February 1847. p.57 and WB 13/14.

JONES, Godfrey and Margaret Jones, spinster, 15 August 1750. Sur. William Jones and Thomas Stith. p. 1.

JONES, Henry E. and Martha E. Wilson, 14 October 1844. Sur. Robert B. Wilson. p. 59.

JONES, John R. and Ann E. Manson, 22 June 1846. Sur. William T. Blackwell. Married 23 June 1846 by John C. Blackwell. p.63 and WB 13/11.

JONES, Pascal and Lucretia Jeffress, 9 November 1804. Sur. Thomas Jeffress. Married by William Ellis, 1 December 1804. p. 19 and WB 6/122.

JONES, Peter, Jr. and Sally G. Bacon, 30 May 1807. Sur. John Taylor. p.21.

JONES, Peter B. and Virginia C. Pilkinton, 27 October 1845. Sur. Elisha B. Jackson. Married 28 October 1845 by William J. Norfleet. p. 59 and WB 12/310.

JONES, Robert and Patsy P. Willson. Married 15 December 1800 by James Shelburne. WB 5/67.

JONES, Robert B. and Elizabeth G. Blackwell. Married 20 December 1815 by Thomas Adams. WB 7/248.

JONES, Stephen and Susanna Burnett, 21 November 1804. Sur. Joseph Rash. p.19.

JONES, Thaddeus C. and Rebecca E. Epes, 2 February 1835. Sur. Willis Gay. Married in 1835 by Thodowick Pryor. p. 47 and WB 11/89.

JONES, Thomas of Lunenburg and Leonna Jones, orphan of Robert Jones, dec'd, 31 July 1760. Sur. Godfrey Jones and Thomas Read. p. 1.

JONES, William of Lunenburg and Anne Tankersley, daughter of John Tankersley, 10 March 1761. Sur. John Tankersely and Thomas Read. p.3.

JONES, William and Nancy G. Denton, 23 February 1835. Sur. Samuel A. Peace. p. 49.

JONES, William and Rebecca Johnson, daughter of Amos S. Johnson, 4 September 1851, at Amos Johnson's residence by Thomas E. Locke. Joel Parrish, witness. p. 5 and St. John's Church Register.

JONES, William R. S. and Martha Stephen Crymes, 12 August 1844. Sur.
Ellison Clark. p. 59.

JORDAN, Archer and Elizabeth Walker. Married 18 September 1795 by William
Ellis. WB 4/124.

JORDAN, Banister and Salley Johnson, 9 July 1807. Sur. Clement Jordan.
Married 23 July 1807 by James Shelburne. p. 21 and WB 6/231.

JORDAN, Baxter and Polly Lipscomb Pettus, 29 December 1803. Sur. Miles
Jordan. p. 17.

JORDAN, Benjamin and Jane Jones, of Nottoway County. Married 19 January
1792 by John Jones. WB 4/20.

JORDAN, Charles E. and Mary E. Williams, 4 August 1838. Sur. Thomas
Hamlin. p. 53.

JORDAN, James J. and Ann E. Johns, 24 January 1843. Sur. John Crymes.
Married 1 February 1843 by Chester Bullard. [The bond gives the
date as 1846, but the endorsement states 1843.] p. 57 and WB 12/145.

JORDAN, Miles, Jr. and Rebecca M. Ellis, 24 March 1825. Sur. Ambrose
Ellis. Married 29 March 1825 by William Hatchett. p. 39 and WB 8/470.

JORDAN, Thomas and Roxany [or Rosary] Wilson. Married 2 August 1831 by
Silas Shelburne. WB 11/2.

JORDAN, William P. and Sophia A. Pettus, 18 September 1836. Sur. Musgrove
L. Pettus. Married 21 September 1836 by James M. Jeter. p.49 and
WB 11/180.

JORDAN, Woodson and Jemime Ragsdale. Married 12 July 1792 by John Neblett.
WB 4/32.

JUSCO, W. and N. Andrews. Married 25 April 1810 by Charles Ogburn.
[Recorded in 1832.] WB 10/181A.

JUSTICE, Daniel and Sarah Ship. Married 27 January 1810 by Thomas Adams.
WB 7/39.

JUSTICE, Daniel J. and Beede Ragsdale, 19 March 1821. Sur. William
Garrett. Married __ March 1821 by Thomas Adams. p. 31 and WB 8/209.

JUSTICE, Stephen and Elizabeth Garrott, 23 December 1806. Sur. Daniel
Taylor. p. 21.

JUSTICE, William and Lucretia Apperson, 3 February 1803. Sur. Frederick
Watkins. p. 17.

JUSTICE, Zachariah and Nancy Matthews. Married 24 July 1795 by John Jones.
WB 4/151.

JUSTIS, Zachariah and Mary Garrett. Married __ December 1816 by Thomas
Adams. WB 7/356.

KEARSEY, John and Frances Hazelwood. Married 16 January 1785 by Thomas
Crymes. WB 3/200.

KEATS, James and Martha Tucker. Married 12 December 1793 by William
Ellis. WB 4/43.

KEELING, John T. and Elizabeth E. Harding, 1 December 1836. Sur. Daniel
W. Parsons. p. 51.

KEESEE, Phillip and Elizabeth Morgan. Married 22 May 1822 by Baxter
Ragsdale. WB 8/263.

KEETH, Marshall M. and Susan E. Gregory. Married 25 March 1831 by Silas
Shelburne. WB 11/2.

KEETON, Charles W. and Frances Elizabeth Chumney, daughter of Robert B.
Chumney who consents, 12 September 1853. p. 13.

KEETON, Edward and Susan Overton, 28 September 1835. Sur. Nathaniel
Pennington. Married by Daniel Petty whose list was dated 10 October
1836. p. 47 and WB 11/179.

KEETON, James W. and Lucy T. Clark, daughter of Hatcher Clark who consents,
13 October 1851. p. 6.

KEETON, John W. and Martha E. Fowlkes. Married 8 August 1827 by Silas
Shelburne. WB 9/161.

KEETON, Joseph and Martha Gregory, 9 February 1829. Sur. William Keeton.
p. 43.

KELLY, Charles and Martha Hitchings, 20 November 1822. Sur. Jesse Hitchings.
Married 21 November 1822 by Thomas H. Jeffress. p. 35 and WB 8/263.

KELLY, Peter and Nancy Hitchens, 20 March 1822 [marriage bond states
March 26, the endorsement states March 20]. Sur. Nancy Hitchens, Sr.
Married 21 March 1822 by Thomas H. Jeffress. p. 33 and WB 8/263.

KEY, Thomas and Martha Ann Lester, daughter of Bolling Lester who consents,
6 December 1850. p. 2.

KING, Everett and Elizabeth Crowder, 7 February 1835. Sur. John J.
Hazelwood. Married by Daniel Petty, on list of 1835. p. 47 and
WB 11/124.

KING, John and Polly Love. Married 15 May 1794 by James Shelburne. WB 4/107.

KING, Nathaniel and Cealy B. Ellis. Married 26 April 1800 by William
Ellis. WB 5/22.

KIRK, George and Polly Satterfield. Married 14 August 1794 by John Rogers.
WB 4/59A.

KIRK, John and Polly Philips. Married 19 February 1799 by John Jones.
WB 5/6A.

KIRKLAND, William and Lucy Moore. Married 9 February 1797 by John Rogers. WB 4/167.

KNIGHT, David H. and Sarah J. Lipscomb, daughter of Ann Lipscomb, 9 February 1852, "on certificate of her mother proved by oath of George T. Knight, a witness." p. 8.

KNIGHT, George T. and Mary E. Lipscomb, 13 November 1848. Sur. John Thompson. p. 65.

KNIGHT, Matthew J. and Cecila A. Ellis, 31 January 1822. Sur. Thomas N. Gregory. Married 31 January 1822 by Joel Johns. p. 33 and WB 8/357.

KNIGHT, Samuel and Sarah Knott. Married 18 May 1809 by James Shelburne. WB 7/3.

KNIGHT, Sherwood W. and Martha Ann Williams, 14 August 1843. Sur. Tarlton W. Knight. p. 57, and DB 33/189-190.

KNIGHT, Tarlton and Elizabeth W. Farmer, 17 December 1806. Sur. Janey Farmer. Married 24 November 1806 by James Shelburne. p. 21 and WB 6/231.

KNOTT, Charles and Mary D. Hayes, 17 December 1821. Sur. John J. Hayes. p.33.

KNOTT, James and Sarah Wade Smithson. Married 13 December 1798 by Matthew Dance. WB 4/244-A.

KNOTT, Richard and Nancy Crenshaw. Married 26 October 1800 by James Shelburne. WB 5/51.

KNOTT, Richard and Nanny Crenshaw, 12 March 1811. Sur. Thomas Bragg. Married 14 March 1811 by James Shelburne. WB 7/15 and p. 23.

LAFFOON, Alexander and Catharine Johnson, 10 November 1823. Sur. Thomas Parrish. p. 35.

LAFFOON, Daniel and Nancy Gee, 14 January 1822. Sur. John Gee. p. 33.

LAFFOON, James and Martha Ann Morgan, 14 December 1846. Sur. George W. Potts. Married by Daniel Petty whose list was returned to court 8 February 1847. p. 63 and WB 13/14.

LAFFOON, Jeremiah and Lucretia Parrish. Married 19 January 1818, but the minister's name not shown. WB 8/38.

LAFFOON, Jessie of Lunenburg, and Catharine Winn, 18 July 1792. Sur. Thomas Scarborough. p.13.

LAFFOON, John and Maria J. Reese, daughter of Polly C. Reese, 16 December 1851. George W. Buckner, witness. p. 7.

LAFFOON, Matthew of Lunenburg and Elizabeth Murrel Samford, 1 April 1814. Sur. James Samford. p. 29.

LAFFOON, Robert and Delpha Stone, 10 May 1825. Sur. Daniel Laffoon.
Married 12 May 1825 by Joshua Featherston. p. 39 and WB 8/572.

LAFFOON, Robert and Eliza Inge, 27 September 1826. Sur. William D.
Parrish. Married 28 September 1826 by Joshua Featherston. p. 41
and WB 9/127.

LAFFOON, Thomas and Sarah F. Matthews, 1 February 1845. Sur. John
Mathews. p. 61.

LAFFOON, William of Lunenburg and Martha Winn, 9 February 1814. Sur.
Freeman Winn. p. 27.

LAFFOON, William and Sarah A.S.H. Rand, 1 November 1824. Sur. Robert B.
Jones. Married 4 November 1824 by John Doyle. p. 37 and WB 8/402.

LAFFOON, William G. and Rebecca J. Winn, 24 December 1846. Sur. Freeman
J. Winn. p. 63.

LAMBERT, Benjamin and Lucy E. Williams, 9 September 1834. Sur. Thomas
Adams. p. 47.

LAMBERT, James and Martha G. Perkins, 25 September 1838. Sur. Chasteen C.
Tisdale. p. 55.

LAMBERT, John A. and Nancy A. Hanks, 1 October 1835. Sur. Freeman J.
Gunn. Married 5 October 1835 by Joshua Featherston. p. 49 and
WB 11/156.

LAMBERT, Joseph and Rebecca Edwards Moore. Married 3 December 1790 by
John Easter. WB 4/7A.

LAMBERT, Sterling and Tabitha Edmondson, 31 July 1826. Sur. William E.
Robertson. p. 41.

LAMBERT, Thomas and Polly Mize, 31 October 1825. Sur. John Mize.
Married 12 November 1825 by Joshua Featherston. p. 39 and WB 8/572.

LAMBERT, Thomas J. and Elizabeth H. Hammock, 20 December 1853. Robert B.
Brydie made oath that Elizabeth was 21 years of age. p. 16.

LAMBERT, William and Constance Edmundson. Married 22 February 1816 by
James Shelburne. WB 7/313.

LANDRUM, James and Nancy Hood. Married 7 July 1808 by Joel Johns. WB 6/244.

LAWRENCE, James and Elizabeth Bragg. Married 8 June, 1783 by James
Shelburne. WB 3/150.

LAY, Rev. Henry Champlin and Elizabeth Withers Atkinson, daughter of
Roger B. Atkinson, 14 April 1847 [endorsement states May 8]. Sur.
David May. Married 13 May 1847 by Edmund Withers. p. 63 and WB 13/83.

LEE, Ambrose of Lunenburg, and Elizabeth White, 14 September 1792. Sur. John White. p. 13.

LEE, Edward and Betsy Robertson. Married 21 February 1805 by John Robertson. WB 6/147.

LEE, Edward and Nany J. Wilson, 9 December 1833. Sur. John R. Buford. p. 45.

LEE, Henderson and Susan S. Hatchett, 3 March 1825. Sur. Richard J. Gaines. p. 39.

LEE, Thomas and Betsey Thompson, 12 February 1807. Sur. William Thompson. p. 21.

LEFOE, Daniel and Molly Tatum, 10 February 1791. Sur. Gravitt Tatum. p. 13.

LeGRAND, William of Lunenburg and Erman Elliott Vaughan, 22 October 1786. Sur. Craddock Vaughan. p. 7.

LEMAY, Lewis and Mary Ussery, 15 October 1804. Sur. Thomas Ussery. Married 16 October 1804 by John Neblett. p. 19 and WB 6/124.

LERTIE, John and Elinor Pointer. Married 22 June 1805 by William Davis WB 6/135.

LESTER, Alexander and Mary Ragsdale. Married 19 April 1785 by Thomas Crymes. WB 3/210.

LESTER, Alexander and Jude Lock. Married 25 December 1807 by James Shelburne. WB 6/230-A.

LESTER, Archibald of Lunenburg and Elizabeth Crymes, 12 May 1785. Sur. George Crymes. Married by James Shelburne who does not give exact date. p. 7 and WB 3/212.

LESTER, Barnett and Jane Vaughan. Married 16 October 1816 by James Robertson. WB 7/280.

LESTER, Elijah J. and Martha A. Matthews, 27 December 1847. Sur. Washington Brown. Married 28 December 1847 by W. S. Wilson. p. 63 and WB 13/220.

LESTER, Frederick of Lunenburg and Dolly Pollard, 5 September 1797. Sur. Daniel Robertson. p. 17.

LESTER, Frederick and Martha Ann Craghead, 27 November 1826. Sur. Patrick H. Hurt. Married 28 November 1826 by Silas Shelburne. p.41 and WB 9/161.

LESTER, George of Lunenburg, and Sarah W. Robertson, 15 November 1806. Sur. Stephen Shelton. p. 21.

LESTER, Henry and Martha Pennington. Married 1 October 1805 by James Shelburne. WB 6/146-A.

LESTER, Isam of Lunenburg and Elizabeth Jones Volentine, 11 December 1789. Sur. Zachariah Volentine. p. 9.

LESTER, Jeremiah and Nancy Spain, 5 March 1838. Sur. John Spain. Married 3 March 1838 by Pleasant Barnes. p. 55 and WB 11/281.

LESTER, Jeremiah and Sarah Finch, 17 October 1821. Sur. James G. Moore. Married 20 October 1821 by James Robertson. p.33 and WB 8/230.

LESTER, John and Sally Rucks. Married 30 January 1808 by William Ellis. WB 6/207-A.

LESTER, John Bryan, Jr. of Lunenburg, and Susanna C. Stone, 29 June 1805. Sur. John Smithson. p. 21.

LESTER, Royall and Nancy Alexander. Married 26 December 1816 by James Robertson. WB 7/309.

LESTER, Whitfield and Elizabeth E. Hatchitt, 9 October 1826. Sur. William Hatchitt. Married 17 October 1826 by Silas Shelburne. p. 41 and WB 9/161.

LESTER, Whitehead of Lunenburg and Sicily Buford, 8 January 1791. Sur. Henry Buford. p. 13.

LETT, Drury H. and Elinor A. Tisdale, 27 October 1841. Sur. Richard K. Tisdale. p. 55.

LETT, William and Amey Williams. Married 20 October 1803 by John Rogers. WB 6/82.

LEWIS, Elam of Lunenburg and Sally Tatum, 21 February 1791. Sur. Gravitt Tatum. Married by James Shelburne, exact date not shown. p.13 and WB 4/12.

LIPSCOMB, Edward B. and Nancy Thompson, 4 September 1826. Sur. Samuel B. Wood. Married 7 September 1826 by William Richards. p.41 and WB 9/81.

LIPSCOMB, William T. and Pamelia J. Tatum, 10 April 1843. Sur. William B. Vaughan. Married 12 April 1843 by Samuel G. Mason. p.57 and WB 12/170.

LOCKE, George and Betsy Crenshaw. Married 7 November 1805 by Rev. Dabbs. WB 6/193.

LOCK, Richard and Mary Thorton. Married 10 December 1783 by James Shelburne. WB 3/150.

LOCKE, Rev. Thomas E. and Lucy Armistead Nelson, 15 December 1841. Sur. William H. Taylor. Married 21 December 1841 by Thomas T. Castleman at Mount Holly. p. 55, WB 12/97 and St.John's Church Register.

LOGAN, Samuel of Lunenburg and Lucy Smith, 10 February 1791. Sur. William Taylor. p. 13.

LOVE, Henry H. of Lunenburg and Mary C. Jeffress, 6 December 1814. Sur. Thomas Jeffress. Married 15 December 1814 by James Shelburne. p.27 and WB 7/227.

LOVE, William H. and Harriet F. Rowlett, 8 May 1846. Sur. Jordan R. Hardy.
p.63.

LOWRY, Thomas of Lunenburg and Fanny Mallery, daughter of William Mallery,
deceased, 2 November 1762. Sur. Thomas Tabb. p.3.

LOWERY, Thomas and Susan C. Bruce, 9 September 1822. Sur. Abner H. Burks.
Married 11 September 1822 by Joel Johns. p. 33 and WB 8/357.

LUCAS, John of Lunenburg and Elizabeth Comer, spinster, daughter of John C.
Comer, dec'd, 27 October 1762. Sur. William Sammons. p. 3.

LYNCH, Abner of Lunenburg and Susanna S. Jordan, 9 June 1791. Sur. Ambrose
Ellis. Married 9 June 1791 by William Ellis. p. 13 and WB 4/14.

MacCADEN, Hugh and Catharine Scot, daughter of John Scot, 11 October 1762.
Sur. John Scot. p. 3.

McALISTER, James and Phebe Couch, 30 November 1826. Sur. Samuel G. Osborn.
Married 7 December 1826 by Silas Shelburne. p. 41 and WB 9/161.

McCARGO, John M. and Mary Ann Ellis, 9 February 1826. Sur. John Williams.
Married 16 February 1826 by Silas Shelburne. p. 41 and WB 9/161.

McCONICO, Garner and Mary Walker. Married 27 November 1789 by James Shelburne.
WB 3/358.

McCONNICO, Jared of Lunenburg and Sally Carter Betts, 7 October 1788. Sur.
Spencer Betts. Married 6 October 1788 by Thomas Crymes. p. 9 and
WB 3/342.

McCUTCHEON, Alexander E. and Jane Jeffress, 4 November 1826. Sur. Thomas H.
Jeffress. Married 19 December 1826 by Thomas H. Jeffress. p.41 and
WB 9/116.

McINTIRE, Thomas and Prudence Chumney, 23 January 1843. Sur. Robert B.
Chumney. Married 26 February 1843 by J.W.D. Creath, "Pas: Baps. Ch.
N.K. Co." p. 57 and WB 12/132.

McKENNEY, John H. and Martha Gee. Married 9 May 1839 by Thomas E. Locke at
Mrs. Bridget Gee's residence, Lunenburg. WB 11/425 and St. John's
Church Register.

McKINNEY, John L. A. and Elizabeth Williams, 10 January 1848. Sur. Cread
T. Scruggs. Married 12 January 1848 by William S. Wilson. p. 63 and
WB 13/220.

McKINNEY, Joshua J. and Frances Jane Jeter, 18 December 1847. Sur. John
L. A. McKinney. Married 22 December 1847 by William S. Wilson. p. 63
and WB 13/220.

McLAUGHLIN, David and Susanna Snead. Married 17 October 1799 by William
Ellis, Sr. WB 5/22.

McLAUGHLIN, Stephen and Alice Armon Williams. Married 30 September 1793
by William Ellis. WB 4/43.

McCLAUGHLIN, William and Martha Winn, 17 March 1829. Sur. Thomas Winn. p.43.

McMACHEN, James and Rebeckah Cunningham, daughter of Mathew Cunningham, 11 May 1753. Sur. Andrew Cunningham and Paul Carrington. p. 1.

McQUIE, Andrew and Amelia Hardy. Married 10 November 1809 by Thomas Adams. WB 7/39.

MACKAN, John S. and Mary Dalton, 17 October 1821. Sur. John T. Foster. Married 18 October 1821 by Joel Johns. p. 33 and WB 8/357.

MADDUX, Washington and Frances Ragsdale, 11 December 1817. Sur. Sterling Lambert. Married __ December 1817 by Thomas Adams. p. 31 and WB 7/356.

MADDUX, Washington and Rebeccah Moore, 22 January 1837. Sur. William E. Wilson. p. 51.

MALONEY, Deleware P. and Catharine C. Cheatham, 26 September 1833. Sur. Eli Cheatham. p. 45.

MANLY, Archibald and Ann Elizabeth Hampton, 8 April 1829. Sur. James S. Peace. Married 9 April 1829 by Joshua Featherston. p. 43 and WB 10/1.

MANLEY, Samuel and Patience Amos, 20 November 1821. Sur. William Kirk. Married 21 November 1821 by John Doyle. p. 33 and WB 8/193.

MANSON, Peter and Jincy M. Edmunds. Married 22 May 1828 by Joshua Featherston. WB 9/389.

MANSON, Richard and Nancy Bennett. Married 19 December 1809 by Joel Johns. WB 7/9.

MARABLE, Champion and Cornealia A. Keeton, 3 October 1849. Sur. William B. Keeton. p. 65.

MARABLE, Hartwell and Sarah B. Smithson, 8 August 1811. Sur. Renneson Tisdale. p. 25.

MARABLE, James H. and Mary E. Ingram, 2 December 1848. Sur. Edward T. Marable. Married 12 December 1848 by Thomas Adams. p. 65 and WB 13/232.

MARABLE, J. and L. Hazlewood. Married 13 October 1818 by Charles Ogburn. WB 10/181-A.

MARABLE, Joseph R. and Mary M. Marable, 27 February 1837. Sur. Benjamin F. Lester. p. 51.

MARABLE, Matthew and Permelia Ragsdale. Married 6 October 1808 by James Shelburne. WB 7/3.

MARABLE, William, the younger, of the Parish of Cumberland in County of Lunenburg, and Judith More, daughter of Thomas More of same Parish and County, 3 October 1760. Sur. Mat. Marable. p. 3.

MARR, John of Lunenburg and Judy Barnes, 2 April 1796. Sur. John Barnes. Married 5 April 1796 by William Ellis. p. 15 and WB 4/168.

MARSHALL, Alexander and Jane C. Webb. Married 12 April 1810 by Matthew
Dance. WB 7/7.

MARSHALL, Archibald and Sally Winn, 14 July 1803. Sur. Richard Stone.
Married 23 July 1803 by William Ellis. p. 17 and WB 6/76.

MARSHALL, Jesse of Lunenburg and Nancey Ingram, 9 July 1789. Sur. John
Moon. p. 11.

MARSHALL, John W. and Louisa Maddux, 21 December 1836. Sur. Joseph
Marshall. p.49.

MARSHALL, Josiah W. and Nancy T. Neal. Married 12 June 1823 by Silas
Shelburne. WB 8/340.

MARSHALL, Thomas and Lucy E. Orgain, 14 July 1823. Sur. Thomas Adams.
Married 24 July 1823 by Littleberry Orgain. p. 35 and WB 8/344.

MARSHALL, William J. and Susan B. Keeton, 13 August 1849. Sur. Thomas G.
Crawley. Married 5 September 1849 by William S. Wilson. p.67 and
WB 13/353.

MARTIN, Robert and Sarah Cunningham, spinster, of County of Lunenburg,
10 February 1752 [bond says Feb. 4.] Sur. James Read and William
Wright. p. 1.

MARTIN, Robert and Sarah E. Hudson, 21 August 1841. Sur. Ethelbert J.
Hudson. p. 55.

MASON, Jordon and Patsey Allen Tisdale, 25 November 1811. Sur. William
Williams. Married 28 November 1811 by James Shelburne. p. 23 and
WB 7/32.

MASON, Thomas and Frances Foster, 12 March 1807. Sur. Robert Foster.
Married 23 March 1807 by William Ellis. p. 21 and WB 6/187.

MASON, William and Polly Crittenden. Married 6 January 1802 by Matthew
Dance. WB 6/29.

MASON, William and Catharine Ragsdale, 4 July 1804. Sur. William Ingram.
Married 13 July 1804 by John Neblett. p. 19.

MASON, William and Salley Tisdale, 17 December 1812. Sur. James Smithson.
p. 25.

MATTHEWS, Cornelius and Lydia Andrews. Married 25 February 1797 by William
Ellis. WB 4/168.

MATTHEWS, Jeremiah and Elizabeth Farguson, 26 December 1804. Sur. William
Farguson. Married 28 December 1804 by John Neblett. p 18 and WB 6/124.

MATTHEWS, John A. and Susan Harris, 20 February 1850. Sur. Drury Matthews.
p. 67.

MATTHEWS, Lewis and Elizabeth Laffoon. Married 15 February 1816 by
Stephen Jones. WB 7/275

MATTHEWS, Lewis and Martha Potts. Married 17 January 1839 by Joshua
Featherston. WB 12/7.

MATTHEWS, Nathaniel and S. J. Hatchett, 14 February 1849. Sur. Colin
Stokes. p. 65.

MATTHEWS, Peter R. and Sarah Frances Gee, 4 December 1852. Andre N.
Moore made oath that Sarah Frances was 21 years of age and is a
witness thereto. p. 11.

MATTHEWS, William and Sally Allen. Married 2 January 1806 by John
Neblett. WB 6/147.

MATTHEWS, William and Rebecca Lafoon, 14 March 1825. Sur. William H.
Brown. Married 17 March 1825 by John Doyle. p.39 and WB 8/550.

MAURY, Matthew Fontaine, of Lunenburg, and Euphan Tabb, 1 December 1780.
Sur. William Downing [or Dowsing]. p. 5.

MAY, Henry and Julianna Jones, 20 October 1830. Sur. Mitchell Clay. p.43.

MAYES, William of Lunenburg, and Mary Nance, 20 October 1790. Sur.
Richard Mayes. Married by John Chappell whose list was returned
to November Court 1790. p. 11 and WB 4/7.

MAYTON, Daniel and Polly Matthews. Married 21 November 1810 by Thomas
Adams. WB 7/39.

MAYTON, David and Elizabeth Grant, 14 July 1825. Sur. Benjamin Zachary.
Married 28 July 1825 by John Doyle. p. 39 and WB 8/550.

MARLEY [or MAXEY], Abner and Polly Ann Knight. Married 1 February 1832
by Silas Shelburne. WB 11/2.

MEADOWS, Archibald and Rhoda Williamson. Married by John Chappell whose
list was returned to the June Court 1791. WB 4/7A.

MEANLEY, Samuel and Elizabeth Hammock. Married 10 February 1796 by John
Jones. WB 4/132A.

MIDDLETON, John and Martha Wachup [Warkup or Walker?], spinster, __August
1752. Sur. Robert Woods, Paul Carrington, Clem Read, William Cabell,
and John Stewart. p. 1.

MILLER, John and Rebecca Bailey, 12 July 1830. Sur. Richard Ellis and
William B. Overton. Married 13 July 1830 by Pleasant Barnes p. 43
and WB 11/281.

MILLER, William B. and Mary C. Williams, 1 May 1837. Sur. John L. Irby. p.51.

MILLS, James S. and Ann Edmund, 14 November 1853, on certification from
his mother. Peter Thompson made oath that Ann was 21 years of age
and is a witness thereto. p. 15.

MILLS, Richard C. and Lucy Satterfield. Married 22 December 1818 by
Joel Johns. WB 8/357.

MILLS, Robert - See Robert WILLS.

MINOR, James and Susanna Maclaughlin. Married 21 August 1794 by William
Ellis. WB 4/75.

MINOR, John, Jr. and Elizabeth Snead, 22 November 1817. Sur. Randolph
Thompson, Jr. p. 29.

MINOR, Joseph and Elizabeth Baines. Married 17 September 1784 by Thomas
Crymes. WB 3/185.

MINOR, Joseph and Edith Cox, spinster, daughter of John Cox, 11 October
1750. Sur. Thomas Stith and Clem Read. p. 1

MINOR, Langston B. Parkes, of Lunenburg, and Elizabeth Burks, 27 December
1825. Sur. Thomas Wilkinson. Married 27 December 1825 by William
Hatchett. p. 39 and WB 9/29.

MITCHELL, James C. and Nancy C. Stokes, 1 September 1846. Sur. Nathaniel
A. Venable. p. 63.

MITCHELL, Robert and Letty Reams. Married by James Shelburne whose list
was returned to court 9 July 1789. WB 3/345.

MIZE, James and Nancy Carroll. Married 23 August 1793 by John Neblett.
WB 4/50.

MIZE, Mark and Permely Stone, 6 February 1827. Married 6 February 1827 by
Baxter Ragsdale. WB 9/349.

MOHORN, John, Jr. and Eliza B. Averett, 12 November 1821. Sur. Peter
Averett. Married 22 November 1821 by James Robertson. p.33 and
WB 8/230.

MOHORN, Thomas and Letsey Hardy, 26 January 1824. Sur. Richard Mohorn.
Married 27 January 1824 by James Robertson. p. 37 and WB 8/534.

MOHORN, William and Elizabeth A. Fowlkes, 18 June 1830. Sur. Coleman
Jeffress, Jr. Married 23 December 1830 by Pleasant Barnes. p.45 and
WB 117/281.

MONDAY, John and Wealthy Tatum. Married 18 December 1793 by James
Shelburne. WB 4/46.

MONROE, James of Lunenburg, and Salley Crews, 11 September 1794. Sur.
William Crews. Married 15 September 1794 by William Ellis. p. 13
and WB 4/75.

MONROE, Johnson and Amelia Hooper. Married 1 December 1781 by James
Shelburne. WB 3/104.

MONROE, Robert and Jannie Puckett. Married 14 December 1786 by Thomas
Crymes. WB 3/268.

MOON. See also MOORE.

MOON, Jesse of Lunenburg and Permelia Farmer, 25 November 1814. Sur.
Littleberry Rutledge. p. 27.

MOON, John of Lunenburg and Mary Dudley, 21 November 1795. Sur. John
Cureton. Married 26 November 1795 by William Ellis. p.15 and WB 4/124.

MOON, Lodowick F. and Kezia Johnson, 7 December 1825. Sur. Thomas N.
Gregory. Married 8 December 1825 by William Hatchett. p. 39 and
WB 9/29.

MOON, Paraham B. and Petronella Wood, 13 November 1830. Sur. William
Wood. Married 22 December 1830 by Silas Shelburne. p. 43 and
WB 10/131.

MOON, Pleasant and Susanna Brown. Married 20 June 1800 by Arch'd McTarbert.
WB 5/28.

MOON, William and Martha R. Glenn. Married 28 September 1791 by James
Shelburne. WB 4/45A. [See William Moss.]

MOORE, Abner H. and Jutuary Farmer. Married 5 October 1786 by Thomas
Crymes. WB 3/268.

MOORE, Alexander and Nancy C. Carter. Married 8 August 1827 by Matthew
Dance. WB 10/129A and WB 9/311.

MOORE, Anderson and Lucy Laffoon. Married 26 December 1840 by Joshua
Featherston. WB 12/7.

MOORE, Asa and Dorothy Laffoon, 4 December 1827. Married 4 December 1827
by Benjamin Watkins. p. 99 and WB 9/349.

MOORE, David and Polly M. Epperson. Married 2 January 1810 by Thomas
Adams. WB 7/39.

MOORE, Elijah and Elizabeth Winn. Married December 1808 by Thomas Adams.
WB 6/253A.

MOORE, Elisha and Elizabeth Jennings Gee. Married 3 February 1810 by
Thomas Adams. WB 7/39.

MOORE, James and Jane Dobbins. Married 9 February 1797 by John Neblett
who reports this marriage again later, listing the date as 10 April.
WB 4/168 and WB 4/232A.

MOORE, Jesse and Rebecca Matthews, 28 February 1829. Sur. Boswell Skinner.
Married 7 March 1829 by Joshua Featherstone. p. 41 and WB 10/1.

MOORE, John J. of Lunenburg, and Sally Willson, 10 March 1814. Sur.
Edward Willson. Married 25 "M" 1814 by Charles Ogburn. p.27 and
WB 10/181.

MOORE, John R. and Martha Inge, 12 April 1847. Sur. John Inge. p. 63.

MOORE, Joseph of Lunenburg and Francis McQuaid, 27 December 1789. Sur. William Neblett. p. 9.

MOORE, Joseph B. and Ann Calaham, 29 January 1851. Thomas Vaden makes affidavit that Ann is more than 21 years old. p. 3.

MOORE, Matthew P. and Jane Parish, 24 June 1836. Sur. Washington Parish. Married 27 June 1836 by James M. Jeter. p.51 and WB 11/180.

MOORE, Mason and Rebecca Parrish. Married 10 December 1810 by Thomas Adams. WB 7/39.

MOORE, Osborne J. and Rebecca N. Gee, 13 February 1834. Sur. Peter Gee. p.47.

MOORE, Richard and Desdemonia Womack, 9 January 1812. Sur. Jacob Womack. p. 25.

MOORE, Robert, Jr. of Lunenburg, and Martha Thomas, 5 November 1789. Sur. Robert Moore, Sr. p. 9.

MOORE, Samuel U. [or W.] and Nelly A. Hicks, 26 April 1825. Sur. John Gee. Married 27 April 1825 by John Doyle. p. 39 and WB 8/550.

MOORE, Samuel and Ann Daniel, 28 September 1835. Sur. James George. Married 1 October 1835 by Joshua Featherston. p. 49 and WB 11/156.

MOORE, Stephen and Polly L. Johnson, 13 February 1811. Sur. Reubin Johnson. Married 13 February 1811 by Thomas Adams. p. 23 and WB 7/40.

MOORE, Thomas G. and Mary C. Laffoon, 23 December 1844. Sur. James Dixon. p. 59.

MOORE, William and Elizabeth Russell, 11 September 1826. Sur. William J. Hightower. Married 14 September 1826 by James Robertson. p.41 and WB 9/127.

MOORE, William and Harriet Satterfield, 22 January 1850. Sur. Robert Crymes. p. 67.

MOORE, William B. and Ann Inge, 15 June 1829. Sur. Joseph Moore. Married 13 June 1829 by Joshua Featherston. p. 43 and WB 10/1.

MOOR, William and Hannah Stone. Married 2 March 1786 by Thomas Crymes. WB 3/263.

MOORE, William H. and Sarah H. Laffoon, 17 February 1842. Sur. Collin Callaham. p. 57.

MOORE, William H. and Mary Ann White, 24 March 1845. Sur. Elijah J. Estes. p. 61.

MOORE, Winfield and Maria Jane Skinner, daughter of Susan Skinner, 8 March 1852. Thomas G. Moore, witness. p. 8.

MORETON, Samuel and Anne Moore, spinster, 2 October 1760. Sur. George Moore. p.3.

MORGAN, Edward and Elizabeth Goodwin, 25 November 1822. Sur. John H.
Booth. Married November 1822 by Thomas Adams. p. 35 and WB 8/271.

MORGAN, Jeremiah, Jr. of Lunenburg, and Sally B. Winn, 23 April 1814.
Sur. George Ragsdale. p. 27.

MORGAN, Jesse, of Lunenburg, and Mary Landrum, 21 December 1789. Sur.
Richard Landrum. p. 11.

MORGAN, Jesse and Rebecca Laffoon, 14 March 1825. Sur. Philip Russell.
p. 39.

MORGAN, Jesse and Hannah B. Peace. Married 31 March 1825 by John Doyle.
WB 8/550.

MORGAN, John and Sarah Neblett. Married 21 December 1797 by John Neblett.
WB 4/232.

MORGAN, John and Patty Betts. Married 26 May 1802 by William Ellis. WB 6/11.

MORGAN, John and Mary Ragsdale. Married 21 October 1839 by Joshua
Featherston. WB 12/7.

MORGAN, Reuben and Celia Bishop, 17 November 1806. Sur. John Bishop.
Married 3 November 1802 by Charles Ogburn who reported this marriage
in 1832. p. 21 and WB 10/181.

MORGAN, Richard J. and Emma Jane Hammock, daughter of Hugh Hammock,
8 November 1852. John S. Hammock, witness. p. 10.

MORGAN, Samuel B. and Nancy Betts, 14 March 1811. Sur. Charles Betts.
Married 8 March 1811 by James Shelburne. p. 23 and WB 7/32.

MORGAN, Samuel B. and Dianah L. Young, 2 February 1847. Sur. John L.
Morgan. p. 63.

MORGAN, Samuel J. and Mary E. [Brydie], 4 May 1835. Sur. Ethelbert J. Hudson.
[Mary's last name omitted in M.R. and in bond. Landon C. Bell in
THE OLD FREE STATE shows the name as Brydie.] p. 47.

MORING, John H. and Martha W. Taylor, 13 November 1849. Sur. C. C. Bishop.
p. 65.

MORISET, John F. and Minerva Crenshaw, 5 November 1850. T. H. Fowlkes, her
guardian, and proved by oath of W. M. Cardwell. p. 2.

MORRIS, Joseph B. and Ann Calaham, 29 January 1851. Thomas Vaden made oath
that Ann was more than 21 years of age. p. 3.

MOSBY, Edward and Sally Sparks. Married 14 December 1798 by Matthew Dance.
WB 4/244A.

MOSBY, Stephen and Abeonaday Minor, spinster, 9 October 1758. Sur. Stephen
Bedford and G. Carrington, Jr. p. 1.

MOSELEY, David of Lunenburg and Mary Hammock, 29 May 1789. Sur. Joseph
Moseley. p. 11.

MOSES, John F. and P. A. Williams, daughter of Clarrissa Williams, 26 November 1849. Sur. William H. H. Williams. Married 18 December 1849
by Samuel G. Mason. p. 65 and WB 13/349.

MOSS, William and Martha R. Glenn, Married 28 September 1791 by James
Shelburne. WB 4/46. [See William Moon.]

MOUNT, John and Susannah Mathews, 11 October 1746. p. 1.

MULLINS, Collin and Jincey Crenshaw. Married 24 December 1802 by Joel
Johns. WB 6/76.

MOURNING, William and Mary Macan, 12 November 1833. Sur. Joshua Byasee
and Prudence Cumbley. p. 45.

MURRILL, Leroy and Martha Jean Yates, 12 December 1848. Sur. Albert H.
Royall. p. 65.

MURRELL, Robert and Catharine Burnett. Married 9 April 1800 by John
Neblett. WB 5/35.

NANCE, Frederick of Lunenburg and Susanna Christopher, 27 September 1775.
Sur. Thomas Starke. p. 5.

NANCE, James of Lunenburg, and Martha Sammons, 11 March 1791. Sur.
William DeGraffenreidt. Married by John Chappell whose list was
returned to June Court 1791. p. 11 and WB 4/8.

NANCE, Johnson T. and Rebecca Pamplin, 23 February 1825. Sur. James L.
Cheatham. Married 24 February 1825 by James Robertson. p. 39
and WB 8/534.

NANCE, Robert and Sarah Walker. Married 14 February 1799 by Matthew
Dance. WB 4/244A.

NASH, John, Jr. and Anna Tabb, 1 November 1780. Sur. James Tabb. p.5.

NASH, William A. and Amanda W. Jackson, 23 October 1849. Sur. William C.
Jackson. p. 65.

NASH, William P. and Mary Johnson, 26 November 1833. Sur. Alfred Thompson.
Married 4 December 1833 by Joshua Featherston. p. 45 and WB 11/54.

NEAL, Alexander R. and Ann E. Hurt, daughter of Patrick H. Hurt, 2 June
1847. "Married about 10 June 1847" by Thomas Adams. p. 63 and
WB 13/105.

NEAL, James of Lunenburg and Mary Stokes, daughter of Henry Stokes,
9 September 1813. Sur. William G. Pettus. Married 13 September 1813
by Richard Dabbs. p.27 and WB 7/124.

NEAL, Joel and Henrietta Davis, 7 December 1821. Sur. John Davis. Married 17 December 1821 by Silas Shelburne. p. 33 and WB 8/270.

NEAL, John H. and Mary A. Jordan, 27 September 1841. Sur. James J. Jordan. Married 29 September 1841 by Albert Anderson. p. 55 and WB 12/72.

NEAL, John P. and Elizabeth Dunn, 23 May 1811. Sur. John Jeter. p. 25.

NEAL, Poindexter and Betsy Dunn. Married 2 May 1811 by James Shelburne. WB 7/32.

NEAL, Thomas and Mary Ann Stokes, spinster, 14 November 1758. Sur. Young Stokes. p. 1.

NEAL, William and Ellman Neal, 20 December 1785. Sur. William Scott. p.7.

NEAL, William Y. and Martha J. Brydie, 7 November 1842. Sur. Thomas Arvin. p. 55.

NEATHERY, Thomas of Lunenburg and Mary Wells, 11 February 1796. Sur. Jesse Wells. Married 12 February 1796 by James Shelburne. p. 15 and WB 4/160.

NEBLETT, Francis and Nancy Elam, 4 January 1803. Sur. Sterling Neblett. p. 17.

NEBLETT, James and A. Fisher. Married 30 September 1802 by Charles Ogburn whose list was recorded in 1832. WB 10/181A.

NEBLETT, Sterling of Lunenburg and Betsey Coleman, 23 September 1797. Sur. Edward Ragsdale. p. 15.

NEBLETT, Sterling, Jr. and Ann Macfarland, 13 August 1821. Sur. Thomas Adams. Married August 1821 by Thomas Adams. p. 31 and WB 8/209.

NEBLETT, Sterling, Jr. and Clarissa R. Green. Married 10 November 1851 by Thomas E. Locke at William B. Green's residence, Charlotte. St.John's Church Register.

NEBLETT, William of Lunenburg, and Sally Love, 18 April 1792. Sur. Sterling Neblett. Married 18 April 1792 by James Shelburne. p. 13 and WB 4/46.

NEBLETT, William and Amey Williams, 5 October 1803. Sur. William Taylor. p.17

NEBLETT, William James and Ann E. Green. Married 27 May 1846 by Thomas E. Locke, at William B. Green's residence, Charlotte County. St. John's Church Register.

NELSON, Doct: R. C. and Mary Scott Watkins. Married 23 December 1847 by T. E. Locke, at Mr. Samuel Watkins' residence, Clarksville. St.John's Church Register.

NELSON, Thomas C. and Maria Louisa Taylor, 15 December 1835. Sur. William H. Taylor. p. 47.

NEVILS, Clement H. and Lucy Ann Davidson, 9 October 1826. Sur. Booker
Nevil. Married 12 October 1826 by James Robertson. p.41 and WB 9/127.

NEVILS, John and Eliza Tatum, 23 November 1822. Sur. Daniel W. Parsons.
Married 1 December 1822 by Silas Shelburne. p. 35 and WB 8/270.

NEWBILL, Henry and Jane Moore, 8 April 1811. Sur. Eddins [Edwin ?] Moore.
p. 23.

NEWBILL, John G. of Lunenburg, and Susanna Parham Winn, 14 October 1795.
Sur. Thomas Newbill. Married 14 October 1795 by Renard Anderson.
p. 13 and WB 4/124.

NEWBILL, John G. and Jincy Estes. Married 15 June 1802 by Will Spencer,
M.G.U.E. Church. WB 6/82.

NEWBILL, Thomas of Lunenburg and Gracey Powell, 12 November 1795. Sur.
John Powell. Married 24 November 1795 by William McKendree. p. 13
and WB 4/116.

NEWBY, Soloman of Lunenburg, and Milley Fowlkes, 8 October 1789. Sur.
John Fowlkes. p. 11.

NOLLEY, John A. and Jane Callis. Married 11 January 1827 by Joshua
Featherston. WB 9/127.

NORMENT, Archilles and Polly Jeffress. Married 5 December 1815 by Joel
Johns. WB 7/280.

NORMENT, Hugh F. and Mary H. Blackwell, 12 October 1829. Sur. John A.
Hatchett. Married in 1829 by Silas Shelburne. p.43 and WB 10/131.

NORTHINGTON, John of Mecklenburg, and Mary Cardon Booker, 30 November
1795. Sur. Jonathan Booker of Lunenburg. p. 15.

NORVELL, John of Lunenburg and Polly Booth, 25 September 1795. Sur.
Nathaniel Booth. Married 26 September 1795 by John Neblett. p.13
and WB 4/116A.

NUNNALLY, Abner and Frances Walthall, 27 February 1844. Sur. Edward B.
Walthall. Married 27 February 1844 by Thomas E. Locke at William
B. Walthall's residence. p. 59.

NUNNERLY, Branch O. and Drusilla Christopher, 20 September 1846 [21st on
bond]. Sur. Morris Montgomery. p. 61.

OGBURN, Benjamin and Sarah Sills, 30 March 1807. Sur. Edward Ogburn.
Married January 1807 by Thomas Adams. p. 21 and WB 6/254.

OGBURN, Charles H. and Jane M. Hite, 26 February 1844. Sur. William H.
Hardy. Married February 1844 by Robert Michaels who shows the bride's
name as Ann M. Hite. p. 59 and WB 12/214.

OGBURN, Edward and Elizabeth Williams. Married December 1807 by Thomas
Adams. WB 6/253A.

OGBURN, John and M. Witt. Married 18 December 1802 by Charles Ogburn. [Recorded in 1832.] WB 10/181A.

OLD, James of Dinwiddie Co. and Louisa Tucker, 2 February 1796. Sur. Nelson Tucker. Married 4 February 1796 by William Ellis. p.15 and WB 4/124.

OLDHAM, Tarpley of Lunenburg and Polly Cabiness, 26 November 1788. Sur. John Bishop. Married 5 December 1788 by Thomas Crymes. p. 9 and WB 3/342.

OLIVER, Benjamin and Pamelia Winn. Married 13 August 1816 by Joel Johns. WB 7/280.

OLIVER, Curtis and Sally Brown, 20 June 1800 by Arch'd. McTarbert. WB 5/28.

OLIVER, Isaac and Judah Betts, 10 August 1775. Sur. Elisha Betts and N. Hobson. p. 5.

OLIVER, John and Jane P. Pulliam. Married 5 December 1827 by Silas Shelburne. WB 9/480.

OLIVER, John G. and Susan Saunders, daughter of Robert Saunders, 10 December 1832. Matthew G. Almond, witness. p. 11.

OLIVER, Joseph M. and Martha J. Young, 5 November 1844. Sur. Ralph Young. p.59.

ORGAIN, Benjamin of Lunenburg, and Susannah Edmundson, 24 February 1792. Sur. William Neblett. p. 13.

ORGAIN, John, Jr. and Ann Craig, 30 December 1834. Sur. Edward Craig. p.47.

OSLIN, Samuel W. and Pamelia F. Callis, 17 April 1843. Sur. Gray Thompson. Married 21 April 1843 by John C. Blackwell. p. 57 and WB 12/177.

OVERBY, Anderson B. and Nancy S. Hines, 22 August 1848. Sur. John H. Bottom. Married 24 August 1848 by Richard E. G. Adams. p. 65 and WB 13/191.

OVERBY, Buckner of Lunenburg, and Sally Hudgins, 29 December 1787. Sur. John Riggins. p. 9.

OVERBY, Edmund and Mildred Ragsdale, 2 December 1835. Sur. Edmund Bishop. p. 47.

OVERBY, Freeman of Lunenburg and Amey Stanley, 2 July 1785. Sur. John Taylor. Married 9 November 1785 by Thomas Crymes. p.7 and WB 3/263.

OVERBY, John W. and Minerva P. Bishop, 12 March 1849. Sur. William J. Robertson and John A. Bishop. p. 65.

OVERTHRONE [or Overthrow], Samuel and Elizabeth Gill, 8 February 1796. Sur. John Moody. Married 9 February 1796 by Charles Ogburn. p.15 and WB 4/147.

OVERTON, William G. and Ann S. Jones. Married 4 July 1818 by Thomas Adams. WB 8/67.

OWEN, John and Obedience Ligon. Married 11 March 1784 by Thomas Crymes. WB 3/156.

OWEN, John and Rebecca White. Married 11 November 1802 by James Shelburne. WB 6/28A.

OWEN, Peter and Harriett Leonard, 10 December 1841. Sur. John Verser. P.55.

OWEN, William and Tabitha Crews. Married 9 December 1781 by Thomas Crymes. WB 3/104.

PAGE, Lewis of Lunenburg, and Sally Justice, 13 February 1778. Sur. Daniel Justice. p. 5.

PAGE, John and Elizabeth Wilkerson. Married 28 November 1782 by David Ellington. WB 3/132.

PALMER, PARMER - See also Farmer

PARMER, Benjamin and Nancy Stokes, 10 February 1845. Sur. Washington Crafton. p. 61.

PALMER, Edward and Esther Marron, daughter of Daniel Marron, dec'd, 12 June 1762. Sur. Richard Wilkins. p. 3.

PARMER [PALMER], John and Elizabeth Crafton. Married 28 May 1801 by William Ellis. WB 5/67.

PALMER, Melkijah and Mary Bohannon, 5 December 1829. Sur. William A. Bohannon. p. 43.

PALMORE, Thomas and Phebe Westbrook. Married 26 December 1782 by Thomas Crymes. WB 3/131.

PAMPLIN, John and Elizabeth Crenshaw. Married 26 April 1810 by Joel Johns. WB 7/9.

PAMPLIN, Robert and Elizabeth Estes. Married 29 December 1803 by William Ellis. WB 6/76.

PAMPLIN, Robert H. and Polly A. Bragg, 15 December 1826. Sur. William T. Abernathy. Married 21 December 1826 by Thomas H. Jeffress. p. 41 and WB 9/116.

PAMPLIN, William T. and Nancy Fowlkes, 27 October 1821. Sur. Sterling Fowlkes. Married 29 October 1821 by Silas Shelburne. p. 31 and WB 8/227.

PARHAM, Lewis and Dicy Moon. Married 28 July 1808 by William Ellis. WB 6/207A.

PARKER, John of Lunenburg and Jenny Wright, 8 April 1797. Sur. Julius Hite. Married 10 April 1797 by John Neblett. p.15 and WB 4/168.

PARKER, John and Martha Wrenn, 29 October 1821. Sur. Manoah Vincent. Married October 1821 by Thomas Adams. p. 33 and WB 8/209.

PARRISH, Charles of Lunenburg and Jenney Williams, 9 February 1789. Sur.
Thomas Ussery. p. 11.

PARRISH, David and Jane Laffoon. Married 27 November 1818. The minister's
name not shown. WB 8/38.

PARISH, Henry Sterling and Susan Pulliam, 18 December 1845. Sur. James M.
Laffoon. Married 18 December 1845 by W. S. Wilson. p. 61 and
WB 13/46.

PARRISH, James of Lunenburg, and Patty Dixon, 27 March 1791. Sur. James
Laffoon. Married 1 April 1791 by Henry Ogburn. p. 11 and WB 4/13.

PARRISH, James of Lunenburg and Mary Tarpley, 25 March 1788. Sur. John
Parrish. p. 9.

PARRISH, Joel of Lunenburg, and Susanah Maury, 16 May 1786. Sur. Metcalfe
DeGraffenreidt. p. 7.

PARRISH, Joel of Lunenburg and Henrietta Laffoon, daughter of Matthew Laffoon,
23 April 1813. Sur. Matthew Laffoon. Married 24 April 1813 by Thomas
Adams. p. 25 and WB 7/248.

PARRISH, Joel M. and Narcissa A. Snead, 16 November 1825. Sur. Thomas R.
Tisdale. Married 8 December 1825 by Silas Shelburne. p. 39 and WB 9/161.

PARRISH, John of Lunenburg, and Nancy Landrum, 3 February 1783. Sur.
Richard Landrum. p. 7.

PARRISH, John of Lunenburg, and Libey [or Lucy] Brindle, 22 December 1790.
Sur. James Parrish. Married 24 December 1790 by Henry Ogburn. p. 11
and WB 4/7.

PARRISH, John and Bethiah Bailey, 31 December 1835. Sur. Branch B. Beach.
Married 31 December 1835 by John Tompson. [Note: John's last name
is illegible and could be PARRIET, PATRICK or POTEAT.] p. 49 and
WB 11/173.

PARRISH, Matthew and Winney Laffoon. Married 23 May 1819 by Stephen Jones
who also shows the date as Mar. 23. WB 8/38 and WB 8/96.

PARISH, Robert and Elizabeth Jeter. Married 15 November 1799 by James
Shelburne. WB 5/51.

PARRISH, Robert D. and Kitturah R. Tisdale, 22 December 1810. Sur. William
Morgan. p. 23.

PARRISH, Sterling and Kitturah Winn, 23 December 1811. Sur. Joel Parrish.
Married 25 December 1811 by Thomas Adams. p. 23 and WB 7/40.

PARRISH, Thomas and Zilpha Johnson, 18 December 1824. Sur. James G. Parrish. p. 37.

PARRIET, John. See John Parrish and Bethiah Bailey.

PARROTT, W. and E. Johnson. Married 15 December 1819 by Charles Ogburn.
WB 10/181A.

PARSONS, Daniel W. and Mary S. Dupree, 27 July 1836. Sur. William A.
Bradshaw. p. 49.

PATRICK, John. See John Parrish, page 91.

PATTESON, Charles of Lunenburg, and Regina DeGraffenreidt, 30 April 1785.
Sur. Tscharner DeGraffenreidt. p. 7.

PATTILLO, Robert C. and Elizabeth A. Hawkins, 8 May 1826. Sur. Tarlton
W. Knight. Married 9 May 1826 by Silas Shelburne. p.41 and WB 9/161.

PAYLOR, David of Lunenburg, and Sally Tombs, 9 November 1786. Sur. William
Tombs. p. 9.

PEACE, James S. and Mary Manly, 9 October 1826. Sur. William Kirk.
Married 11 October 1827 by Howel Sims. p. 41 and WB 9/195.

PEACE, John J. and Elizabeth Peace. Married 11 October 1832 by Henry
Reeves. WB 11/5.

PEACE, Joseph of Lunenburg, and Elizabeth Bishop Garrott, 7 February 1791.
Sur. Mason Garrott. p. 11.

PEACE, Samuel of Lunenburg, and Betsey Landers Jones, 11 October 1797. Sur.
Lemuel Jones. Married 12 October 1797 by John Neblett. p. 15 and
WB 4/232.

PEACE, Samuel A. and Ann E. Hawthorne, 9 January 1843. Sur. Peter W.
Hawthorne. Married 8 February 1843 by Joshua Featherston. p. 57 and
WB 12/161.

PEARCY - See Piercy page 95

PEARCY, Algernon and Polly Gill. Married October 1817 by Thomas Adams.
WB 7/356.

PEARCEY, Peter R. and Olive W. Smith, 19 November 1842. Sur. Parks Tucker.
Married by Daniel Petty whose list was returned to court 8 February
1847. p. 57 and WB 13/14.

PEASELEY, William and Lucy Sanders, 8 November 1764. Sur. Richard Swepson
and B. Anderson. p. 3.

PEEBLES, Jesse and Harriett Powell, both of Lunenburg, 10 March 1828 by
Silas Shelburne. WB 9/480 and DB 28/30.

PEGRAM, William and Agness Rhodes, 29 January 1779. Sur. William Rhodes.
p. 5.

PENN, Jesse of Lunenburg, and Amey Rudder, 25 October 1796. Sur. Benjamin
Rudder. Married 27 October 1796 by John Neblett. p. 15 and WB 4/168.

PENN, William P. and Tabitha Hardy, 23 March 1835. Sur. Harris Edmundson.
p. 47.

PENNINGTON, Charles S. and Drucilla Smithson. Married 4 March 1828 by Silas Shelburne. WB 9/480.

PENNINGTON, Josephus and Elizabeth M. Marshall, daughter of William J. Marshall who consents and is a witness, 14 September 1853. p. 14.

PENNINGTON, Nathaniel and Lucy Overton, 9 August 1824. Sur. William S. Overton. Married 12 August 1824 by Silas Shelburne. p.37 and WB 8/492.

PENNINGTON, William of Mecklenburg, and Drusela Smithson, 25 November 1780. Sur. William Walker. p. 5.

PEOPLES, R. R. and E. Whalepool. Married 2 December 1820 by Charles Ogburn. WB 10/181A.

PERKINS, Benjamin and Polly Vaughan. Married 7 February 1798 by Matthew Dance. WB 4/233.

PERKINS, David W. and Mary Ann Laffoon, 22 July 1851, "on certification of her mother [not named] and proved by Mortimore Laffoon. p. 5.

PERKINSON, Coleman and Nancy Chandler, 13 December 1810. Sur. James R. Brooks. Married 15 December 1810 by Joel Johns. p. 23 and WB 7/60.

PETTEFORD, David and Elizabeth C. Cooper, 27 June 1848. Sur. Benjamin W. Cooper. p. 65.

PETTUS, Allen G. and Tabitha W. Marable, 1 April 1841. Sur. John J. Wood. p. 55.

PETTUS, David, Sr. and Elenor Willson. Married 25 September 1802 by James Shelburne. WB 6/146-A.

PETTUS, David, Jr. and Eliz^a Boswell. Married 24 December 1802 by James Shelburne. WB 6/146-A.

PETTUS, George W. and Elizabeth S. Eubank, 8 January 1841. Sur. Wyatt Pettus. p. 55.

PETTUS, James H. and Martha A. Smithson, 21 November 1849. Sur. Wyatt H. Pettus. Married 28 November 1849 by Samuel G. Mason. p. 67 and W3 13/349.

PETTUS, John of Lunenburg, and Sarah Pettus, 14 July 1785. Sur. John Pettus. p. 7.

PETTUS, John and Martha Ragsdale, 26 February 1805. Sur. Nathaniel Ragsdale. p. 21.

PETTUS, John R. and Mary E. Smith, 3 June 1841. Sur. William A. Stone. p.55.

PETTUS, Matthew of Lunenburg and Hannah Willson, 12 February 1795. Sur. Valentine Brown. p. 13.

PETTUS, Thomas and Susanna Gregory. Married 24 December 1816 by James Shelburne. WB 7/313.

PETTUS, Walker and Nancy Jordan, 10 June 1822. Sur. Labon Jordan. Married 27 June 1822 by Silas Shelburne. p. 33 and WB 8/270.

PETTUS, William G. of Lunenburg and Jane C. Lamkin, 1 December 1814. Sur. William H. Taylor. p. 27.

PETTUS, William W. and Martha A. Davis, 10 December 1849. Sur. Joseph E. Davis and Thomas F. Pettus. Married 19 December 1849 by Samuel G. Mason. p. 67 and WB 13/349.

PETTUS, Wyatt H. and Harriet F. Eubank, 11 January 1836. Sur. Philip G. Eubank. p. 49.

PETTY, Daniel and Dorothea J. Hardy, 22 October 1829. Sur. Henry G. Hardy. Married 3 November 1829 by Silas Shelburne. p. 43 and WB 10/131.

PETTYPOOL, Edward and Sarah Wrenn, Married 29 November 1800 by James Shelburne. WB 5/51.

PETTYPOOL, Henry of Lunenburg and Jenny Green, 11 October 1788. Sur. John Richie. p. 9.

PETTYPOOL, Isham of Lunenburg, and Rhody Bowers, 8 April 1795. Sur. John Bowers. p. 15.

PETTYPOOL, John of Lunenburg, and Lucy Clarke, 11 February 1790. Sur. Benjamin Clarke. p. 11.

PETTYPOOL, Seth of Lunenburg, and Elizabeth Ladd, 28 January 1792. Sur. Thomas Ladd. Married 6 February 1792 by James Shelburne. p.13 and WB 4/46.

P'POOL, Stephen and Susanna Moon, 18 May 1824. Sur. Josiah B. Wilson. Married 18 May 1824 by Silas Shelburne. p. 37 and WB 8/492.

PETTYPOOL, William of Lunenburg and Katharine Moore, 2 August 1794. Sur. Ussery Moore. Married 7 August 1794 by John Neblett. p. 13 and WB 4/88.

PETTIPOOL, William of Lunenburg and Frances Brooks, 15 February 1775. Sur. David Burton and Martha Taylor. p. 5.

PEWETT, John and Nancy Crenshaw, 9 September 1812. Sur. William Davis. p. 25.

PEWETT, Robert and Nancy T. Johnson, 18 June 1823. Sur. Patrick A. Erskine. Married 26 June 1823 by Silas Shelburne. p. 35 and WB 8/340.

PHILLIPS, Anthony of Lunenburg and Lillian Beuford, 26 March 1779. Sur. Thomas Walker. p. 5.

PHILIPS, Charles M. and Sarah A. E. Crowder, 22 December 1834. Sur.
John R. Crenshaw. p. 47.

PHILLIPS, Dabney P. and Jane E. Fisher, 4 March 1826. Sur. Turner
Abernathy. Married 4 March 1826 by James McAden. p. 41 and WB 8/560.

PHILLIPS, Dyer of Lunenburg, and Letty Hurt, 18 July 1781. Sur. Moses
Hurt, Jr. p. 5.

PHILLIPS, George and Anne Brown, 9 February 1768. Sur. Robert Blackwell
and Nicho. Hobson. p. 5.

PHILLIPS, John and Mary C. Willson, 1 December 1823. Sur. James Wilson.
Married 18 December 1823 by Silas Shelburne. p. 35 and WB 8/340.

PHILLIPS, Martin and Emily M. Pilkinton, 1 May 1836. Sur. James A.
Pilkinton. p. 49.

PHILLIPS, Norbourn D. and Elizabeth E. Daniel, 11 February 1850. Sur.
James W. Stone. p. 67,

PHILLIPS, Robert of Lunenburg, and Lucy Meanly, 8 August 1793. Sur. John
Kirk. Married 27 August 1793 by John Jones. p. 13 and WB 4/40.

PHILIPS, Robert and Wilen Lester [bond states Wilen Lesley], 17 September
1806. Sur. Reuben Cooper. p. 21.

PHILLIPS, Robert and Sally Andrews, 27 February 1821. Sur. Henry Gee.
Married February 1821 by Thomas Adams. p. 33 and WB 8/209.

PHILIPS, Robert and Nancy Stone, 21 May 1823. Sur. Randolph Thompson, Sr.
p. 35.

PHILLIPS, William W. and Louisa Townsend, 23 July 1853. Joseph P. Townsend
proved Louisa was over 21 years of age and is a witness. p. 13.

PIERCE, John and Elizabeth Matthews, 11 March 1813. Sur. Stephen Morgan.
Married 11 March 1813 by Thomas Adams. p. 27 and WB 7/248.

PIERCY - See PEARCY page 92.

PIERCY, John and Margaret P. Raney. Married 1 April 1819 by Thomas Adams.
WB 8/67.

PIERCY, Peter A. and Virginia A. Gee, 22 December 1851, "certification of
Matthew A. Rainey and Sarah A. Rainey, proved by oath of Dennis Gee,
a witness thereto and the fact that Virginia Gee is the daughter of
said Sarah A. Rainey." p. 7.

PIERCY, Thomas and Jane G. Raney. Sur. William Raney. Married December
1817 by Thomas Adams. p. 29 and WB 7/356.

PIERCY, Thomas S. and Elizabeth Hawthorn, 22 December 1851. James Hawthorn,
father of Elizabeth makes affidavit that she is over 21 years. p. 7.

PIKE, Thomas of Lunenburg, and Elizabeth Haymore of Lunenburg, 20 March
1786. Sur. John Taylor. p. 7.

PILKINTON, Willis and Elizabeth A. Bagley. Married 23 June 1813 by
Thomas Adams. WB 7/248.

PILLAR, John H. and Martha Ann Smith. Married 27 June 1839 by Thomas E.
Locke at David Smith's residence, Lunenburg. WB 11/425 and St.John's
Church Register.

PITMAN, John of Lunenburg and Sally Farmer, 9 March 1787. Sur. Jeffery
Murrel. Married 21 March 1787 by Thomas Crymes. p. 9 and WB 3/269.

POINDEXTER, John of Lunenburg, and Nancey Neal, 11 October 1792. Sur.
William Hepburn. p. 13.

POINDEXTOR, Philip of Lunenburg, and Sarah Crymes, daughter of George
Crymes, 15 August 1761. Sur. George Crymes. p. 3.

POLLARD, Edward S. and Frances W. Thompson, 27 April 1848. Sur. George W.
Thompson. Married 10 May 1848 by William S. Wilson. p. 65 and
WB 13/220.

POLLARD, William of Lunenburg, and Amey Clarke, 2 January 1787. Sur.
George Clarke. Married 16 January 1787 by Thomas Crymes. p.9 and WB 3/268.
WB 3/268.

POLLOCK, John M. and Clemar A. Brown. Married by Daniel Petty whose return
is dated 7 December 1833, exact date of marriage not shown. WB 11/32.

POOL, Edward A. and Julia N. Jeffress, 29 August 1836. Sur. Thomas H.
Staples. p. 49.

POPHAM, John of Lunenburg, and Wineforth Heath, daughter of James Heath,
6 July 1761. Sur. James Heath. p. 3.

PORTWOOD, Thomas and Elizabeth Sullivant, 19 May 1757. Sur. Henry Isbel
and G. Carrington, Jr. p. 1.

POTEAT, John. See John Parrish and Bethiah Bailey, page 91.

POTTER, John of Lunenburg, and Mary Hawkins, 16 October 1759. Sur. Thomas
Moore. p. 1.

POTER, John and Molly Dixon. Married 13 March 1805 by John Neblett.
WB 6/124. [See John Potts.]

POTTER, Matthew. See Matthew Pettus and Hannah Willson, page 93.

POTTS, George and Elizabeth Buckner, 23 May ___*___. Sur. Edmund H. [or F.]
Taylor and Claiborne Mills. [* Marriage Bond #1508 states 23 May 1874.
The bond was made during the term of James Barbour, Esq., Governor of
Virginia. His term was from January 4, 1812-December 11, 1814. There-
fore, this marriage date is probably 23 May 1814.]

POTTS, John. See John Poter and Molly Dixon. Last name not clear.

POTTS, John and Susanna Laffoon, 11 December 1817. Sur. James Brintle.
Married 23 December 1817 by Stephen Jones. p. 31 and WB 7/357.

POTTS, Peter of Lunenburg, and Gracey Broadway, 13 November 1793. Sur. Robert Manden. p. 13.

POTTS, Peter and Polly Reese. Married 17 October 1799 by John Paup. WB 5/2A.

POTTS, Stephen of Brunswick County, and Molly Potts Kirkland, 11 February 1796. Sur. Benjiman Kirkland. Married 13 February 1796 by John Rogers. p. 15 and WB 4/127.

POWEL, William H. and Martha C. McKee. Married 15 December 1802 by John Jones. WB 6/14A.

POWERS, James and Lucretia Turner, 21 December 1846. Sur. Richard W. Turner. Married 24 December 1846 by John C. Blackwell. p. 61 and WB 13/11.

POWERS, Samuel and Selah Zachary. Married 1 April 1802 by James Shelburne. WB 6/28.

POWERS, William of Lunenburg and Dosha Farley, 8 December 1796. Sur. Edward Farley. Married 10 December 1796 by James Shelburne. p.11 and WB 4/160.

POWERS, William and Elizabeth Parmer, 10 November 1808. Sur. Woodson Knight. Married 12 November 1808 by William Ellis. p. 23 and WB 6/256.

PREWIT, Robert and Nancy T. Johnson. Married 26 June 1823 by Silas Shelburne. WB 8/340.

PRICE, George and Elizabeth Gordon, 15 December 1806. Sur. John Gordon. Married 18 December 1806 by Matthew Dance. p. 21 and WB 6/181.

PRICE, James T. and Lucretia J. Fowlkes, 18 December 1848. Sur. William Doswell. Married 18 December 1848 by William Doswell. p. 65 and WB 13/232.

PRIEST, Miles of Lunenburg and Fanny Gossee, 22 December 1790. Sur. David Priest. M. B. #254.

PRITCHETT, Armstead and Mary M. Neblett, 9 December 1830. Sur. Thomas B. Green. p. 45.

PRITCHETT, John and Susan Blackwell. Married 24 December 1827 by James McAden. WB 9/292.

PROCISE, John D. and Elizabeth E. Walker, daughter of Mary Walker, 24 December 1850. James H. Sullivan, witness. p. 3.

PROCISE, John D. and Mary E. McKinney, 12 December 1853. William J. Marshall makes oath that Mary is over 21 years of age and is a witness thereto. p. 15.

PROCISE, Mark [or Mack] and Sarah Hazlewood, 5 December 1825. Sur. Samuel Snead and Amos S. Johnson. Married 6 December 1825 by William Hatchett. p. 39 and WB 9/29.

PROCISE, Mack [or Mark] D. and Elizabeth F. Lester, 27 October 1846. Sur. James J. Jordan and Ts. Woodson. p. 63.

PUCKETT, James and Polly Franklin. Married 20 November 1795 by James Shelburne. WB 4/159A.

PUGH, James of Lunenburg, and Nancey George, 19 February 1784. Sur. William Wrenn. p. 7.

PULLY, John A. and Sally Slaughter, 10 May 1842. Sur. John Rash. Married 12 May 1842 by George A. Bain. p. 55 and WB 12/90.

PULLY, Thomas and Gerusha [or Genesha] Brown, 24 September 1821. Sur. James Brown. Married 27 September 1821 by James Robertson. p. 31 and WB 8/230.

PULLY, William of Lunenburg and Lucy Thompson, 4 October 1790. Sur. David Thompson. p. 11.

PULLY, William S. and Mary B. Brown, 22 January 1829. Sur. Joseph A. Brown. p. 43.

QUEENSBERRY, William and Nancey Robertson, 8 May 1817. Sur. Frederick N. Robertson. p. 31.

RADFORD, James of Lunenburg, and Anne Shelburne, 5 July 1789. Sur. William Bush. p. 11.

RAGSDALE, Baxter and Sally Morgan. Married 26 February 1799 by John Neblett. WB 5/2A.

RAGSDALE, David of Lunenburg and Francis Brammer, 26 December 1781. Sur. Richard Hite. p. 5.

RAGSDALE, Drury of Lunenburg and Elizabeth Sturdivant, 30 January 1790. Sur. Joseph Dunnman (?). p. 11.

RAGSDALE, Edward and Sally B. Ragsdale, 11 December 1823. Sur. Thomas Booth [M.B. shows Thomas Rooff.] p. 35.

RAGSDALE, George and Julia A. Roe, 25 December 1846. Sur. Henry Ragsdale. p. 61.

RAGSDALE, Henry and Milly R. Hite. Married December 1807 by Thomas Adams. WB 6/253A.

RAGSDALE, Henry and Rebecca Chavous [or Chavouz - Deed Book states Chavens], 13 January 1830. Sur. David Ballentine and Stephen McLaughlin. Married 14 January 1830 by Baxter Ragsdale. p. 45, WB 10/71 and DB 29/87.

RAGSDALE, Joel M. and Susan C. Baker, 23 May 1829. Sur. Josiah B. Wilson. p. 43.

RAGSDALE, John of Lunenburg and Patience Williams, 4 May 1780. Sur. William Taylor. p. 5.

RAGSDALE, John of Lunenburg and Sally Scarbery, 25 December 1783. Sur. William Ragsdale. p. 7.

RAGSDALE, John of Lunenburg and Mary Jones, 3 December 1792. Sur. Thomas Garland. p. 13.

RAGSDALE, John of Lunenburg, and Martha Gee, 18 December 1792. Sur. Nathan Gee. p. 13.

RAGSDALE, Joseph of Lunenburg, and Sarah Shelburne, 17 November 1791. Sur. Richard Ragsdale. p. 11.

RAGSDALE, Joshua of Lunenburg, and Leuiza [Louisa] Maddox, 2 December 1789. Sur. John Ragsdale. p. 11.

RAGSDALE, Richard of Lunenburg, and Rebecca Pollard, 5 November 1785. Sur. William Burchett. Married by James Shelburne whose list was "from October 1785 to May 1786." p. 7 and WB 3/252.

RAGSDALE, William of Lunenburg and Milley Gee, 29 January 1794. Sur. John Tisdale of Lunenburg. p. 13.

RAGSDALE, William, Jr. and Olive J. Ashley, 25 March 1822. Sur. William Davis. Married March 1822 by Thomas Adams. p. 33 and WB 8/271.

RAMSEY, Newett and Elizabeth Waller, 12 March 1814. Sur.George Gee. p.29.

RANDOLPH, William E. and Mary S. Lavinia Epes, daughter of John C. Epes, 10 May 1853. William P. Epes, witness. p. 13.

RANEY, Buckner M.D. and Jane Tomlinson, 10 December 1821. Sur. Howel P. Crowder. Married 13 December 1821 by Baxter Ragsdale. p. 33 and WB 8/263.

RAINEY, Francis and Cissly M. Gee. Married by Daniel Petty whose return was dated 8 February 1847, but the date of marriage not shown. WB 13/14.

RANEY, Matthew A. and Sally A. Gee. Married by Daniel Petty whose return was dated 8 June 1840, but the date of marriage not shown. WB 11/415.

RANEY, Peter, Jr. and Julia A. Crowder, 16 February 1826. Sur. Green W. Crowder. Married by Charles Ogburn 11 February 1825 and reported in 1832. M.R. index states 11 February 1824. p. 41 and WB 10/181.

RAINEY, Theopilus A. and Ann M. Piercy, 25 March 1853. William A. Rainey proves that Ann is 21 years of age. p. 12.

RASH, Alexander B. and Lucy A. Jackson, 21 December 1852. Gray Thompson proves Lucy is more than 21 years of age and is a witness. p. 12.

RASH, Jacob B. and Agnes S. Hines, 26 January 1830. Sur. William Rash. Married 28 January 1830 by Joshua Featherston. p. 43 and WB 10/101.

RASH, James and Sarah D. Jackson, daughter of Dorothy A. Jackson, 1 May 1852. A. J. J. Brown, witness. p. 9.

RASH, John and Catharine Leonard, 27 December 1824. Sur. William Brown and Randolph Thompson. p. 37.

RASH, John and Elizabeth Carl [or Earl]. Married 14 March 1833 by Joshua Featherston. WB 11/8.

RASH, John and Nancy Brown, 10 December 1836. Sur. James W. Hudson. Married 14 December 1836 by Matthew Dance. p. 51 and WB 11/336.

RASH, Robert and Rebecca Sills. Married 17 December 1809 by Thomas Adams. WB 7/39.

RASH, Robert Jr. and Elizabeth Robertson, 2 October 1822. Sur. William Williams, Jr. p. 35.

RAWLINS, Peter of Lunenburg and Mary Early, widow, 23 April 1761. Sur. Mathew Watson. p. 3.

READ, Clement, Jr. and Mary Nash, spinster, 22 December 1757. Sur. George Carrington, Jr. and Thomas Read. p. 1.

READ, Melanethon H. and Jane Christian Burwell. Married 11 October 1842 by Thomas E. Locke at Randolp Burwell's residence, Mecklenburg. St. John's Church Register.

REAVES, Peter of Lunenburg and Anne Tucker, 22 February 1793. Sur. Daniel Clay. p. 13.

REDFORD, Francis and Elizabeth Wood. Married 27 November 1816 by William Richards. WB 7/307.

REDFORD, William and Susannah Shelburn. Married 26 November 1782 by Thomas Crymes. WB 3/131.

REESE, Freeman Harper of Lunenburg and Fanney Brown, 23 January 1797. Sur. William Brown. p. 15.

REESE, James and Barbara Caudil, 8 March 1804. Sur. Jeremiah Lambert. Married 13 March 1804 by John Neblett. p. 19 and WB 6/123.

REESE, Joseph A. and Sally Moore, 23 December 1822. Sur. Joseph Moore. p.35.

REESE, Parham and Polly Skinner, Married 25 December 1818. Minister's name not shown. WB 8/38.

REESE, Samuel U. W. and Evalina Winn, daughter of Booker Winn, 4 April 1853. William J. Robertson, witness. p. 12.

REESE, Washington and Elizabeth Calliham, 14 January 1846. Sur. William C. Robertson. p. 61.

REESE, William S. and Mary E. Ragsdale, daughter of Thomas M. Ragsdale, 9 September 1851. Samuel U. Reese, witness. p. 5.

RHODES, Elisha of Lunenburg and Salley Pewett [or Perrett], 28 December 1785. Sur. Joel Perrett. p. 7.

RICHARDS, Henry B. and Angelina L. Barnes, 9 May 1836. Sur. Enos H. Barnes. p. 51.

RICHARDS, William of Lunenburg, and Ermin Lester, 9 October 1788. Sur. Bryant Lester, Jr. p. 9.

RICHARDS, William H. and Nancey Jeffress, 23 December 1823. Sur. John Y. Richards. Married 23 December 1823 by Silas Shelburne. p. 35 and WB 8/340.

RICHARDSON, Henry and Margarett Kelly, 25 December 1844. Sur. Drury
Cooper. Married by Daniel Petty whose return was recorded 8 February
1847, exact date of marriage not shown. The minister shows the
bride's name as Mary Ann Kelly. p. 59 and WB 13/14.

RICHARDSON, James G. and Eliza Smith, 24 October 1823. Sur. Joshua
Smith. Married 29 October 1823 by Silas Shelburne. p. 37 and WB 8/340.

RICHARDSON, James G. and Mary Maddux, 23 November 1844. Sur. Ed. B. Gee.
p. 59.

RICHARDSON, John of Lunenburg and Elizabeth Gunn, 21 December 1795. Sur.
Daniel Winn. Married 21 December 1795 by John Neblett. p. 15 and
WB 4/124.

RICHARDSON, John and Sally N. Coleman, 19 April 1824. Sur. Anthony W.
Smith. Married 20 April 1824 by Silas Shelburne. p. 37 and WB 8/340.

RICHARDSON, Jonathan and Louisa Brown, 3 October 1829. Sur. David
Valentine. Married 10 December 1829 by Baxter Ragsdale. p. 43,
WB 10/71, and DB 29/87.

RICHARDSON, Robert and Sarah Gregory, 8 October 1838. Sur. William Keeton.
p. 53.

RICHIE, David and Hannah Ingram, 1 October 1803. Sur. Matthew Calliham.
p. 17.

RITCHEE, John of Lunenburg and Patty Green, 22 November 1788. Sur. Henry
Pettypool. p. 9.

RIGGINS, John and Betsey Smith, 23 August 1811. Sur. Thomas Cole. Married
24 August 1811 by Jesse Brown. p. 23 and WB 7/60.

RIGGONS, Thomas and Jean Whitworth, 10 April 1811. Sur. Richard Jeffress.
Married 21 April 1811 by Joel Johns. p. 25 and WB 7/60.

RIVERS, William and Susan Womack, 10 April 1817. Sur. Jacob Womack. p. 31.

ROACH, John R. and Temperance A. Wallace, daughter of Anderson Wallace,
14 October 1850. William Townsend, witness. p. 2.

ROACH, William and Martha Jackson, 25 January 1811. Sur. William Bohannon.
Married 30 January 1811 by Joel Johns. p. 23 and WB 7/60.

ROADS, William and Dosha Blankinship. Married 30 September 1784 by David
Ellington. WB 3/185.

ROBERTS, Alexander and Susanna Wills. Married 3 October 1833 by Mathew
Dance. WB 8/254.

ROBERTS, Benjiman A. and Maria Wilson, 8 March 1847. Sur. Robert B.
Wilson. Married 12 Jany. 1847 by William S. Wilson. p.63 and WB 13/46.

ROBERTS, George W. and Maria S. Pettus, 28 October 1833. Sur. Allen Stephen Pettus. p. 45.

ROBERTS, John of Lunenburg and Susanna Pettus, 21 January 1788. Sur. William Hatchett. p. 9.

ROBERTS, John of Lunenburg and Rebacha Sammons, 12 November 1789. Sur. James Sammons. Married 16 November 1789 by James Shelburne. p. 11 and WB 3/358.

ROBERTS, John and Elizabeth Gregory, 5 December 1822. Sur. David Y. Gregory. Married 12 December 1822 by Silas Shelburne. p. 35 and WB 8/270.

ROBERTS, Peter P. and May Wyatt, 13 January 1812. Sur. Overstreet Wyatt. Married 14 January 1812 by Thomas Adams. p. 25 and WB 7/40.

ROBERTS, Philip of Lunenburg and Elizabeth Davis, 2 January 1796. Sur. Nevil Gee. Married 4 January 1796 by John Neblett. p. 15 and WB 4/124.

ROBERTS, Robert and Eliza Smithson, 10 September 1838. Sur. Charles Smithson. p. 53.

ROBERTS, Robert and Mary E. Harvy, 30 June 1849. Sur. John C. Harvy. Married 5 July 1849 by William S. Wilson. p. 67 and WB 13/353.

ROBERTS, Thomas and Susanah Dozer, 12 December 1766. Sur. Leonard Dozer and Nick Holmes. p. 3.

ROBERTS, William T. of Charlotte County, and Martha A. Saunders, of Lunenburg County, 12 September 1845. Sur. David C. Hutcheson. Married 17 September 1845 by Louis Dupree. p. 61 and WB 12/286.

ROBERTSON, Christopher of Lunenburg and Constant Edmundson, 22 March 1787. Sur. William Taylor. p. 9.

ROBERTSON, Christopher and Polly Rudder. Married 2 April 1805 by John Neblett. WB 6/123A.

ROBERTSON, Daniel of Lunenburg, and Elizabeth Edmundson, 12 October 1797. Sur. Christopher Robertson. p. 15.

ROBERTSON, Daniel H. and Martha Edmundson, 12 November 1821. Sur. Edward Lee. Married November 1821 by Thomas Adams. p. 33 and WB 8/209.

ROBERTSON, Edward and Martha Ann Tomlinson, 14 October 1846. Sur. Samuel W. Snead. p. 61.

ROBERTSON, Francis of Lunenburg, and Elizabeth Street, widow and relict of Col. Waddy Street, 16 April 1821. Married 19 April 1821 by Charles Ogburn. p. 33, WB 10/22, and DB 25/222.

ROBERTSON, Frederick N. and Martha F. Ellis, 23 January 1815. Sur. Johnson F. Nance. Married 26 January 1815 by James Shelburne. p. 29 and WB 7/227.

ROBERTSON, George C. and Serena A. Cox, daughter of Thomas W. Cox, 22 September 1852. William J. Cox attests that Serena is more than 21 years of age and is a witness thereto. p. 10.

ROBERTSON, James of Lunenburg and Charity Tatom, 8 January 1795. Sur. Frederick Nance. Married 21 January 1795 by James Shelburne. p. 15 and WB 4/107.

ROBERTSON, John and Mary Poindexter, daughter of Philip Poindexter, 6 December 1752. Sur. Richard Witton and Paul Carrington. p. 1.

ROBERTSON, John of Lunenburg and Molly Weatherford, 27 July 1781. Sur. Benjamin Weatherford. p. 5.

ROBERTSON, John and Betsy Rudd. Married 1 May 1800 by Matthew Dance. WB 5/22.

ROBERTSON, John and Nancy Jeffress. Married 15 November 1800 by James Shelburne. WB 5/51.

ROBERTSON, John and Polly Thompson, 14 December 1803. Sur. William Taylor. p. 17.

ROBERTSON, John and Elizabeth C. Bishop, 26 February 1821. Sur. Phillip H. Bowers. Married February 1821 by Thomas Adams. p. 31 and WB 8/209.

ROBERTSON, John J. and Mary M. Green, 2 February 1825. Sur. Branch B. Beach. Married 3 February 1825 by James Robertson. p. 39 and WB 8/534.

ROBERTSON, Jonas. See Jonas Robinson.

ROBERTSON, Peter and Mary Ann L. Gregory, 30 October 1822. Sur. Patrick A. Erskine. Married 31 October 1822 by Silas Shelburne. p. 35 and WB 8/270.

ROBERTSON, Richard and Frances C. Estes. Married 26 February 1801 by William Ellis. WB 5/67.

ROBERTSON, Thomas and Polley Hammons. Married September 1821 by Thomas Adams. WB 8/209.

ROBERTSON, William B. and Mary A. P. Betts, 6 February 1826. Sur. Mont. S. Bacon. Married 7 February 1826 by Thos. H. Jeffress. p.41, WB 8/551, and DB 27/157.

ROBERTSON, William E. and Mary E. Stainback, 10 July 1826. Sur. Sterling Lambert. p. 41.

ROBERTSON, William E. and Sally G. Hardy, 13 March 1844. Sur. George H. Lee. Married March 1844 by Robert Michaels. p. 59 and WB 12/215.

ROBINSON, Jonas and Francis Bailey, 23 October 1817. Sur. Edward S. Bailey. Married 29 October 1817 by James Robertson. [The marriage bond states the name Robertson, but the signature on the bond is Robinson.] p. 29 and WB 8/1.

ROBINSON, Thomas and Polly Hammonds, 10 September 1821. Sur. Richard Hammonds. Married September 1821 by Thomas Adams. p. 31 and WB 8/209.

ROBINSON, Thomas C. and Sally P. Cordle, daughter of Julia Cordle, 23 December 1851. William C. Robertson, witness. p. 7.

ROBINSON, William and Milly Hammons, 26 December 1848. Sur. Garrott Waller. p. 65.

RODGERS, John W. and Polly Moon, 8 October 1814. Sur. James Farmer. Married 11 August 1814 by James Shelburne. p. 27 and WB 7/227.

ROGERS, John W. and Susan Dagnall, 8 September 1823. Sur. Richard Dagnall. Married 11 September 1823 by William Hatchett. p. 35 and WB 8/336.

ROGERS, Reuben and Martha Chappell. Married 28 January 1800 by John Jones. WB 5/56.

ROSS, William and Salley C. Pritchett, 28 November 1812. Sur. John Pritchett. Married 29 November 1812 by Thomas Adams. p. 25 and WB 7/248.

ROWLETT, Jesse W. and Mary W. Smith, 13 January 1841. Sur. Thomas W. White. p. 55.

ROWLETT, John M. and L. G. Jeffress. Married 17 August 1832 by Silas Shelburne. WB 11/2.

ROWLETT, John and Polly Hudson. Married 30 December 1819 by Thomas H. Jeffress. WB 8/139.

ROWLETT, Matthew J. and Elizabeth Pettus, 6 January 1794. Sur. Stephen Johnson. Married 6 January 1794 by William Creath. p. 13 and WB 4/46.

ROWLETT, Stephen D. and Eliza. Fowlkes, 21 March 1814. Sur. Sterling Fowlkes. Married 12 April 1814 by James Shelburne. p.29 and WB 7/110.

ROWLETT, William and Martha Willson, daughter of Edward Willson, 9 October 1817. Sur. William G. Pettus. p. 31.

ROWLETT, William B. and Eliza Clay, 2 November 1835. Sur. Charles B. Clay. Married 5 November 1835 by Matthew M. Dance. p.47 and WB 11/336.

RUCKES - See Rux

RUCKES, Benjiman of Lunenburg and Carrarhan [also shown Keranhappuchi] Crafton, 14 April 1785. Sur. Seth Farley. Married 21 April 1785 by Thomas Crymes. p. 7 and WB 3/210.

RUCKS, James and Barthena Young, 13 January 1814. Sur. John C. Branagin. Married 19 January 1814 by James Robertson. p. 29 and WB 7/124.

RUDD, Joseph and Mary W. Willson. Married 22 December 1802 by James Shelburne. WB 6/29.

RUDD, Joseph and Susanna Hardwicke. Married 18 October 1805 by James Shelburne. WB 6/147.

RUDD, Thomas and Elizabeth Ingram, 6 March 1783. Sur. Sylvanus Walker. p. 7.

RUDD, William S. and Amelia M. Ingram, 12 November 1849. Sur. James H. Marable. p. 65.

RUDDER, Benjamin and Frances Freeman. Married 25 December 1801 by John Neblett. WB 5/67A.

RUDDER, Charles of Lunenburg and Lucretia Matthis, 15 August 1785. Sur. John Matthes. p. 7.

RUDDER, Edward of Lunenburg and Jincy Chambers, 17 December 1787. Sur. John Chambers. p. 9.

RUDDER, Epaphroditus and Sally Freeman. Married 20 December 1820 by Thomas Adams. WB 8/67.

RUDDER, John of Lunenburg and Martha Garrott, 15 December 1779. Sur. John Garrott. p. 5.

RUDDER, John H. and Mariam Turner. Married 12 December 1833 by Joshua Featherston. WB 11/54. See William Turner and Myram Turner, page 125.

RUSSELL, Henry J. and Harriet T. Johnston, 18 October 1837. Sur. John Williams. p. 53.

RUSSELL, Jeremiah B. and Nancy F. Throckmorton, 7 December 1852. Samuel E. Tucker guardian of Nancy. John Hazelwood, witness. p. 11.

RUSSELL, John of Lunenburg and Pheby Hudson, 13 June 1787. Sur. Stephen Smith. p. 9.

RUSSELL, John and Martha Hightower. Married 28 July 1808 by Joel Jones. WB 6/244.

RUSSELL, John J. and Elizabeth Pewett, 18 October 1837. Sur. John Williams. p. 51.

RUSSELL, Phillip and Elizabeth Morgan, 23 May 1822. Sur. Claiton Russell. Married 22 May 1822 by Baxter Ragsdale. p. 35 and WB 8/263.

RUSSELL, Richard of Parish of St. James in County of Lunenburg, and Elizabeth Carlton, spinster of same county and Parish, daughter of Thomas Carlton who personally gave his consent, 7 July 1761. Sur. Robert Munford. p. 3.

RUSSELL, Thomas L. and Martha R. Bohannon, 10 November 1845. Sur. Philip R. Bohannon. p. 61.

RUSSELL, Thornton and Rebecca J. Pulliam, 31 September 1830 [endorsement on bond states September 20]. Sur. George W. Pulliam. Married October 1830 by Silas Shelburne. p. 43 and WB 10/131.

RUSSELL, William and Susanna Hightower. Married 9 October 1804 by James Shelburne. WB 6/146A.

RUTHERFORD, John A. H. and Catharine Jane Hurt, 18 November 1835. Sur. Patrick H. Hurt. p. 49.

RUTLEDGE, Blanks and Polly Clay. Married 17 October 1805 by William Ellis. WB 6/136.

RUTLEDGE, James and Frances W. Stone, 17 June 1845. Sur. William H. Moore. Married 18 June 1845 by James W. Hunnicut. p. 61 and WB 12/253.

RUTLEDGE, Littleberry and Nancy Farmer, 26 December 1812. Sur. Matthew Filbert. Married 30 December 1812 by James Robertson. p. 25 and WB 7/59.

RUTLEDGE, Peter and Mary Borum. Married 26 December 1828 by Thomas H. Jeffress. WB 9/212.

RUTLEDGE, Robert and Nancy Smithson. Married 4 January 1800 by James Shelburne. WB 5/51.

RUTLEDGE, William and Elay Bowen, 3 September 1811. Sur. Thomas Rutledge. p. 23.

RUTLEDGE, William and Sarah Sheffield, 16 September 1850. David Moon makes affidavit that Sarah is more than 21 years of age. Married 18 September 1850 by William Doswell. p. 1 and WB 13/411.

RUX, John and Elizabeth Verser, 22 November 1841. Sur. William Arvin, Jr. p. 55. [See Rucks]

RYAN, Phillip H. and Sarah Sowdon, daughter of Sarah Y. Sowdon, 17 March 1852. Matt. G. Williams, witness. p. 8.

RYLAND, John and Susanna Hawkins, 22 December 1817. Sur. James Smith, Jr. p. 29.

RYLAND, John T. and Mary B. Carter, 23 June 1848. Sur. Thomas C. Averett. p. 65.

SADLER, Thomas and Nancy S. Robertson, 8 March 1804. Sur. James Roberts. Married 10 March 1804 by James Shelburne. p. 19 and WB 6/147.

SALE, John and Mary Ann Betts. Married 15 January 1808 by William Ellis. WB 6/209A.

SAMMONS, Robert and Elizabeth Crafton. Married 10 April 1789 by Thomas Crymes. WB 3/342.

SANDS, Phillips and Martha Hardy. Married 2 November 1797 by Charles Ogburn. WB 4/232 and WB 10/181A.

SANDS, Samuel and Margaret Craghead. Married 20 July 1786 by Thomas Crymes. WB 3/263.

SATTERFIELD, James W. and Ann Eliza Coleman, 18 June 1850. Sur. Robert
Crymes. p. 67.

SATTERWHITE, John and Frances Cockerham, spinster, 15 May 1756. Sur.
Henry Cockerham, Thomas Nash, and G. Carrington, Jr. p. 1.

SAUNDERS, John H. and Pamelia W. Pettus, 14 October 1833. Sur. Albert
G. Smith. p. 45.

SCARBROUGH, Thomas and Sally Callihan. Married 12 July 1792 by John
Neblett. WB 4/32A.

SCARBROUGH, Thomas G. and Sarah Jane Hudson, 14 December 1835. Sur.
Littleberry Williams. Married 23 December 1835 by Joshua Featherston.
p. 49 and WB 11/156.

SCOGGIN, James L. and Ann E. Shell, 5 June 1847. Sur. William T. Blackwell. Married 7 June 1847 by John C. Blackwell. p. 63 and WB 13/132.

SCOTT, James H. and Michell Branch Scott, 21 November 1823. Sur. Robert
Scott. Married 26 November 1823 by Joel Johns. p. 35 and WB 8/357.

SCOTT, John of Lunenburg and Dicey Farmer, 14 February 1811. Sur.
Lodowick Farmer. p. 23.

SCOTT, Robert and Jane Ragsdale. Married 27 February 1782 by James
Shelburne. WB 3/104.

SCOTT, Robert and Eliza Chambers, 19 November 1803. Sur. Edward Chambers.
p. 17.

SCOTT, Robert and Mary E. Marshall, daughter of John Marshall, 11 October
1852. A. W. Marshall, witness. p. 10.

SCOTT, William and Martha Burton. Married 19 November 1816 by James
Shelburne. WB 7/313.

SEAY, George N. and Petronella S. Hatchett, 9 September 1844. Sur.
Richard J. H. Hatchett. p. 59.

SEWAL, Benjamin and Sarah Smith. Married 30 January 1783 by Thomas Crymes.
WB 3/131.

SHACKELTON, George W. and Matilda A. Arkin [or Aikin], 13 July 1829. Sur.
Joseph Arkin. Married 14 July 1829 by John Thompson. p.43 and WB 10/66.

SHACKELTON, Robert L. and Mary A. R. Fuqua, 22 May 1841. Sur. Josiah B.
Cox. p. 55.

SHACKELTON, Thomas T. and Nancy C. Street, 23 October 1847. Sur. James
C. Mitchell. p. 63.

SHARP, Richard H. and Lucy O. Hardy, 17 February 1843. Sur. Griffin O.
Hardy. Married 22 February 1843 by John C. Blackwell. p.57 and WB 12/177.

SHAW, John and Caroline A. Bagley, 13 May 1825. Sur. Charles Smith. p.39.

SHEERES, David and Nancy Thompson. Married 10 February 1785 by David
Ellington. WB 3/207.

SHELBURN, Augustine and Jane Bush. Married 6 April 1782 by James
Shelburne. WB 3/118.

SHELBURNE, Cephas and Mary Ann M. Fowlkes, 1 April 1836. Sur. Henry W.
Tisdale. p. 49.

SHELBURNE, Cephas and Lucy J. Wriglesworth, 13 March 1843. Sur. Paul
Wilson. Married 15 March 1843 by Chester Bullard. p. 57 and WB 12/145.

SHELBURN, James and Sally Crafton. Married 22 December 1802 by James
Shelburn. WB 6/29.

SHELBURN, James and Mary Jane R. Clarke, 10 June 1844. Sur. Mastin Barnes.
Married 12 June 1844 by Chester Bullard. p. 59 and WB 12/246.

SHELBORNE, John and Elizabeth Willis. Married 4 March 1784 by James
Shelburne. WB 3/169.

SHELBORNE, Samuel and Sally Pampton. Married 26 November 1789 by James
Shelburne. WB 3/358.

SHELBURNE, Silas of Lunenburg and Mary Stone, 10 November 1814. Sur.
Asher Stone. Married 18 November 1814 by William Richards. p. 27
and WB 7/226.

SHELBURNE, Silas and Margaret M. Knott, 27 November 1822. Sur. W. O. Gee.
Married 2 December 1822 by Silas Shelburne. p. 35 and WB 8/270.

SHELBURN, Silas W. and Rebecca S. J. [or G.] Wood, 5 November 1846. Sur.
Paul K. Wood. Married 9 November 1846 by Samuel G. Mason, Charlotte
C.H. p. 61 and WB 13/10.

SHELBURNE, Simeon and Nancy B. Smithson, 14 May 1812. Sur. Christopher T.
Smithson. Married 17 May 1812 by James Shelburne. p. 25 and WB 7/124.

SHELBURN, Thomas and Polly Crenshaw, 8 November 1804. Sur. John Fram.
Married 19 November 1804 by James Shelburne. p. 19 and WB 6/147.

SHELTON, James and Obedience Worsham, spinster, 22 May 1756. Sur. Henry
Isbell. p. 1.

SHELTON, John W. and Jane Jordan. Married 8 April 1818 by James Robertson.
WB 8/1.

SHELTON, William F. and Mary S. Ashworth, Married 4 December 1845 by William
S. Wilson. WB 13/46.

SHELTON, Young and Henrietta Shelton. Married 13 December 1784 by Thomas
Crymes. WB 3/200.

SHENEBERY, George Peter and Mary Thompson, 20 December 1806. Sur. James
   Newberry. Married 26 December 1806 by Matthew Dance who shows George's
   name as Shinneburg. p. 23 and WB 6/181.

SHIP, Mack and Sally Matthews. Married 18 January 1794 by John Neblett.
   WB 4/50.

SHIP, Robert and Eliza Pettypool. Married January 1794 by James Shelburne.
   WB 4/46.

SHIP, William and Nancy Niblett, 14 September 1803. Sur. Francis Neblett.
   p. 17.

SHORTER, George and Parthena Thompson, 20 January 1844. Sur. Edwin P.
   Thompson. Married January 23, 1844 by William G. Wilson. p. 59 and
   WB 12/177.

SHORTER, Thomas H. and Lucy A. Thompson, 29 October 1844. Sur. Clement J.
   Thompson. p. 59.

SHULE, Andrew and Mary Anders. Married by James Shelburne whose list was
   return "for November Court 1790 to May Court 1791." WB 4/11A.

SIKES, Thomas Aldridge and Sally Willis. Married 28 October 1783 by James
   Shelburne. WB 3/150.

SIMMONS, Benjamin and Martha Hood. Married 25 December 1800 by William
   Ellis. WB 5/67.

SIMMONS, George and Prudence Roads. Married 17 April 1783 by David Ellington.
   WB 3/139.

SIMMONS, John and Nancy Ryland, 3 September 1822. Sur. Thomas Ryland. Married
   3 September 1822 by James Smith. p. 33 and WB 8/267.

SIMMONS, John W. and Jane Lucas Willson, 11 August 1834. Sur. Wilson
   Harris. p. 47.

SIMMONS, William [or Williamson], and Elizabeth Claughton. Married
   12 August 1809 by Richard Dabbs. WB 7/9.

SIMMONS, Williamson and Mary R. Fowlkes, 24 September 1823. Sur. Christopher
   Anderson. Married 3 October 1823 by Silas Shelburne. p. 35 and WB 8/340.

SINGLETON, Robert and Jane E. Matthews, 14 January 1845. Sur. Freeman J.
   Winn. Married 28 January 1845 by Joshua Featherston. WB 12/238.

SINGLETON, Zebelon and Jincey Taylor. Married 19 March 1816 by Thomas
   Adams. WB 7/249.

SKELTON, John T. and Martha E. Abernathy, 4 August 1817. Sur. James
   Fisher. Married August 1817 by Thomas Adams. p. 29 and WB 7/356.

SKELTON, William F. and Mary S. Ashworth, 20 December 1845. Sur. Robert H. Ashworth. Married 4 December 1845 by W. S. Wilson. p. 61 and WB 13/46.

SKINNER, Ashley and Mary Garland, 22 December 1834. Sur. John Inge and William H. Taylor. p. 47.

SKINNER, Blackwell and Mary Laffoon, 18 December 1841. Sur. Freeman J. Winn. p. 55.

SKINNER, Gholson and Jane [or June] Moore, 29 February 1844. Sur. James N. Skinner. p. 59 and DB 33/259A.

SKINNER, James and Martha Moore, 8 December 1834. Sur. James Inge. p. 47.

SKINNER, John and Polly Inge. Married 21 December 1799 by John Neblett. WB 5/2A.

SKINNER, Reuben and Sally Inge. Married December 1808 by Thomas Adams. WB 6/253A.

SKINNER, Samuel and Betsy Cammell, Married 16 March 1793 by John Neblett. WB 4/36.

SKINNER, Samuel and Patsy Inge. Married 23 April 1797 by John Neblett. W5 4/233.

SKINNER, Samuel and Eliza Skinner, 2 February 1835. Sur. Gholson Skinner. p. 47.

SKINNER, Vincent and Katy Chandler. Married 22 April 1802 by Joel Johns. WB 6/11.

SKINNER, Vincent and Sally Riggin. Married 7 February 1820 by Stephen Jones. WB 8/96.

SKINNER, Vincent and Eudocia A. Garland, 25 February 1824. Sur. John Skinner. Married 25 February 1824 by Baxter Ragsdale. p. 37 and WB 8/336.

SKINNER, William and Elizabeth Byars. Married 24 January 1816 by Stephen Jones. WB 7/275.

SKINNER, William B. and Martha J. Stone, 1 November 1836. Sur. John Skinner. Married 2 November 1836 by Joshua Featherston. p. 51 and WB 11/182.

SKINNER, William B. and Lucy J. Reese, ward of John J. Peace, 31 October 1853. James W. Moore, witness. p. 14.

SLAUGHTER, Henry and Siller Haley. Married 18 August 1799 by James Shelburne. WB 5/51.

SLAUGHTER, Isaiah and Mary G. Stone. Married by Daniel Petty whose list was returned 8 June 1840. WB 11/415.

SLAUGHTER, Isaiah and Amelia E. Wilkes, 12 December 1853. Edward Goodwyn certifies that Amelia is 21 years of age. p. 15.

SLAUGHTER, Jeremiah and Elizabeth Stembridge. Married by James Shelburne whose list was returned to court 9 July 1789. WB 3/345.

SLAUGHTER, John and Mary Williams. Married 20 January 1790 by James Shelburne. WB 3/358.

SLAUGHTER, John and Meria L. Slaughter, 14 October 1822. Sur. Henry P. Crenshaw. p. 35.

SLAUGHTER, Josephus and Lucenda Watkins, 13 April 1835. Sur. Ezekiel Slaughter. p. 47.

SLAUGHTER, Manly and Sally Ford. Married 29 July 1810 by James Shelburne. WB 7/15.

SMITH, Anthony and Polly Harris Valentine, 28 February 1807. Sur. John Going. Married January 1807 by Thomas Adams. p. 23 and WB 6/254.

SMITH, Benjamin E. and Mary A. B. Hardy, 12 December 1825. Sur. Larkin Hardy. p. 39.

SMITH, Charles and S. Thompson. Married 2 August 1802 by Charles Ogburn whose list was recorded in 1832. WB 10/181A.

SMITH, Charles and Eliza B. Neblett, 12 May 1830 [endorsement states May 11]. Sur. William G. Overton. p. 45.

SMITH, Charles and Mrs. Rebecca E. Jones, 11 September 1846. Sur. Thomas Taylor, Henry Stokes, and F. W. Epes. Married 15 September 1846 by Thomas E. Locke at the residence of Mrs. Rebecca Epes. p. 61 and St. John's Church Register.

SMITH, Clement and Lucy Stembridge. Married 10 December 1795 by James Shelburne. WB 4/159A.

SMITH, Daniel and Elizabeth A. Townsend, 10 December 1838. Sur. William Townsend. p. 53.

SMITH, David and Betty Gee. Married 28 October 1816 by Charles Ogburn. WB 10/181A.

SMITH, Drury A. and Jane Jones. Married 13 December 1832 by Matthew M. Dance. WB 11/19.

SMITH, Griffin and Sally G. Jeffress, 18 July 1814. Sur. Richard Jeffress. Married by James Shelburne whose lists states, "from March Court 1814 to February Court 1816." p. 27 and WB 7/227.

SMITH, J. and C. Andrews. Married 30 December 1810 by Charles Ogburn. WB 10/181A.

SMITH, James and Ann W. Degraffenreid. Married 15 September 1815 by James Shelburne. WB 7/227.

SMITH, James and Nancy Parke Street, 13 May 1803. Sur. John Taylor. p. 17.

SMITH, James Thomas and Celia Townsend, 11 May 1846. Sur. James P. Smith and Archibald Townsend. Minister's return states, "12 May 1846 - James Thomas Townsend as in the face of license, but should have been Smith ... on the 31st of March. William S. Wilson." p.63 and WB 13/46.

SMITH, John of Lunenburg and Cicily W. Andrews, 28 December 1812. Sur. William Hightower. p. 25.

SMITH, John and Clarary Neele. Married 26 March 1794 by James Shelburne. WB 4/107.

SMITH, John and Salley Street. Married 21 January 1795 by James Shelburne. WB 4/107.

SMITH, John and Sally Fisher, 13 February 1809. Sur. James Fisher. p. 23.

SMITH, John and Martha Wyatt, 28 November 1811. Sur. John Wyatt. Married 29 November 1811 by Thomas Adams. p. 25 and WB 7/40.

SMITH, John A. and Sally A. Richardson. Married 1 September 1818 by Matthew Dance. WB 8/59.

SMITH, Joseph and Elizabeth Garrett. Married 22 December 1789 by James Shelburne. WB 3/358.

SMITH, Joseph and Levena Moon. Married 21 January 1795 by James Shelburne. WB 4/107.

SMITH, Joseph and Sarah Tunstall. Married 25 May 1815 by Joel Johns. WB 7/280.

SMITH, Joshua and Mary E. Lanier, 12 June 1817. Sur. Sam Jefferson. Married June 1817 by Thomas Adams. p. 29 and WB 7/356.

SMITH, Paschal and Nancy Young. Married 29 March 1820 by James Robertson. WB 8/99.

SMITH, Redman and Hannah Hamlet. Married 26 January 1786 by Thomas Crymes. WB 3/263.

SMITH, Robert B. and Harriett Ann Mize, daughter of Mark Mize who consents, 3 May 1851. p. 4.

SMITH, Stephen and Agnes Hix. Married 19 November 1795 by John Neblett. WB 4/116A.

SMITH, Sterling and Ann J. Blackwell. Married December 1820 by Thomas Adams. WB 8/151.

SMITH, Thomas and Nancy B. Leonard. Married 31 May 1808 by William
Ellis. WB 6/256.

SMITH, Thomas H. and Elizabeth G. Smithson, 8 May 1848. Sur. Henry G.
Hardy. p. 65.

SMITH, Thomas and Mary P. Matthews, 12 December 1853. John Matthews
proves that Mary is 21 years of age, and is a witness. p. 15.

SMITH, William and Mary White. Married May 1785 by David Ellington.
WB 3/211.

SMITH, Williamson and Betsey Steagall, 27 March 1807. Sur. Aaron
Steagall. p. 21.

SMITH, William H. and Catharine Estes, 12 August 1844. Sur. Robertson
Freeman. p. 59.

SMITH, WILLIAMSON and Patsey Thompson. Married September 1819 by Thomas
Adams. WB 8/67.

SMITHSON, Allen and Lina Neville. Married 5 May 1786 by James Shelburne.
WB 3/252.

SMITHSON, Christopher Todd and Elizabeth Shelburne, 19 June 1797 by
William Ellis. WB 4/180

SMITHSON, Clement and Nancy Pettus. Married 18 December 1792 by James
Shelburne. WB 4/45A.

SMITHSON, Clement and Mary A. Smithson, 19 August 1836. Sur. Eleazer
Cheatham. p. 51.

SMITHSON, David and Nancy Wood. Married 29 December 1808 by Edward Almond.
WB 7/1.

SMITHSON, David and Beatrice E. Middleton, both of Lunenburg. Married
3 December 1828 by Silas Shelburne. WB 9/480 and DB 28/237.

SMITHSON, Francis and Martha Wood. Married 21 February 1782 by James
Shelburne. WB 3/104.

SMITHSON, Francis and Mary Lester, 10 November 1803. Sur. Robert
Rutledge. p. 17.

SMITHSON, Frederick S. N. and Louisa P. C. Wood, 21 November 1846. Sur.
Paul Wood. p. 61.

SMITHSON, James A. and Elizabeth W. Tisdale. Married 17 December 1816 by
James Shelburne. WB 7/313.

SMITHSON, John and Betsy Knott. Married 17 December 1801 by Joel Johns.
WB 6/11.

SMITHSON, John and Fanny Bayne, 15 September 1804. Sur. Nathaniel
Smithson. Married 7 October 1804 by Joel Johns. p. 19 and WB 6/128.

SMITHSON, John and Polly Wood, 28 January 1807. Sur. Stephen Wood.
Married 29 January 1807 by Edward Almond who states Betty Wood. p.23
and WB 6/265.

SMITHSON, John C. and Sarah A. Smithson, 3 November 1842. Sur. Bartley C.
Smithson. p. 55.

SMITHSON, John P. and Mary A. R. Smithson, daughter of Nancy Smithson,
8 November 1852. William H. Eubank, witness. p. 10.

SMITHSON, Lewis and Elizabeth Smithson, 10 March 1803. Sur. Christopher
Robertson. Married 16 March 1803 by James Shelburne. p.17 and WB 6/29.

SMITHSON, Marion Cox and Phebe Carter White. Married 27 December 1782 by
James Shelburne. WB 3/132.

SMITHSON, Nathaniel and Polly Cheatham. Married 30 March 1797 by Matthew
Dance. WB 4/181A.

SMITHSON, Nicholas and Nancy Cheatham, 14 March 1807. Sur. Nathaniel
Smithson. Married 4 April 1807 by James Shelburne. p. 21 and WB 6/231.

SMITHSON, Stephen and Sally Wood, 7 May 1824. Sur. Patrick A. Erskine.
Married 7 May 1824 by Silas Shelburne. p. 37 and WB 8/340.

SMITHSON, Sterling T. of Lunenburg, and Elizabeth A. Staples, 21 August 1813.
Sur. Allen Love. Married 1 September 1813 by Mathew Dance. p.27 and WB 7/81.

SMITHSON, William B. and Jane Campbell, 13 August 1845. Sur. Thomas
Tomlinson. p. 61.

SMITHSON, William C. and Mary B. Morgan. Married 22 September 1828 by
Silas Shelburne. WB 9/480.

SMITHSON, William G. and Mary A. E. Crenshaw, 12 December 1836. Sur.
William A. Bradshaw. Married 22 December 1836 by M. M. Dance. p. 51
and WB 11/336.

SNEAD, Benjamin and Polly Tisdale. Married 26 January 1797 by James
Shelburne. WB 4/160.

SNEAD, Edmund H. and Jane S. Robertson, 19 December 1848. Sur. James E.
Jeter. p. 65.

SNEAD, George W. and Elizabeth W. Smithson, 18 January 1837. Sur. John
Matthews. p. 53.

SNEAD, Harrison and Polly Scira (?). Married 11 October 1810 by Matthew
Dance. WB 7/9

SNEAD, James J. and Eliza A. Snead, 7 November 1837. Sur. Leonard Goodwyn.
p.53.

SNEAD, John H. and Minerva O. Walthall, 23 October 1845. Sur. Chatten C. Bishop. p. 61.

SNEAD, Joseph H. and Martha P. Roberta Ingram, 29 January 1851. William L. Rudd made oath that Martha was over 21 years of age. Married 4 February 1851 by T. E. Locke at Mrs. Ingram's residence. p. 3 and St. John's Church Register.

SNEAD, Richard and Jane Winn, 9 December 1812. Sur. Alexander Winn. Married 10 December 1812 by Joel Johns. p. 25 and WB 7/120.

SNEAD, Samuel W. and Mary C. Bishop, 28 November 1846. Sur. John E. Robertson. p. 61.

SNEAD, William and Susanna W. Winn. Married 5 August 1819 by Joel Johns. WB 8/357.

SNEAD, William C. and Cornelia E. Winn, 14 August 1843. Sur. Enos H. Barnes. p. 57.

SOMERVILLE, John and Betsey Ann DeGraffenreidt, 9 April 1807. Sur. Charles Brydie. p. 21.

SPENCER, Matthew L. and Louise S. Neal, 26 March 1838. Sur. Alex R. Spencer. p. 53.

SPENCER, William and Mary Newbill. Married 1 November 1797 by John Easter. WB 4/211.

STANLEY, Joshua and Elizabeth Johnson, 19 March 1804. Sur. John Ryland. p. 19.

STAPLES, Joshua and Elmira Jeffress, 5 November 1826. Sur. John M. Rowlett. Married 15 November 1826 by Matthew M. Dance. p. 41 and WB 9/159.

STAPLES, Levitius Addison and Ann Eliza Arvin, daughter of Thomas who consents, 10 October 1853. p. 14.

STAPLES, Thomas and Sarah Smithson, 21 May 1814. Sur. Joseph Yarbrough. Married by James Shelburne whose lists is from March Court 1814 to February Court 1816. p. 27.

STAPLES, Thomas, JR. and Elizabeth Jeffress, 18 December 1823. Sur. Thomas A. Filbert. Married 23 December 1823 by Silas Shelburne. p. 35 and WB 8/340.

STAPLES, Thomas H. and Jane C. McCutcheon, 8 February 1830. Sur. John A. Hatchett. Married 23 February 1830 by Thomas H. Jeffress. p. 43 and WB 10/112.

STEAGALL, Frederick and Susey Cole, 18 June 1804. Sur. Nun Cole. Married 19 June 1804 by Joel Johns. p. 19 and WB 6/128.

STEAGALL, Griffin and Elizabeth Ann Wrenn. Married 25 December 1815 by Thomas Adams. WB 7/249.

STEAGALL, Hartwell and Jane Steagall, 1 July 1826. Sur. Randolph Steagall. p. 41.

STEAGALL, Ralph and Luand Nolley. Married 19 March 1818 by Thomas Adams. WB 8/67.

STEAGALL, Samuel and Nancy Gee, 8 January 1821. Sur. Nelson W. Gee. Married January 1821 by Thomas Adams. p. 31 and WB 8/209.

STEGAR, Thomas T. and Elizabeth A. Jennings. Married 2 February 1840 by Albert Anderson. WB 11/418A.

STEMBRIDGE, William and Kindness Breedlove. Married 22 January 1785 by David Ellington. WB 3/207.

STEVENSON, William and Sally C. Bigger, 9 September 1822. Sur. Thomas Lowry. Married 10 September 1822 by William Hatchett. p. 33 and WB 8/262.

STEWART, Anderson and Blanch Epps. Married 19 December 1827 by Baxter Ragsdale. WB 9/349.

STEWART, Anderson and A. Potts. Married 30 December 1832 by Joshua Featherston. WB 11/8A.

STEWART, Branch and Sarah Jane Edmonds, 15 March 1845. Sur. Henry Dinkins. p. 61.

STEWART, Haley and Franky Eppes, 21 September 1822. Sur. John Eppes. p.35.

STEWARD, John and Jene [Jean on bond] Weakly, spinster, 22 May 1756. Sur. James Stewart and Clem Read. p. 1.

STEWART, John and Elizabeth Gill. Married 2 June 1816 by Thomas Adams. WB 7/248.

STEWART, John G. and Sarah Kelly, daughter of Nancy Kelly, 14 February 1853. Richard R. Crenshaw, witness. p. 12.

STEWART, Norris and Susan E. Gee, 14 March 1848. Sur. Joseph B. Moore. Married 14 March 1848 by Richard E. G. Adams. p. 63 and WB 13/191.

STOKES, Bartlett and Martha W. Blanton. Married 30 April 1802 by James Shelburne. WB 6/28.

STOKES, David R. and Sarah H. Stokes, 9 February 1846. Sur. Peter W. Street. Married 17 February 1846 by Thomas E. Locke at Peter W. Street's residence. p. 61 and St. John's Church Register.

STOKES, Drury Y. and Seluda A. Jeffress, 11 August 1823. Sur. Richard Jeffress. p. 35.

STOKES, Hamlin T. and Kitturah Hardy. Married 15 December 1800 by William Ellis. WB 5/67.

STOKES, Henry and Susanna Reaves Pettypool. Married 5 February 1795 by
William Ellis. WB 4/106A.

STOKES, Henry and Ann E. Hatchett, 19 November 1841. Sur. William H.
Hatchett. p. 55.

STOKES, John and Susanna R. Jones, 19 May 1814. Sur. William G. Pettus.
p. 27.

STOKES, Morriss and Martha Jane Meadows, 18 November 1835. Sur. Francis
Meadows. p. 47.

STOKES, Richard and Sarah J. Cralle, 10 December 1849. Sur. Henry Stokes.
p. 65.

STOKES, Richard A. and Bettie L. Farmer, ward of George W. Hardy who consents,
12 September 1853. p. 14.

STOKES, Richard H. and Lucinda Farmer, 9 January 1817. Sur. David Street.
Married 13 January 1817 by Joel Johns. p. 31 and WB 7/346.

STOKES, William and Nancy Lock. Married 5 May 1786 by James Shelburne.
WB 3/252.

STOKES, William A. of Lunenburg and Martha Tarry Lowry, 3 January 1814.
Sur. Langston Bacon, Jr. p. 29.

STOKES, William A. and Lucy Ann Street. Married 16 October 1827 by Matthew
M. Dance. WB 9/311.

STONE, Anderson and Betsey Stone, 4 June 1811. Sur. John Stone. Married
6 June 1811 by Joel Johns. p. 23 and WB 7/60.

STONE, Asher and Sally Craighead. Married 15 October 1809 by James
Shelburne. WB 7/3.

STONE, Benjamin and Frances Gordon. Married 18 August 1800 by Matthew
Dance. WB 5/17.

STONE, Robert and Jency Blankenship. Married 28 November 1799 by Matthew
Dance. WB 5/17.

STONE, Daniel and Mary Dobbyns, 13 February 1821. Sur. Boller Dobbyns.
Married 15 February 1821 by Silas Shelburne. p. 33 and WB 8/140.

STONE, Isaac and Rebecca Whitworth. Married in 1793 by William Creath.
WB 4/46.

STONE, James W. and Harriet Moore, 26 January 1846. Sur. Washington Reese.
Married 20 February 1846 by Joshua Featherston. p. 61 and WB 13/5.

STONE, Peter and Delphia Inge, 14 August 1817. Sur. Robert H. Bentley.
Married 29 August 1817 by Stephen Jones. p. 29 and WB 7/357.

STONE, Peter W. and Elizabeth Snead, 10 July 1826. Sur. Joseph E. Winn.
p. 41.

STONE, Peter W. and Letty Winn, 13 November 1837 [endorsement states
November 15]. Sur. William C. White. p. 53.

STONE, Thomas and Mary J. Hughes. Married 12 August 1816 by Joel Johns.
WB 7/280.

STONE, Thomas and Francis G. Tisdale. Married 6 December 1809 by James
Shelburne. WB 7/3.

STONE, Thomas and Martha Waller, 13 September 1825. Sur. Robert Phillips.
Married 15 September 1825 by Joshua Featherston. p. 39 and WB 8/572.

STONE, William and Hannah Love. Married 27 September 1781 by James
Shelburne. WB 3/92.

STONE, William of Mecklenburg County, and Tabitha Neal. Married 22 November
1791 by William Creath. WB 4/34.

STONE, William A. and Clarisa A. Pettus, 12 August 1822. Sur. Asher Stone.
Married 14 August 1822 by William Richards. p. 33 and WB 8/270.

STOUT, John Hoff and Ann Beasley, 25 June 1792. See footnote 1, and footnote
on page 33.

STRANGE, Benjamin and Charlotte Shelton. Married 11 February 1819 by
Thomas Adams. WB 8/67.

STRANGE, Benjamin and Sarah J. E. V. Callis, 4 November 1836. Sur. Peter
Thompson. Married 10 November 1836 by Joshua Featherston. p.51 and
WB 11/182.

STREET, James P. and Sarah E. Williams, 23 May 1843. Sur. Lewis H. Averett.
p. 57.

STREET, John T. and Anna Stokes, 9 January 1817. Sur. William Stokes. p.29

STURDIVANT, Edward C. and Rebecca Dicks, 14 March 1811. Sur. John Daley.
Married 15 March 1811 by Thomas Adams. p. 25 and WB 7/40.

STURDIVANT, Henry W. and Lucy Farguson. Married November 1807 by Thomas
Adams. WB 6/253A.

STURDIVANT, James and Fanny Callis. Married 12 January 1797 by John
Neblett. WB 4/168.

STURDIVANT, James and Nancy Brintle, 8 June 1811. Sur. Allan Steagall.
Married 8 June 1811 by Thomas Adams. p. 25 and WB 7/40.

---

1 - John Hoff Stout was born Jan. 20, 1767, Quakertown, N. J., d. Sept. 17, 1814. He was the son of
Joseph Stout and wife Theodocia and grandson of Benjamin Stout. Joseph Stout d. Sept. 4, 1777,
age 35 at Battle of Brandywine. Ann Beasley was b. May 13, 1772, Nottoway Co., Va., daughter
of William and Ann (Hurt) Beasley. William Beasley d. Dec. 4, 1802, age 52 years. Ann (Hurt)
Beasley d. Oct. 8, 1777, age 25. (From Bible on file at the Virginia Historical Society Mss 6:4,
D2894:1)

STURDIVANT, John and Lettitia Callis. Married 26 December 1798 by John Neblett. WB 5/2A.

SULLIVANT, Charles of Lunenburg and Mary Johnson, widow, 8 May 1761. Sur. Owen Sullivant. p.3.

SULLIVANT, Robert D. and Lucy Colly, 11 December 1843. Sur. Samuel G. Jefferson. p. 57.

SULLIVANT, Woodson and Susanna Stone, 18 December 1804. Sur. Robert Stone. Married 16 December 1804 by James Shelburne. p. 19 and WB 6/147.

SUMMERS, Benjamin and Martha Hood. Married 25 March 1800 by William Ellis. WB 5/67.

SWANSBERRY, John and Mary Christopher. Married 27 November 1815 by Stephen Jones who gives John's name as Swanbur. WB 7/276.

SYDNOR, William and Elizabeth Cross. Married 27 January 1795 by John Jones. WB 4/87.

SYME, Wythe and Nancey Fisher. Married 18 November 1810 by Thomas Adams. WB 7/39.

TALBERT, David G. and Patsy Jennings. Married June 1791 by John Chappell. WB 4/7A.

TALLY, John and Sally Dizmang. Married 22 December 1796 by John Neblett. WB 4/167A.

TANNER, Ludwell and Rebecca H. Ragsdale, 20 January 1823. Sur. Washington Maddux. p. 37.

TERRY [or TARRY], Benjamin and Lucy P. Smith, 20 December 1834. Sur. John A. Smith. p. 47.

TARRY [or TERRY], Edwin C. and Nancy Smithson, 16 August 1830. Sur. Chas. Smithson. Married 18 August 1830 by Silas Shelburne. p.43 and WB 10/131.

TARRY, Edwin C. and Mary E. Wood, 6 January 1821. Sur. William Wood. Married 10 January 1821 by Silas Shelburne. p. 31 and WB 8/140.

TERRY, George W. and Eliza E. Smith, daughter of Joshua Smith who consents, 11 November 1850. p. 2.

TERRY, Larkin and Julia Dodson. Married 30 March 1820 by Silas Shelburne. WB 8/140.

TATUM, Absalom of Lunenburg and Salley Green, 12 July 1813. Sur. Richard Bragg. Married 28 July 1813 by James Robertson. p. 27 and WB 7/124.

TATUM, Benjamin and Elizabeth Beasley. Married 25 June 1818 by James Robertson. WB 8/1.

TATOM, Crafton and Susanna Fullilove. Married January 1794 by James
Shelburne. WB 4/46.

TATUM, William and Mary Crenshaw. Married 11 March 1784 by Thomas Crymes.
WB 3/156.

TAYLOR, Alro [or Alec]and Sally Hicks. Married 23 February 1797 by John
Neblett who reports this marriage the second time giving the bride's
name as Luccy Hicks [also spelled Hix]. WB 4/232A and WB 4/168.

TAYLOR, Benjamin and Mary Brintle, 3 December 1803 [1804 on endorsement].
Sur. William Edmunds. p. 19.

TAYLOR, Charles of Lunenburg and Mary J. Williams, 10 January 1815. Sur.
John Knight. Married 11 January 1815 by James Shelburne. p. 29 and
WB 7/227.

TAYLOR, Cary and Patsey Callis, 17 January 1817. Sur. Jabez Lambert. p.31.

TAYLOR, Daniel and Rebecca Johnson. Married 23 July 1795 by John Neblett.
WB 4/88.

TAYLOR, Daniel and Susanna Williams. Married 20 December 1810 by James
Shelburne. WB 7/15.

TAYLOR, Davis and Sally Toombes. Married 30 November 1786 by Thomas Crymes.
WB 3/268.

TAYLOR, Edmund F. and Petronella Lamkin, 13 February 1809. Sur. William
H. Taylor. p. 23.

TAYLOR, Frederick and Narcissa P. Crenshaw, 22 March 1852. Richard L. B.
Williams certifies that Narcissa is over 21 years of age, and is a
witness thereto. p. 9.

TAYLOR, George and Narcissa Williams, 19 January 1807. Sur. David H.
Williams. Married 20 January 1807 by Edward Almond. p. 23 and WB 6/265.

TALOR, Giles and Lina Stokes. Married 6 July 1786 by Thomas Crymes.
WB 3/263.

TAYLOR, James W. and Minerva Singleton, 8 February 1841. Sur. Thornton
Russell. Married 8 February 1841 by Joshua Featherston. p. 55 and
WB 12/54.

TAYLOR, James W. and Susan A. Bowen, 20 November 1848. Sur. Robert Bowen.
Married 2 November 1848 by Richard E. G. Adams. p. 65 and WB 13/334.

TAYLOR, John and Elizabeth Jones, 14 November 1803. Sur. Peter Jones, Jr.
p. 17.

TAYLOR, Littleton L. and Mary F. Cralle, 13 February 1837. Sur. Edmund
F. Taylor. p. 53.

TAYLOR, Miles and Sally Taylor, 23 February 1829. Sur. James Taylor. Married 25 February 1829 by Joshua Featherstone. p. 43 and WB 9/389.

TAYLOR, William and Jane Hilton, 1 September 1848. Sur. Daniel L. Riggin. Married 4 September 1848 by Richard E. G. Adams. p. 65 and WB 13/191.

TAYLOR, William H. and Narcissus Bacon. Married 30 November 1812 by Thomas Adams. WB 7/248.

TAYLOR, William and Mary Pride. Married October 1820 by Thomas Adams. WB 8/151.

THACKER, Putman W. and Araminta D. Rowlett, 29 September 1849. Sur. Charles R. Steare. p. 65.

THACKSTON, Benjamin and Sarah C. Smithson. Married 7 August 1828 by Silas Shelburne. WB 9/480.

THACKSTON, James and Flora Bell. Married July 1796 by James Shelburne. WB 4/160.

THACKLETON, George W. and Matilda Akin. Married 14 July 1829 by John Thompson. WB 10/66.

THOMAS, Samuel and Martha S. Collier, 19 December 1829. Sur. Henry G. Hardy. p. 43.

THOMAS, Samuel and Martha Jane White, 15 February 1837. Sur. Francis T. Jackson. p. 53.

THOMAS, Spencer and Nancy Stainback, 29 February 1812. Sur. Benjamin Jenkins. Married 3 March 1812 by John Jones. p. 25 and WB 7/60.

THOMAS, William and Dolly W. Stainback, 13 February 1817. Sur. Benjamin Jenkins. Married 18 February 1817 by John Jones. p. 29 and WB 7/353.

THOMAS, William [also shown John] and Petronella Kelly, daughter of Nancy Kelly, 27 February 1850. Sur. William Holmes. p. 67.

THOMPSON, Archer W. of Lunenburg and Martha George, 10 November 1814. Sur. Thomas George. p. 27.

THOMPSON, Benjamin of Lunenburg and Lucy Gill, 10 December 1813 [endorsement states December 9th]. Sur. James Wilson. Married 16 December 1813 by Milton Robertson. p. 27 and WB 7/82.

THOMPSON, Clement J. and Mary A. Fowlkes. Married 25 October 1831 by Silas Shelburne. WB 11/2.

THOMASON [or Thompson] Flemming and Rachel Landrum. Married 9 January 1801 by John Neblett. WB 5/68.

THOMPSON, Gray and Minerva A. Callis, 18 December 1838. Sur. Benjamin Strange. Married 20 December 1838 by Joshua Featherston. p.53 and WB 12/7.

THOMPSON, John and Susan Williams, 14 November 1826. Sur. John Smith. p.41.

THOMPSON, Randolph, Jr. and Lamenta White, 5 November 1822. Sur. Carter White. p. 33.

THOMPSON, Robert and Mary Hitchins. Married 4 November 1819 by Thomas H. Jeffress. WB 8/139.

THOMPSON, Spotswood and Eliza Andrews. Married by Daniel Petty whose list was recorded 8 June 1840. WB 11/415.

THOMPSON, William and Nancy Vaughan. Married 12 October 1799 by John Neblett. WB 5/2A.

THOMPSON, William and Martha Callis, 15 March 1811. Sur. James Callis. Married 16 March 1811 by Thomas Adams. p. 23 and WB 7/40.

THORNTON, William and Patsy Owen. Married 5 May 1786 by James Shelburne. WB 3/252.

THORNTON, William and Nancy Osborne. Married 11 June 1806 by John Jones. WB 6/187.

TISDALE, Daniel W. and Susan Dean Yates, 30 October 1849. Sur. William Thompson. Married 31 October 1849 by William S. Wilson. p. 65 and WB 13/353.

TISDALE, Henry and Frances Smithson,* 9 July 1807. Sur. William Taylor. Married 15 July 1807 by James Shelburne. p. 21 and WB 6/231.

TISDALE, Henry W. and Martha C. Tarry, 27 September 1842. Sur. Drury W. Lett. p. 57.

TISDALE, Hinchey M. and Jane Tucker, 15 January 1825. Sur. Lew Allen Tucker. Married 20 January 1825 by Silas Shelburne. p. 41 and WB 8/490.

TISDALE, John and Charlotte Johnson. Married 1 December 1789 by James Shelburne. WB 3/358.

TISDALE, John H. and Mary E. Yates, 10 November 1851. Daniel W. Tisdale certifies that Mary is more than 21 years of age. p. 6.

TISDALE, John R. B. and Narcissa Dobbyns. Married by Daniel Petty whose return was dated 7 December 1833, the exact date of marriage not shown. WB 11/32.

TISDALE, Thomas and Francis G. Winn. Married 5 January 1804 by William Ellis. WB 6/76.

TISDALE, Thomas R. and Jane E. Collier. Married 13 January 1825 by Silas Shelburne. WB 8/492.

---

* Frances Smithson, widow of John Smithson. See John Smithson and Fanny Bayne marriage, page 114. She was daughter of Karon Bayne. O.B. 20, p.241 and W.B. 6, p. 52.

TISDALE, William and Jenny Brizentine. Married 29 January 1789 by Thomas
Crymes. WB 3/342.

TISDALE, William A., Jr. and Mary Ford, 1 May 1822. Sur. George H. Ford.
Married 2 May 1822 by Silas Shelburne. p. 33 and WB 8/270.

TODD, William of Lunenburg and Sarah McKie, daughter of Michael Mackey,
6 October 1761. Sur. John Bracey [signed John Bressie]. p. 3.

TOMLINSON - See Bible record on this family in the Archives, V.S.L.

TOMLINSON, Benjamin and Nancy Gee, 21 December 1816*. Married 21 December
1814 by Thomas Adams. [* Note: The first marriage on the minister's
list was dated 2 March 1814 and the last one was 12 June 1816. The
return was recorded 13 June 1816, therefore, the typed M.B. and the
M.R. must be in error.] p. 29 and WB 7/249.

TOMLINSON, Harris M. and Maria Ward, 31 December 1833. Sur. William Ward
and Elish. Arnold. p. 45.

TOMLINSON, Thomas Bonner and Elizabeth T. Pamplin, 28 May 1824. Sur.
Miles Crowder. p. 37.

TOMLINSON, Thomas R. and M. Pamplin. Married 1 January 1824 by Charles
Ogburn whose return was recorded at June Court 1832. WB 10/181A.

TOONE, John and Dicey Jeter Winn, 22 December 1811. Sur. Orsanus Winn.
Married 18 December 1811 by James Shelburne. p. 23 and WB 7/32.

TOONE, John and Frances Parker Winn. Married 29 December 1815 by Joel
Johns. WB 7/280.

TOWERS, Thomas and Martha Crafton. Married 22 December 1802 by James
Shelburne. WB 6/28A.

TOWLER, William and Hannah A. Watson, 11 February 1813. Sur. Joseph
Yarbrough. Married 14 February 1813 by Richard Dabbs. p. 27 and WB 7/124.

TOWNSEND, Archer and Elizabeth Townsend, 21 December 1824. Sur. Daniel
Townsend. Married 23 December 1824 by Silas Shelburne. p. 37 and
WB 8/492.

TOWNSEND, Daniel and Nancy L. Williams, 13 May 1850. Sur. William
Townsend. p. 67.

TOWNSEND, David and Jincy Townsend. Married 13 December 1799 by Matthew
M. Dance. WB 5/16.

TOWNSEND, Drewry and Lucy Slaughter. Married 20 September 1809 by Edward
Almond. WB 7/1.

TOWNSEND, James Thomas. See James Thomas Smith, page 112.

TOWNSEND, Joseph and Lucy Stone. Married 27 March 1800 by William Ellis.
WB 5/28.

TOWNSEND, Joseph and Rebecca E. Elmore, 11 January 1836 [endorsement states
12 January 1836]. Sur. William Townsend. p. 51.

TOWNSEND, Joseph and Ann R. Perkinson, 19 November 1850. John J. Townsend makes oath that Ann is over 21 years of age. p. 2.

TOWNSEND, Richard and Fanny Jordan. Married 4 December 1783 by James Shelburne. WB 3/150.

TOWNSEND, William and Amey Booth. Married 18 January 1794 by John Neblett. WB 4/50.

TRAYNUM, Clement and Elizabeth Malone, 29 December 1786. Sur. Robert Hardin. Married 4 January 1787 by Thomas Crymes. p. 7 and WB 3/268.

TROTTER, Henry and Elizabeth Morgan. Married 13 May 1818 by Thomas Adams. WB 8/67.

TROTTER, Isham and Agnes T. Manson. Married December 1816 by Thomas Adams. WB 7/356.

TUCKER, Archibald M. and Dosha [or Dortia] Farley. Married 17 December 1816 by James Robertson. WB 7/309.

TUCKER, C. and L. E. H. Tomberlinson. Married 1 March 1827 by Charles Ogburn. WB 10/181A.

TUCKER, Charles A. and Lucy T. Dicks, 10 October 1836. Sur. James Dicks. Married 18 October 1836 by Joshua Featherston. p. 51 and WB 11/182.

TUCKER, Charles A. and Martha A. Hawthorn, 25 November 1837. Sur. Edward P. Buford. p. 53.

TUCKER, Charles S. and Elizabeth B. Jordan, 23 February 1811. Sur. John G. W. Holloway. Married 24 February 1811 by Thomas Adams. p. 23 and WB 7/40.

TUCKER, Lew and Assula Pettipool. Married 24 January 1788 by Thomas Crymes. WB 3/309.

TUCKER, L. A. and M. A. Barnes. Married 18 January 1827 by Charles Ogburn. WB 10/181A.

TUCKER, Parks and Celia A. Raney, 24 April 1838. Sur. Peter Raney, Jr. p. 55.

TUCKER, Pleasant and Rebecca Daniel. Married 4 May 1831 by Joshua Featherston. WB 10/151A.

TUCKER, Robert and Sarah Smith. Married 27 November 1787 by Thomas Crymes. WB 3/309.

TUCKER, Robert H. and Harriett Harrison, 16 March 1835. Sur. Joseph J. Perriman. p. 47. [See Roy G. Tucker.]

TUCKER, Robert W. and Martha Gunn. Married 10 February 1819. Minister's name not shown. WB 8/38.

TUCKER, Roy G. and Harriet Harrison. Married 2 July 1835 by Pleasant
Barnes. WB 11/281. [See Robert H. Tucker.]

TUCKER, Stephen and Frances Wells Glascock. Married 8 April 1782 by James
Shelburne. WB 3/118.

TUCKER, William and Sarah Cheatham, 22 April 1834. Sur. Thomas Cheatham.
p. 47.

TUCKER, William and Martha P. Hazlewood, 10 June 1850. Sur. James E.
Hazelwood. p. 67.

TUCKER, William H. and Mary Jane Rux, 30 October 1845. Sur. John Rux. p. 61.

TUCKER, Worsham and Sarah Potts, 31 December 1821. Sur. Littleton Potts.
Married 1 January 1822 by John Doyle. p. 33 and WB 8/258.

TUNSTILL, Littleberry and Nancy Foster, 12 December 1825. Sur. Meriweather
Tunstill. Married 21 December 1825 by Thomas H. Jeffress. p. 39 and
WB 8/551.

TUNSTILL, Meriweather and Elizabeth Tunstill, 12 December 1825. Sur.
Littleberry Tunstill. Married 22 December 1825 by Thomas H. Jeffress.
p. 39 and WB 8/551.

TUNSTILL, Stokes and Eliza Balden [also shown Baldwin], 2 April 1822. Sur.
William Tunstill. Married 4 April 1822 by Thomas H. Jeffress. p. 35
and WB 8/263.

TUNSTILL, William and Mary Gafford, 3 September 1821. Sur. Thomas Vaughan.
Married 5 September 1821 by Joel Johns. p. 31 and WB 8/357.

TURLEYFIELD, John and Rebecca Janes Parham. Married 23 December 1799 by
William Ellis, Sr. WB 5/22.

TURNER, William and Polley Denton, 19 December 1803. Sur. Theophilus
Denton. p. 17.

TURNER, William and Myram Turner, 9 December 1833. Sur. John H. Rudder.
[See John H. Rudder and Mariam Turner, page 105.] p. 45

TURPIN, Henry and Mary Wilson, 21 December 1833. Sur. Rob. Wilson. p. 45.

USSERY, John and Nancy Green. Married 23 December 1797 by John Neblett.
WB 4/232.

USSERY, Pleasant and Susanna D. Irby, 1 January 1810. Sur. Thomas Hamlin.
Married 1 January 1810 by Thomas Adams. p. 23 and WB 7/39.

USSERY, Samuel and Nancy Hurt. Married 11 February 1801 by John Neblett.
WB 5/68.

USSERY, Samuel and Matilda Ussery, 27 November 1804. Sur. John Brown. p.19.

USSERY, William and Sally Williams. Married 21 December 1797 by John
Jones. WB 4/209

VADEN, Isham W. and Eliza W. Steagall, 14 April 1823. Sur. Alexander Laffoon. p. 37.

VADEN, Thomas and Patsey Calliham, 1 September 1835. Sur. Henry Calliham. Married 3 September 1835 by James M. Jeter. p. 49 and WB 11/169.

VALENTINE, David and Fillis Ragsdale, 16 August 1826. Sur. James Chavers. Married 26 July 1826 by Baxter Ragsdale. p. 41 and WB 9/74.

VAUGHAN, Coleman A. and Polly Y. Beasley, 10 April 1817. Sur. John C. Beasley. Married 17 April 1817 by James Robertson. p. 29 and WB 7/309.

VAUGHAN, George and Polly Hardwick, 13 October 1803. Sur. Alfred Cralle. p. 17.

VAUGHAN, Henry and Amelia Ann Fowlkes. Married July 1832 by David Wood. WB 10/200A.

VAUGHAN, John N. and Henrietta Farmer, ward of Tarlton W. Knight who consents, 12 May 1851. p. 4.

VAUGHAN, Pleasant and Mourning E. Dance, 27 August 1822. Sur. Stephen Dance. Married 27 August 1822 by Matthew Dance. p. 33 and WB 8/254.

VAUGHAN, Thomas and Martha Gafford, 2 October 1821. Sur. William Tunstill. Married 4 October 1821 by Joel Johns. p. 31 and WB 8/357.

VENABLE, James and Judith Moreton, spinster, 3 October 1757. Sur. Robert Weakly, James Taylor, and G. Carrington, Jr. p. 1.

VINCENT, Manoah and Nancy G. Duniman. Married December 1807 by Thomas Adams. WB 6/253A.

WADE, Isaac W. and Alice W. Smithson, 15 December 1837 [bond states October 15]. Sur. Benjamin Thackston. p. 51.

WALKER, Allen and Sarah Ann Parrish. Married 23 November 1797 by John Jones. WB 4/209.

WALKER, Benjamin of Lunenburg and Ann Wilson, daughter of Edward Wilson, 25 January 1813. Sur. Josiah Wilson. Married 24 June 1813 by James Shelburne. p. 27 and WB 7/124.

WALKER, Benjamin J. and Mildred A. C. McLaughlin, 28 November 1846. Sur. Henry H. Love. Married by Daniel Petty whose list was returned to court 8 February 1847, exact date of marriage not shown. p. 61 and WB 13/14.

WALKER, Charles P. and Nancy P. Tisdale, 15 December 1821. Sur. James A. Smithson. Married 24 December 1821 by Matthew M. Dance. p. 33 and WB 8/283.

WALKER, Edmund W. and Mary R. Simmons, 11 January 1836. Sur. George L. Bayne. p. 51 and DB 30/389.

WALKER, James and Rebecca Johnson. Married 5 May 1786 by James Shelburne. WB 3/252.

WALKER, James T. and Mary R. Blackwell, daughter of James G. Blackwell, 8 March 1852. James G. Blackwell consents and is a witness. p. 8.

WALKER, Michael of Lunenburg, and Mary Edmundson, 29 December 1814. Sur. Benjamin Edmundson. Married 30 "D." 1814 by Charles Ogburn. p. 27 and WB 10/181.

WALKER, Nicholas E. and Eliza Richardson. Married 2 March 1819 by Silas Shelburne. WB 8/67.

WALKER, Richard and Mary Johnson. Married 13 December 1793 by James Shelburne. WB 4/46.

WALKER, Thomas and Susanna Johnson. Married 20 December 1783 by James Shelburne. WB 3/150.

WALKER, Thomas and Polly Jordan. Married 27 September 1795 by James Shelburne. WB 4/160.

WALKER, Vincent and Delilah Thrift. Married 30 November 1782 by James Shelburne. WB 3/132.

WALKER, William E. and Mary W. [or M.] Hines, 14 December 1846. Sur. William L. Hite. Married 5 January 1847 by John C. Blackwell. p. 61 and WB 13/11.

WALL, Charles F. and Judith T. Johns. Married 23 April 1818 by Joel Johns. WB 8/357.

WALL, Joel G. and Ann S. Petty, daughter of D. J. Petty, 29 August 1850. J. R. Hardy witness. p. 1.

WALLACE, Anderson and Mildred H. Smithson, 19 May 1824. Sur. William Griffin. Married 20 May 1824 by Silas Shelburne. p. 37 and WB 8/492.

WALLACE, Benjamin of Lunenburg and Letty Wilkes, 11 February 1813. Sur. Richard Wilkes. Married 11 February 1813 by Thomas Adams. p. 27 and WB 7/248.

WALLACE, Christopher and Ann P. Rash, 19 November 1836. Sur. William Wallace, Jr. p. 51.

WALLACE, Collin of Lunenburg, and Elizabeth H. Brown, 9 October 1817. Sur. Washington Brown. Married 30 October 1817 by Stephen Jones. p. 29 and WB 7/357.

WALLACE, Hugh Jr. and Sally Pully. Married 5 April 1800 by John Neblett. WB 5/35.

WALLACE, Hugh and Nancy Brown, 25 August 1817. Sur. John Brown, Jr. p.29.

WALLACE, Hugh and Martha Morgan, 27 February 1822. Sur. Collin Wallace. p. 35.

WALLACE, Joseph and Jincey Hardaway Alexander. Married 24 October 1805 by Matthew Dance. WB 6/138.

WALLACE, Phillip J. and Mildred A. F. Wood, 9 December 1850. John Warner made oath that Mildred is more than 21 years of age. p. 3.

WALLACE, Robert and Phebe Wilkes, 25 November 1811. Sur. Richard Wilkes. Married 26 November 1811 by Jesse Brown. p. 23 and WB 7/60.

WALLACE, Ussery and Elizabeth Wrenn, 12 November 1821. Sur. Joseph Morgan. Married 22 November 1821 by John Doyle who shows Elizabeth's name as Weaver. p. 31 and WB 8/193.

WALLACE, William J. and Nancy V. Wallace, 26 May 1845. Sur. Richard M. Wallace. p. 61.

WALLER, James and Sarah Mathes. Married 22 January 1787 by Thomas Crymes. WB 3/268.

WALLER, James and Elizabeth Smith, 4 October 1817. Sur. Samuel Moore. Married October 1817 by Thomas Adams. p. 29 and WB 7/356.

WALLER, Price and Elizabeth Lambert. Married 5 April 1792 by John Rogers. WB 4/19.

WALLER, William and Elizabeth S. Kelly, 20 December 1824. Sur. Joseph B. Barnes. Married 22 December 1824 by Joshua Featherston. p. 39 and WB 8/431.

WALLER, William R. and Mary Jane Russell, 12 November 1849. Sur. David W. Perkins. p. 65.

WARD, Benjamin U. and Lucinda B. Crenshaw, ward of said Benjamin U. Ward, 1 March 1853. p. 12.

WARD, James and Eliza Ann Wilkinson, 1 December 1834. Sur. Thomas Wilkerson. Married 2 December 1834 by Robert J. Carson. p. 47 and WB 11/63.

WARD, John and Salley Burton. Married 14 November 1782 by James Shelburne. WB 3/132.

WARD, Nathan and Rebecca Hudson, 27 June 1838. Sur. Charles A. Carter. p.53.

WARD, Richard and Mary Johns, both of Parish of Cornwall in County of Lunenburg, 2 May 1759. Sur. Charles Cupples and Thomas Read. p. 1.

WARD, Robert and Polly McLaughlin, 24 August 1804. Sur. Samuel Carsons. Married 15 August 1804 by William Ellis. p. 19 and WB 6/122.

WARD, Robert and Sally Stokes. Married 22 December 1808 by William Ellis. WB 6/256.

WARD, Seth and Mary Hudson. Married 30 May 1793 by James Shelburne. WB 4/45A.

WARD, William A. and Mary A. Willard, 13 January 1825. Sur. William J. Hightower. Married 14 January 1825 by James Robertson. p. 39 and WB 8/534.

WARNER, Choral P. and Martha A. F. Gee, 18 December 1834. Sur. George W. Gee. Married by Daniel Petty whose list was returned to court 13 July 1835, but the date of marriage not shown. p. 47 and WB 11/124. [Note: The M.B. and minister's return states Charol P. Warner. The M.B. is signed Charol P. Winn, and the marriage register states Winn.]

WARNER, Ira and Jane J. Wood, 8 December 1834. Sur. Green A. Wood. p. 47.

WARREN, Benjamin and Prudence W. Thornton, 31 December 1812. Sur. Lew Jones. Married 1 January 1813 by Joel Johns. p. 25 and WB 7/120.

WARREN, Robert H. and Harriet S. Crowder. Married 26 September 1827 by James McAden. WB 9/292.

WATKINS, Abner of Cumberland County, and Sebella A. Hatchett of Lunenburg, widow and relict of the late William Hatchett, between September 19, 1827 and February 11, 1828. DB 28/5-8.

WATKINS, Edward and Amanda W. Farmer. Married 29 July 1832 by Matthew M. Dance. WB 11/19.

WATKINS, John of Lunenburg and Mary Moore, daughter of George Moore, 23 February 1762. Sur. George Moore. p. 3.

WATSON, Elisha M. and Nancy Parsons, 8 January 1821. Sur. Joseph Akin. Married 10 January 1821 by Silas Shelburne. p. 31 and WB 8/140.

WATSON, Elisha M. and Mary A. Cole, 8 March 1841. Sur. William H. Cole. p. 55.

WATSON, Jesse and Sarah Ann Thompson, 14 February 1821. Sur. Davis Thompson. Married 1 March 1821 by Silas Shelburne. p. 33 and WB 8/140.

WATSON, John A. and Nancy Hamlett. Married 26 December 1816 by James Robertson. WB 7/309.

WATSON, Joseph A. and Jane C. Bruce, daughter of Mary Bruce, 1 April 1817. Sur. Mitchell Clay. Married 3 April 1817 by James Shelburne. p. 29 and WB 7/313.

WATSON, Joseph E. and Mary A. Williams, 8 August 1846. Sur. John E. Rawlings. Married 9 September 1846 by Samuel G. Mason, Charlotte, C.H., Va. p. 61 and WB 13/10.

WATSON, William and Sarah R. Averitt, 18 November 1850. Thomas C. Averitt certifies that Sarah is over 21 years of age. p. 2.

WATSON, William O. and Mary F. Crafton, daughter of Ebenezer Crafton who consents, 27 August 1850. Married 27 August 1850 by W. Doswell. p. 1 and WB 13/411.

WATTS, Gill W. and Sarah W. Lester, 12 March 1838. Sur. Fred. Lester. p.53.

WEATHERFORD, Burnal and Susan P. Ward, 21 December 1829. Sur. Richard Brown. Married 22 December 1829 by Silas Shelburne. p. 43 and WB 10/131.

WEATHERFORD, John and Lucretia E. Brown, 17 February 1824. Sur. Gricon Brown. Married 19 February 1824 by Silas Shelburne. p. 37 and WB 8/340.

WEATHERFORD, John S. and Sarah B. Bailey, 17 January 1834. Sur. Richard Brown and German Bailey. p. 47.

WEATHERFORD, John S. and Amanda W. Hardy, 12 June 1843. Sur. John Hardy. Married 13 June 1843 by Samuel G. Mason who shows Amanda's last name to be Harding. p. 57 and WB 12/170.

WEATHERFORD, Major of Lunenburg and Mary Edwards, daughter of William Edwards, 26 May 1760. Sur. John Lee. p. 1.

WEATHERFORD, William and Catharine C. Clabourn. Married 19 June 1827 by Silas Shelburne. WB 9/161.

WEAVER, Thomas and Susan Chumney, 2 September 1837. Sur. Robert B. Chumney. p. 53.

WEBB, Green W. and Elizabeth F. Gee, 20 December 1825. Sur. Walker Dodd. p. 39.

WELLS, Daniel and Polly R. Williams, 11 July 1821. Sur. James M. Williams. Married July 1821 by Thomas Adams. p. 33 and WB 8/209.

WELLS, Elija and Pheby Nance, 3 July 1753. Sur. George Walton. Marriage Bond #13.

WELLS, Robert and Sally W. Fullilove. Married 15 May 1794 by James Shelburne. WB 4/107.

WELSHE, Joshua and Fanny Lester. Married 25 December 1794 by James Shelburne. WB 4/107.

WESTBROOK, Josiah and Sally Bradley. Married 30 January 1783 by Thomas Crymes. WB 3/131.

WESTMORELAND, Edmund and Sally Hawkins. Married 30 December 1789 by James Shelburne. WB 3/358.

WHITE, Benjamin J. and Martha Morgan, 5 June 1830. Sur. Jacob White. p.45.

WHITE, Carter and Betsy Winn Cockerham. Married November 1790 by James Shelburne. WB 4/11A

WHITE, Carter and Mary Cockerham. Married 16 May 1799 by William Ellis. WB 5/22.

WHITE, Cephas A. and Mary Winn, 24 February 1837. Sur. Isham W. Vaden. p. 53.

WHITE, Daniel G. and Martha Wood, 8 August 1811. Sur. Stephen Wood. Married 15 August 1811 by James Shelburne. p. 23 and WB 7/32.

WHITE, David and Nancy Stone, 13 February 1812. Sur. Amos T. Johnson. Married 20 February 1812 by James Shelburne. p. 25 and WB 7/32.

WHITE, Fritz Carter, Jr. and Betty Wood. Married 30 January 1794 by John Williams. WB 4/87A.

WHITE, Jacob and Mary Rogers. Married 2 January 1817 by Stephen Jones. WB 7/357.

WHITE, James of Lunenburg and Chriscleany Ussery, 8 April 1813. Sur. Richard Wilkes. Married 13 April 1813 by Matthew Dance. p. 27 and WB 7/60.

WHITE, James and Elizabeth Slaughter, 16 September 1830. Sur. William C. White. p. 45.

WHITE, Robert and Elizabeth Edmunds. Married September 1819 by Thomas Adams. WB 8/67.

WHITE, Thomas and Frances Cockerham. Married 7 November 1810 by Joel Johns. WB 7/60.

WHITE, Thomas W. and Phebe Crafton, 4 September 1841. Sur. James H. Vaughan. p. 55.

WHITE, William and Elizabeth Cockerham, 12 July 1804. Sur. Richard Stone. Married 14 July 1804 by William Ellis. p. 19 and WB 6/122.

WHITE, William B. and Susan W.Thompson, 26 April 1837. Sur. Benjamin W. Wilkes. p. 53.

WHITEHEAD, Benjamin of Lunenburg and Elizabeth Swepstone, daughter of Richard Swepstone, 31 March 1761. Sur. Phillip Goode and Thomas Read. p.3.

WHITLOCK, John and Christain Beaseley, 12 January 1786 by Thomas Crymes. WB 3/263.

WHITTEN, William H. and Ann M. Carter, 26 January 1846. Sur. Leonard Crymes. p. 63.

WHITTLE, Doctor Conway D. and Gilberta M. Sinclair. Married 2 November 1845 by Thomas E. Locke at Lieut. William C. Whittle's residence, Mecklenburg. St. John's Church Register.

WHITTLE, Doctor John S. and Jane A. Patterson, 9 December 1843. Sur.
Conway D. Whittle. Married 12 December 1843 by Thomas E. Locke at
"Wood End", Mrs. Ann P. Patterson's residence. p. 57, WB 12/206 and
St. John's Church Register.

WHITWORTH, Thomas of Lunenburg and Susanna M. Winn, 7 November 1813. Sur.
Edward Winn. p. 27.

WILBORN, Robert of Goochland County and Sally Billups. Married 25 December 1782 by Thomas Crymes. WB 3/131.

WILKES, Benjamin and Polly Wilkes. Married 18 October 1795 by James
Shelburne. WB 4/160.

WILKES, Benjamin W. and Catharine White, 23 October 1837. Sur. Peter W.
Stone. p. 53.

WILKES, John of Lunenburg and Jerushia Stone, 11 November 1813. Sur.
Richard Stone. p. 25.

WILKES, John C. and Elizabeth Thompson, 17 December 1844. Sur. Thomas M.
Smith. p. 59.

WILKES, Minor and Susanna Hazlewood. Married 5 May 1786 by James
Shelburne. WB 3/252.

WILKES, Minor and Phebe White. Married 13 January 1791 by William Ellis.
WB 4/14.

WILKES, Minor and Nancy Tisdale. Married 3 December 1796 by James Shelburne. WB 4/160.

WILKES, Minor and Elizabeth Smith, 9 August 1804. Sur. Joseph Bohannon.
Married 11 August 1804 by William Ellis. p. 19 and WB 6/122.

WILKES, Richard and Jincy Stone. Married 22 August 1805 by William Ellis.
WB 6/135A.

WILKES, Richard and Polly Wallace. Married 15 December 1810 by Thomas
Adams. WB 7/39.

WILKES, Thomas and Jincy Winn, 29 December 1803. Sur. Minor Winn. Married
31 December 1803 by Joel Johns. p. 17 and WB 6/76.

WILKES, William and Phebe Winn. Married 5 September 1809 by Joel Johns.
WB 6/264A.

WILKINS, Edmund W. and Mary Jane Davis, daughter of Nicholas E. Davis who
consents, 9 November 1853. p. 14.

WILKINS, James and Arrabella Marrow, widow, 20 June 1751. Sur. Valentine
W. Mullens [Molins in signature] and Thomas Stith. p. 1.

WILKINS, Richard and Rebecca Twitty, spinster, daughter of John Twitty, dec'd, 27 July 1756. Sur. John Addams, Wm. Jones and G. Carrington,Jr. p.1.

WILKINSON, Benjamin J. and Polly Ann S. Wilkinson, 19 March 1849. Sur. John R. Featherson. Married 11 April 1849 by Richard E. G. Adams. p. 65 and WB 13/334.

WILKINSON, Thomas and Martha Satterfield. Married 28 January 1815 by Thomas Adams. WB 7/248.

WILKINSON, William and Mary H. Blackwell. Married September 1820 by Thomas Adams. WB 8/151.

WILLIAMS, Abraham and Polly Hudson. Married 25 December 1798 by John Neblett. WB 5/2.

WILLIAMS, Absalom and Jean Taylor. Married 4 August 1796 by John Neblett. WB 4/133.

WILLIAMS, Alexander Leonard and Nancy Smith. Married 25 November 1800 by James Shelburne. WB 5/51.

WILLIAMS, Algernon S. and Louisa E. Minor, 27 November 1848. Sur. John D. Tisdale. p. 65.

WILLIAMS, Charles and Martha Jones. Married 5 October 1816 by James Robertson. WB 7/309.

WILLIAMS, Daniel and Sally A. F. Dunman, 11 April 1814. Sur. Henry W. Sturdivant. Married 11 April 1814 by Thomas Adams. p. 27 and WB 7/249.

WILLIAMS, David H. and Betsey W. Knight. Married 27 September 1810 by James Shelburne. WB 7/15.

WILLIAMS, David and Mary Townsend. Married 3 November 1831 by Silas Shelburne. WB 11/2.

WILLIAMS, David and Mary A. Townsend, 28 December 1844. Sur. William Townsend. p. 59.

WILLIAMS, James M. and Sally O. Wyatt, 19 September 1817. Sur. John Smith. Married September 1817 by Thomas Adams. p. 29 and WB 7/356.

WILLIAMS, John and Martha Ambrose. Married 10 April 1792 by John Neblett. WB 4/19A.

WILLIAMS, John and Polley Page, 31 October 1803. Sur. Robert Sammons. Married 2 November 1803 by William Ellis. p. 17 and WB 6/76.

WILLIAMS, John of Lunenburg and Polly Slaughter, 12 November 1813. Sur. Money L. Slaughter. Married 13 November 1813 by James Shelburne. p. 27 and WB 7/110.

WILLIAMS, John F. and Charlotte W. Betts, 27 October 1817. Sur. William
Gooch. p. 29.

WILLIAMS, John H. and Ann E. Brown, 21 October 1844. Sur. Jesse Brown.
p. 59.

WILLIAMS, John L. and Salley B. Morgan, 9 November 1811. Sur. William
Williams. Married 9 November 1811 by Thomas Adams. p. 23 and WB 7/40.

WILLIAMS, John T. and Lucy J. Townsend, 4 December 1849. Sur. William
Townsend. Married 6 December 1849 by William Doswell. p. 67 and
W3 13/375.

WILLIAMS, John W. and Eliza T. Williams, 1 June 1838. Sur. Sherwood W.
Knight. p. 53.

WILLIAMS, Joseph and Eliza Parrish. Married 24 June 1819 by Thomas Adams.
WB 8/67

WILLIAMS, Littleberry and Susan M. Callis, 1 September 1830. Sur. Robert
Morris. Married 2 September 1830 by Joshua Featherston. p. 45 and
WB 10/101.

WILLIAMS, Nicholas and Alse Armon Love, Married 24 October 1782 by James
Shelburne. WB 3/132.

WILLIAMS, Richard of Lunenburg and Clarissa Harlow Pettus, 21 February 1811.
Sur. Thomas Wyatt. p. 23.

WILLIAMS, Richard L. B. and Louisa J. Crenshaw, 13 November 1843. Sur.
Henry P. Crenshaw. Married 12 December 1843 by Samuel G. Mason. p.57
and WB 12/171.

WILLIAMS, Robert and Anne Redman, spinster, 25 January 1762. Sur. William
Redman and Thomas Read. p. 3.

WILLIAMS, Robert and Polly Eubank. Married 18 November 1800 by Edward
Almond. WB 6/81.

WILLIAMS, Robert H. and Burtha J. Ellis, 3 April 1835. Sur. John Thompson.
p. 47.

WILLIAMS, Robert M. and Marietta E. P. Hardy, 6 December 1845. Sur. Samuel
M. Brown. p. 61.

WILLIAMS, Samuel G. and Gracie Bowie Cowan, 11 July 1807. Sur. Peter
Randolph, Jr. p. 21.

WILLIAMS, Thomas and Ann Burge, 12 March 1812. Sur. Tazewell T. Burge.
Married 18 March 1812 by James Shelburne. p. 25 and WB 7/32.

WILLIAMS, Thomas and Elizabeth Slaughter, 8 August 1821. Sur. William M.
Ford. Married 8 August 1821 by Silas Shelburne. p. 31 and WB 8/227.
[See Thomas Fowlkes and Elizabeth Slaughter, page 46.]

WILLIAMS, Thomas and Jane Johnson, 13 February 1822. Sur. William Hightower. Married 14 February 1822 by William Hatchett. p. 33 and
WB 8/262.

WILLIAMS, William and Polly Moody. Married 31 October 1795 by John
Neblett. WB 4/116A.

WILLIAMS, William and Sukey Tisdale. Married 20 March 1810 by James
Shelburne. WB 7/15.

WILLIAMS, William and Eliza J. Blackwell. Married 21 December 1819 by
Thomas Adams. WB 8/67.

WILLIAMS, William H. and Martha F. Townsend, daughter of Drury Townsend,
11 November 1850. William Townsend, witness. p. 2.

WILLIAMSON, George H. and Virginia A. Sterne, 22 July 1841. Sur. Charles
R. Sterne. p. 55.

WILLIAMSON, Jacob and Salley Ragsdale. Married 25 December 1795 by James
Shelburne. WB 4/107.

WILLIAMSON, John and Martha Davis. Married 5 November 1786 by Thomas
Crymes. WB 3/268.

WILLIAMSON, Joseph and Ann Brown. Married 6 September 1781 by James
Shelburne. WB 3/92.

WILLIS, Henry and Mary Taylor, 21 January 1815. Sur. James Burton. p.29.

WILLIS, John and Sarah Powel, 10 January 1825. Sur. Jesse Peebles. Married
10 January 1825 by Thomas H. Jeffress. p. 39 and WB 8/431.

WILLS [or Wiles], Daniel and Polly R. Williams. Married July 1821 by
Thomas Adams. WB 8/209.

WILLS, Elijah and Elizabeth Ragsdale. Married 1 December 1798 by Matthew
Dance. WB 4/245.

WILLS, Robert and Polly Potts, 10 July 1812. Sur. Jesse Laffoon. Married
12 July 1812 by Thomas Adams. WB 7/39.

WILLSON, E. and N. W. Esters. Married 18 December 1818 by Charles Ogburn.
WB 10/181A.

WILLSON, John and Mary B. Morgain, 14 December 1809 by Matthew Dance.
WB 7/1.

WILLSON, Josiah and Jane A. Morrison. Married November 1819 by Thomas
Adams. WB 8/67.

WILSON, Miles A. and Susan Elizabeth Stone, 19 October 1846. Sur. John
S. Wilson. p. 63.

WILSON, Paul and Philadelphia C. F. Wiggleworth, 29 October 1838. Sur.
Fredk. Lester. Married 31 October 1838 by W. S. Wilson. p. 53 and
WB 11/328.

WILSON, Robert and Elizabeth Walker. Married 24 February 1784 by James
Shelburne. WB 3 /169.

WILSON, Samuel and Martha C. Jeffress. Married 27 April 1831 by Matthew
Dance. WB 10/129.

WILMOTH, James W. and Mary Turner, daughter of Wilmoth Turner, 1 December
1851. Vinis Turner, witness. p. 6.

WIMBISH, Benjamin and Elizabeth Watson, 13 December 1761. Sur. Peter
Rawlings and Thomas Read. p. 3.

WINN, Alexander of Lunenburg County, and Jane Stone, widow and relict of
Richard Stone, late of Lunenburg County. Married 5 July 1816 by Joel
Johns. WB 7/280 and DB 24/234.

WINN, Banister and Sally M. Winn. Married 30 November 1801 by William
Ellis. WB 6/11.

WINN, Bass F. of Lunenburg and Mary E. Jordan, 8 October 1813. Sur.
Orasamus Winn. p. 27.

WINN, Bass F. and Lucy Winn. Married 27 April 1827 by Thomas H.Jeffress.
WB 9/212.

WINN, Booker and Lucy Reese, 14 January 1822. Sur. Edmund P. Winn.
Married Thursday, 18 January 1822 by John Doyle. p. 33 and WB 8/258.

WINN, Charol P. and Martha A. F. Gee. See Charol P. Warner on page 129.

WINN, Daniel and Martha McLaughlin. Married 23 May 1801 by William Ellis.
WB 5/67.

WINN, Daniel and Nancy Wilkes. Married 15 October 1805 by James Shelburne.
WB 6/147. [See William Winn and Nancy Wilkes, page 138.]

WINN, Edmund Jr. of Lunenburg and Nancey Singleton, 9 February 1814. Sur.
Freeman Winn. p. 27.

WINN, Edmund and Sarah A. Snead. Married 1 May 1818 by Joel Johns. WB 8/357.

WINN, Edmund P. and Judith Reese, both of Lunenburg. Married 27 December
1819 by Caleb N. Bell. WB 8/66.

WINN, Edmund C. and Martha A. Boswell, 27 September 1830. Sur. Samuel
Arnold. p. 45.

WINN, Edward G. and Sarah Winn. Married 4 March 1801 by William Ellis.
WB 5/67.

WINN, Francis J. and Mary E. Laffoon. Married 15 October 1836 by James M.
Jeter. WB 11/272. [See Freeman Winn and Mary E. Laffoon, page 137.]

WINN, Freeman and Caty Moore, 13 December 1803. Sur. William Farguson.
Married 14 December 18<u>04</u> [1803] by John Paup. p. 17 and WB 6/82.

WINN, Freeman and Lucy Reese, 25 December 1843. Sur. Robert Reese. p.57.

WINN, Freeman J. and Mary E. Laffoon, 12 December 1836. Sur. James George. p. 51. [See Francis J. Winn and Mary E. Laffoon, page 136.]

WINN, Hinchey and Martha Gooch, 10 December 1803. Sur. William H. Robertson. Married 15 December 1803 by William Ellis. p. 19 and WB 6/76.

WINN, Horatio and Patty Pettypool. Married 4 January 1800 by James Shelburne. WB 5/51.

WINN, James and Betsey Powell, 10 January 1804. Sur. Richard Elliott. Married 12 January 1804 by Matthew Dance. p. 19 and WB 6/73.

WINN, John and Myrtila Minor. Married 14 December 1787 by Thomas Crymes. WB 3/309.

WINN, John, Jr. and Charlotte Powell, 3 February 1804. Sur. Eddins Moore. p. 19.

WINN, John and Martha F. Christopher, 20 March 1835. Sur. Henry Winn. p.47.

WINN, John R. and Martha Winn. Married 23 December 1828 by John Thompson. WB 9/444.

WIN[N], Lewellin and Eliza Jane Tunstill, daughter of Littleberry Tunstill, 12 May 1851. John H. Crafton, witness. p. 4. [See Lewellin Wise.]

WINN, Lyddal and Susanna McLaughlin, 24 November 1804. Sur. James Winn. Married 29 November 1804 by William Ellis. p. 19 and WB 6/122.

WINN, Nicholas and Lucy Taylor, 2 May 1829. Sur. John H. McKinney. Married 7 May 1829 by Joshua Featherston. p. 43 and WB 10/1.

WINN, Patrick Henry and Amanda A. Wilkes, 21 December 1835. Sur. Benjamin W. Wilkes. p. 49.

WINN, Richard and Polly Stone, 9 March 1804. Sur. Richard Stone. p. 19.

WINN, Richard and Elizabeth James Floyd. Married 24 November 1840 by Joshua Featherston who also records this marriage the second time stating the date as 15 December 1840. WB 12/7 and 12/54.

WINN, Robert and Susanna Jordan. Married 11 February 1796 by John Neblett. WB 4/124.

WINN, Thomas and Ann Snead. Married 17 August 1809 by Matthew Dance. WB 7/1.

WINN, Thomas and Martha Ann Waller, 20 July 1836. Sur. James Dirk. Married 5 July 1836 by James M. Jeter. p. 51 and WB 11/180.

WINN, Thomas and Catharine Pulliam, 18 December 1845. Sur. James M. Laffoon. Married 18 December 1845 by W. S. Wilson. p. 61 and WB 13/46.

WINN, William and Nancy Wilkes, 9 October 1806. Sur. Lyddall Winn. Married 15 October 1806. [See Daniel Winn and Nancy Wilkes.]

WINN, William B. and Louisa M. Pulliam. 25 April 1838. Sur. George W. Pulliam. p. 53.

WINN, William B. and Mary S. Pulliam, 11 April 1853. Samuel Saunders, witness. p. 13.

WINN, William E. and Sarah A. Snead, 21 December 1846. Sur. William Snead, Jr. Married "about the 23 December 1847" by Thomas Adams. [Note: The minister intended 1846, as the next couple on his list was married in January 1847.] p. 61 and WB 13/105.

WYNN, William H. and Elvira A. White, 13 August 1853. David M. White, witness. p. 13.

WISE, Lewellen and Eliza Jane Tunstill, daughter of Littleberry Tunstill, 12 May 1851. John H. Crafton, witness. p. 4. [See Lewellen Winn.]

WISE, Thomas and Sally Tucker, 17 November 1806. Sur. William Averitt. Married 27 November 1806 by James Shelburne, who states Polly Tucker. p. 21 and WB 6/231.

WOMMACK, Jacob and Nancy Bates, 12 April 1824. Sur. Joel Hood. Married 13 April 1824 by Pleasant Barnes. p. 37 and WB 8/492.

WOMACK, William and Margarett Ellis. Married 4 February 1790 by James Shelburne. WB 3/358.

WOOD, Christopher and Susanna Tatum. Married 29 December 1802 by James Shelburne. WB 6/28.

WOOD, Christopher and Martha J. Staples, 11 January 1830. Sur. John W. Rowlett. Married 14 January 1830 by Silas Shelburne. p. 45 and WB 10/131.

WOOD, George and Betsey White [or Whitt] Married 27 December 1809 by Edward Almond. WB 7/1.

WOOD, Green A. and Mary Jane Tisdale, 12 June 1843. Sur. William M. Wood. p. 57.

WOOD, Jehue [or John] and Francis S. Goode, 8 September 1823. Sur. Thomas Wood. Married 11 September 1823 by Silas Shelburne. p. 37 and WB 8/340.

WOOD, John and Milly Smithson. Married 16 December 1802 by James Shelburne. WB 6/28.

WOOD, John and Lucy C. Smithson. Married 23 December 1818 by Silas Shelburne. WB 8/67.

WOOD, John H. and Rebecca A. F. Smithson, 30 August 1842. Sur. Bartley C. Smithson. p. 55.

WOOD, Johnson and Faney Thompson. Married 21 November 1783 by David Ellington. WB 3/185.

WOOD, Robert and Rebecca Bates, 4 January 1823. Sur. Pleasant Bates. M.B. #822.

WOOD, Silas and Eliza Jane Hawkins. Married 23 December 1840 by James W. Hunnicut. WB 12/7.

WOOD, Stephen of Lunenburg and Constance Robertson, 20 July 1805. Sur. Edward Lee. Married 25 July 1805 by James Shelburne. p.21 and WB 6/147.

WOOD, Thomas and Mary Johnson, 27 January 1812. Sur. Edward Jones. p.25.

WOOD, William and Martha Evans. Married 27 October 1799 by James Shelburne. WB 5/51.

WOOD, William and Mary J. Watts, 16 November 1838. Sur. Gill W. Watts. p. 53.

WOOD, William and Mildred T. Chappell, 17 January 1844. Sur. Elisha B. Jackson. p. 59.

WOODING, Robert and Mary Marrable, daughter of William Marrable, 5 June 1753. Sur. Thomas Hawkins and Field Jefferson. p. 1.

WOODSON, Tscharner and Mary E. Beverly. Married 10 October 1843 by Thomas E. Locke, at the residence of F. W. Epes. St. John's Church Register.

WOODSON, William M. and Lucy M. Woodson. Married 14 September 1831 by Matthew M. Dance. WB 11/19.

WOOTTON, John T. and Frances Ann Brydie, 1 June 1825. Sur. Nathan Fowlkes. Married 2 June 1825 by Thomas H. Jeffress. p. 39 and WB 8/529.

WOOTON, John P. and Mary E. Williams. Married 31 August 1831 by Silas Shelburne. WB 11/2.

WOOTTON, Lucius T. and Agness E. Bayne, 13 January 1841. Sur. Clement J. Thompson. [The M.B. endorsement shows the month as December.] p.55.

WOOTON, Samuel and Polly Ellis. Married 20 January 1815 by James Shelburne. Sur. William Ellis. WB 7/227.

WOOTON, William H. and Hannah S. Wilson, daughter of William E. Wilson, 21 April 1853. Paul Wilson, witness. p. 13.

WRENN, James and Patsey Tubbyfill, 13 November 1806. Sur. William Tubbyfill. Married 27 November 1806 by Matthew Dance. p. 21 and WB 6/181.

WRENN, John and Martha Estes. Married 5 May 1786 by James Shelburne. WB 3/252.

WRENN, Matthew and Nancy George. Married 1 July 1815 by Thomas Adams. WB 7/248.

WRIGHT, Charles and Nancy Wright. Married 22 December 1791 by John Rogers. WB 4/19.

WRIGHT, Robert and Salley Wright. Married 5 March 1805 by John Neblett. WB 6/123.

WYATT, Harris T. and Elizabeth F. Webb, 20 May 1831. Sur. Mont S. Bacon. p. 45.

WYATT, John and Elizabeth Williams, 19 December 1803. Sur. Eldred Williams. p. 17.

WYATT, Richard and Martha Wilkinson. Married 24 October 1802 by John Neblett. WB 6/11.

WYATT, Thomas and Priscilla Hardy. Married 23 November 1814 by Thomas Adams. Sur. Nicholas E. Davis. WB 7/248. [Note: M.B. #1507 is dated 21 November 18_74_ - "bound unto James Barbour, Esq., Governor or Chief Magistrate of the Commonwealth of Virginia." James Barbour was Governor Jan. 4, 1812 - Dec. 11, 1814; therefore, the M.B. is incorrectly dated.]

YANCEY, James G. and Martha P. Crenshaw, 14 November 1842. Sur. Henry P. Crenshaw. Married 20 December 1842 by Samuel G. Mason. p. 55 and WB 12/171.

YARBROUGH, William and Leanner Andrews. Married 26 June 1792 by James Shelburne. WB 4/45.

YATES, John M. and Ann E. Boswell, 12 February 1844. Sur. Robert C. Hardy. Married February 1844 by Robert Michaels. p. 59 and WB 12/215.

YOUNG, Clement and Amy Landrum. Married 18 December 1799 by John Neblett. WB 5/2.

YOUNG, Elijah and Anna Farler. Married 28 December 1794 by James Shelburne. WB 4/107.

YOUNG, Josiah M. and Mary A. E. Anderson, 17 November 1835. Sur. James A. Foster. p. 49.

YOUNG, Ralph [also shown Richard] and Lucintha Bennett, 26 September 1823. Sur. John Rash. Married 9 October 1823 by John Doyle who shows the bride's name as Lucretia Burnette. p. 37 and WB 8/316.

YOUNG, Richard. See above marriage.

YOUNG, William and Sally Eastham. Married 17 December 1791 by William Ellis. WB 4/27.

ZACKARY, Jonathan and Jane Allen Gordon. Married 11 December 1787 by Thomas Crymes. WB 3/309.

ZACHARY, Joshua and Elizabeth Stokes. Married 13 January 1791 by William Ellis.. WB 4/14.

I N D E X
to
Brides', Sureties', and other names

Bennett, Elizabeth	4		Blackwell, Joel	10,50,52
Lucintha	140		Lewis	10
Nancy	79		Martha E.	44
Bentley, Anny	2		Martha H.	59
Robert H.	117		Mary H.	88,133
Betts, Charles	64,85		Mary R.	127
Charlotte W.	134		Nancy	11
Elisha	29,89		Nancy J.	3
Elizabeth A.	39		Robert	11,95
Judah	89		Robert Jr.	11
Judith K.	20		Sally Gunn	10
Mary A.	58		Susan	97
Mary A. P.	103		Thomas	55
Mary Ann	106		W. Thweatt	60
Nancy	85		William F.	58
Pamelia	57		William H.	10
Patty	85		William T.	71,107
Sally	57		Blagrave, Blagrove	
Sally Carter	78		Anne	51
Spencer	78		Mary Newsteys	59
Beverley, Mrs. Frances Susan	40		Nancy	65
Maria Rosalie	40		Blankenship, Blankinship	
Martha A.	59		Dosha	101
Mary E.	139		Jency	117
Bigger, Sally C.	116		Lucy	41
Billups, Christopher	19,26		Martha	41
Mary	26		Blanks, Hannah	19
Sally	132		Thomas	19
Bird, Caty	67		Blanton, Jane C.	28
Bishop, Alfred	9		Martha W.	116
Angelina	12		Bohannon, Dicey M.	61
C. C.	9,66,85		Elizabeth	61
Celia	85		Joseph	132
Chatten C.	31,43,115		Martha R.	105
Edmund (Edmond)	9,36,89		Mary	90
Elizabeth C.	103		Milley	45
James H.	35		Nancy	61
John	85,89		Philip H.	61,68
John A.	51,89		Philip R.	105
Joseph	12		William	45,101
Joseph S.	13		William A.	90
Mary C.	115		Booker, Jonathan	32,88
Minerva P.	89		Mary Carden	88
Molly	47		Booth, Amey	124
Permelia (Pamela)	13		John H.	85
Rebecca	9		Nathaniel	88
Robert L.	31		Polly	88
Blackwell, Ann J.	112		Thomas	98
Christianna	68		Borum, Mary	106
Eliza J.	135		William A.	68
Elizabeth G.	34,71		Boswell, Ann E.	140
Elizabeth Goodwin	52		Elizabeth	93
James	34		Fanny	53
James G.	127		Lucy W.	38

Cralle, Craulle, Crawley,	
Sterling	31
Thomas G.	40,80
Crenshaw, Betsy	77
Christian	54
Cornelius	50
Daniel	54
Elizabeth	90
Henry P.	111,134,140
Jincey	86
John R.	95
Louisa J.	134
Lucinda B.	128
Martha J. M.	13
Martha P.	140
Mary	45,120
Mary A. E.	114
Minerva	85
Nancy	74,94
Nanny	74
Narcissa P.	120
Polly	108
Richard R.	116
Susannah	54
Unity	13
Crews, Salley	82
Tabitha	90
William	82
Crittenden, Polly	80
Cross, Elizabeth	119
Martha	20
Mary	31
Crow, Martha	54
Martha S.	37
Rebecca Ann	32
Sterling L.	32
Crowder, Elizabeth	73
Green W.	71,99
Harriet S.	129
Howel P.	99
Julia A.	99
L. G.	59
Martha J.	49
Miles	123
Sarah A. E.	95
Crymes, Alice	19
Elizabeth	76
Elizabeth W. M.	22
George	76,96
Jane M.	68
John	30,72
Kezia W.	33
Leonard	43,68,131

Crymes,	
Martha Stephen	72
Mourning	49
Nancy	43,52
Patsy	49
Polly	4
Rebecca	23
Robert	84,107
Sarah	52,96
Thomas	23
Cumbley, Prudence	86
Cumby, Elizabeth L.	37
Cunningham, Andrew	79
Mathew	79
Rebeckah	79
Sarah	80
Cupples, Charles	11,128
Cureton, John	83
Cuttaloe, Elizabeth	40
Dagnal(1), Nancy	8
Richard	104
Susan	104
Dalton, Mary	79
Daly, Daley, Dailey,	
Daniel	50
John	118
Patsey	64
Dance, M. M.	63
Martha F.	10
Matthew	35
Mourning E.	126
Rebecca	58
Rebecca E.	63
Stephen	126
Daniel, Ann	84
Drury M.	53
Elizabeth E.	95
Nancy	6
Rebecca	124
Davidson, Lucy Ann	88
William R.	31
Davis, Davies,	
Alice	53
Ann H.	66
Diana	17
Eliza	36
Elizabeth	102
Evelina V.	51
Hannah	30
Henrietta	87
Isbell	22
John	87

Edmondson, Edmundson,
Constance (Constant)	75,102
Elizabeth	102
Harris	92
Lucinda H.	37
Martha	102
Mary	127
Polly	10
Susannah	89
Tabitha	54,75
Upton A.	7

Edwards, Mary 130
| Thomas | 38 |
| William | 130 |

Elam, Nancy 87
| Phebe | 21 |

Elder, John 17
| Margaret J. | 17 |

Ellington, Sally 37
Elliott, Richard 137
Ellis, Ambrose 72,78
Burtha J.	134
Caroline	58
Catharine E.	26
Cealy B.	73
Cecila A.	74
Charlotte Jane	39
Eliza	6
Eliza B.	46
Ellison W.	39,58
John	23
John F.	46
Joseph F.	40,64
Louisa	27
Lucretia	23
Margaret	138
Martha F.	102
Mary A.C.S.	7
Mary Ann	78
Polly	139
Prudence	20
Rebecca M.	72
Richard	6,81
Richard C.	9
Sarah A. R.	58
Susanna Stokes	52
Thomas B.	16
William	139

Elmore, John 32
Patsey	50
Rebecca E.	123
Sarah W.	11
William E.	39

Embry, Elizabeth 34

Epes, Eppes, Epps,
Blanch	116
Elizabeth	21
F. W.	40,59,111,139
Franky	116
Freeman	40
John	116
John C.	8,99
Mary S. Lavinia	99
Rebecca (Mrs.)	59,111
Rebecca E.	71
Richard J.	36
Virginia A. M.	59
William P.	99

Epperson, Polly M. 83
Erskine, Patrick A. 94,103,114
Estes, Esters,
Abraham	8
Alley	1
Benjamin	41
Catharine	113
Elijah J.	64,69,84
Elisha	1,9,41
Elizabeth	90
Frances C.	103
Jincy	88
Malissa B.	30
Martha	139
Martha Ann	64
Mary	9,13,41
Matthew	24
N. W.	135
Nancy	24
Narcissa B.	52
Sally P.	24
Sarah	1
Susanna	40
Thomas	40

Eubank, Elizabeth S. 93
Harriet F.	94
Martha A.	53
Philip G.	94
Polly	134
William H.	114

Evens, Evans,
Elizabeth	34
John	34
Joshua	34
M.	42
Martha	139
Mary Ann	65
Peggy	53
Sally	23
William	23

Grigg, Eliza	48	Hardin, Harding, Hardying,	
William	48	Frances	23
Gunn, Elizabeth	101	John	2,57
Freeman J.	75	Lucy	28
Martha	124	Martha J.	5
Nancy	65	Mary Susan	2
Sally B.	10	Nancey	43
Tabitha	45	Peggy	67
Gurney, Daniel	50	Polly	2,43
		Robert	43,124
Haines, Martha	55	Sarah	21,68,69
Haley, Polly	61	Thomas, Sr.	23
Siller	110	Thomas J.	5
Wealthy	27	William	63
Hamlet, Hannah	112	Hardwick, Elizabeth	27
Nancy	2,129	Jincey	5
Hamblin, Hamlin,		Polly	126
Martha A.	53	Susanna	104
Mary Jane	44	Hardy, Amanda W.	130
Tabitha	7	Amelia	79
Thomas	72,125	Catharine	9
Hammock, Elizabeth	81	Charles	57
Elizabeth H.	75	Cornelius	6,10
Emma Jane	85	Dorothea J.	94
Hugh	85	Elijah D.	64
Irwin	52	Elisha	7,10,16
James	2,56	Emma Jane	16
John S.	85	George H.	57
John T.	56	George W.	117
Mary	86	Griffin O.	107
Nancy	56	Henry G.	57,94,113,121
Permelia Ann	66	J. R.	127
Hammonds, Elizabeth	31	John	130
Milly	104	John C.	57
Polly	103,104	Jordan R.	12,78
Raleigh	19	Joseph G.	57
Rebecca	19	Joshua	4,62
Richard	104	Julia A.	26
William	56	Kitturah	116
Hampton, Ann Elizabeth	79	Larkin	57,111
Haney, Molley	29	Letsey	82
Hanks, Caty	56	Lucy O.	107
Dicy	56	Manerva E.	10
Nancy A.	75	Marietta E. P.	134
Hanna, John	34	Martha	106
Hardin, Harding, Hardying,		Martha A.	11
Amanda W.	130	Mary A. B.	111
Benny	43	Nancy F.	50
Doshe	64	Permelia	10
Elizabeth	43	Permelia Henry	10
Elizabeth E.	73	Petronella S.	58
Emily S.	57	Priscilla	140
		Robert C.	140

Nance, Mary	15,81	Overby, Ann	15
Pheby	130	Edward	5
Polly	27	Fanny	5
Sally	25	George	15
Susanna	44	Mary	32
William	15	Nelly	58,61
Nash, Mary	100	Overthrow, Samuel	89
Thomas	1,19,60,63,107	Overton, Edward	28
Neal, Neele,		Elizabeth	21
Ann E.	65	John E.	7,69
Clarary	112	Lucy	93
Elizabeth W.	9	Mary	32
Ellman	87	Mary Jane	71
James	65	Samuel, Jr.	48
Louisa S.	115	Sarah	28
Mary Ann	32	Sarah T.	69
Mary C.	4	Susan	73
Nancey	96	William B.	81
Nancy T.	80	William G.	111
Tabitha	118	William S.	93
Neblett, Niblett,		Owen, Patsy	122
Ann A.	67	Richard	7
Ann E.	53		
Betsy	9	Page, Polley	133
Eliza B.	111	Palmer, Parmer, Palmore,	
Elizabeth C.	39	Elizabeth	97
Francis	109	John	90
Mary M.	97	Polly	57
Mary S.	57	Pamplin, Pampline, Pampton,	
Nancy	109	Elizabeth	41
Rebecca	65	Elizabeth T.	123
Sarah	85	Jinney	38
Sterling	87	John	38
William	84,89	M.	123
Nelson, Lucy Armistead	77	Rebecca	86
Nevil, Booker	88	Robert	41
Lina (Neville)	113	Sally	108
Newberry, James	109	Sally W.	4
Newbill, Mary	27,115	Unity	28
Nancy	35	Parham, Rebecca Janes	125
Thomas	88	Parker, Edward W.	6
Newby, John	46	Parish, Parrish,	
Nancy	46	David	20
Nolley, Luand	116	Eliza	134
Norment, Archillis J.	59	Elizabeth	2,6
North, John C.	29	Henry S.	6
		James	91
Ogburn, Edward	88	James G.	91
Orgain, Benjamin	37	Jane	24,84
Lucy E.	80	Joel	28,71,91
Minerva C. S.	13	Joel M.	16
Osborn, Nancy	122	John	91,92
Samuel G.	78	Lucretia	74

www.ingramcontent.com/pod-product-compliance
Lightning Source LLC
Chambersburg PA
CBHW070429270326
41926CB00014B/2996